Emerging Trends in Education Policy: Unapologetic Progressive Conversations

Emerging Trends in Education Policy: Unapologetic Progressive Conversations

Theodore S. Ransaw
Brian Boggs

INFORMATION AGE PUBLISHING, INC.
Charlotte, NC • www.infoagepub.com

Library of Congress Cataloging-In-Publication Data

The CIP data for this book can be found on the Library of Congress website (loc.gov).

Paperback: 979-8-88730-228-7
Hardcover: 979-8-88730-229-4
E-Book: 979-8-88730-230-0

Printed in the United States of America

CONTENTS

SECTION III
ROLE OF COLLEGES

SECTION IV
ROLE OF PHILANTHROPY

SECTION V
ROLE OF SOCIAL JUSTICE

PREFACE

William Schmidt

Michigan State University

The world has changed. Today countries are facing a seismic shift as the 20th-century economy is transformed into the digital, knowledge, and service economy of the 21st century. Analogous to the changes in work, life, schooling, and society triggered by the industrial revolution, and countries today face substantially new contexts in each of these areas. One such context in the area of schooling that is changing is mathematics. It is becoming an increasingly essential literacy, second only to textual reading comprehension, which is critical for all citizens as it provides a logical structure that illuminates and brings clarity to many situations citizens regularly encounter in the everyday real world. For example, mathematics yields a greater understanding of the ubiquitous amount of data to which citizens are exposed in their personal lives on their jobs, family finances, medical decisions, and many other areas of everyday life. Citizens are increasingly challenged to understand and to be informed about major national issues such as the national debt, climate change and its effects upon the economy, and the economics and consequences of decisions around national healthcare policy.

The current situation created by the COVID-19 pandemic illustrates the need for change in education policy with respect to mathematics. The misunderstandings that developed among a large segment of the society regarding the spreading

Emerging Trends in Education Policy: Unapologetic Progressive Conversations,
pages vii–viii.
Copyright © 2023 by Information Age Publishing
www.infoagepub.com

of the disease itself, the nature of the experiments leading to the new vaccine, how statistical modeling is based on data and as a result changes as new data become available, as well as what appear to be such simple concepts as what denominator to use in making various comparisons. That lack of knowledge led to irrational behaviors such as refusing to be vaccinated, believing the vaccines were not generally safe, misunderstanding which areas in the US had more cases than others and the linguistic emergence of the newly created oxymoron, "false facts."

Such occurrences point to the fundamental role that education needs to play in society—that of providing all children, no matter their social-class background, with not only traditional literacy, but also with other literacies such as quantitative literacy (e.g., mathematics, statistics, and geometry).

Schooling must address this issue by providing students not only with the basics of mathematics but also with opportunities to apply mathematics to real-world situations thus developing the use of mathematical and statistical reasoning. Typical word problems do not make the grade; they are vacuous, overly simplistic, boring, repetitive, and lack the true nature of real-world issues. What is needed are opportunities for students to engage in real-world exercises that reflect the truly messy nature of the world and demand a careful examination of the information and definition of what the problem is as well as the relevant mathematics needed to find the answer. Knowing this to be true, is not enough. Public education policy must demand it and ensure that all children are given those learning experiences that will help them develop mathematics reasoning and in turn, mathematical literacy thus providing a stronger and better-educated citizenry in years to come. Over the past year, the response to the worldwide pandemic by citizens has made clear and given another reason for the importance of this necessary change in educational policy.

Such misunderstandings, and false information warrant a serious reconsideration of our educational policy and what it means to provide *all* of our students with a set of fundamental literacies that enable them to make intelligent choices. We must make sure that gaps in the educational system and the resulting inequalities do not occur as that would only further disadvantage lower social class and minority children. This is not only disquieting, inequitable and immoral but portends a real threat to democracy. Educational policy is not only about education but is also critical to public policy more generally as reflected in our response as a nation to the recent election and to the pandemic. It is the foundation of democracy.

EMERGING TRENDS IN EDUCATION POLICY

Unapologetic Progressive Conversations

Brian Boggs and Theodore S. Ransaw

Michigan State University

From the moment society first conceived an education system, there has been a need to have critical discussions about how best to provide education, and how best to create education policy. The purpose of *Emerging Trends in Education Policy: Unapologetic progressive conversations,* is to highlight impactful policies, strategies initiatives, and approaches to educational reform in an edited volume.

We start off this volume with a section we hope articulates the role of policy education. Addressing issues surrounding students with disabilities is especially important to the both of us. Starting off with Rosanne Renauer's chapter titled *An Inclusive Society for All through Inclusive Education for Students with Disabilities* seemed like a natural place to start this volume. While we are far and away from the days where students with disabilities are not shunned and made to attend classes in a separate room from so called 'normal' students, we are still not at a place that mirror's the civil rights initiative of the Rolling Quads of the 60s. The Rollings Quads embraced and simultaneously embodied the spirit of the Civil

Emerging Trends in Education Policy: Unapologetic Progressive Conversations,
pages ix–xiv.
Copyright © 2023 by Information Age Publishing
www.infoagepub.com

Rights Movement by making access equitable for all people through legislation. Yes. Students with disabilities is indeed a fitting matter of policy to start off this volume.

Renauer starts her chapter by highlighting the fact that disabilities appear in all shapes and sizes. Students with disabilities includes religion, gender, sexuality, and race. Supporting students with special needs is a step in the right direction toward inclusivity. We have all heard of Critical Race Theory, CRT by now. CRT advances the idea that looking at how the impact of policy and legislation effects some but not others is a way to identify systemic problems. Renauer grounds her chapter with a similar theory Critical Disability Theory, CDT is a tool to help improve the human condition by amplifying the unique and complex voices of students with a disability. Separating students by labeling them disabled and non-disabled is both an ideology and policy that must be changed if we are to lead all students to systemic, economic, social, cultural, and political change that liberates rather than oppresses.

Most of us has struggled with issues of identity, judgement, and mistreatment by others at some point in our lives. LGBTQ students are especially mistreatment just for being who they are. And just like students with disabilities, LGBTQ students need to be protected also. Amanda Miller, & Brian Boggs have a policy recommendation to support LGBTQ students by supporting through one of America's most fundamental laws, the First Amendment which includes the right to free speech the right to assemble peacefully, among others. Miller and Boggs on short, argue that students have the right to express themselves and associate freely with whoever they want. Free speech and the freedom to assemble are supposed to be fundamental to our way of life. Schools often struggle with the application of student's inalienable rights in school. In fact, the younger a student is, the less right that student has. *No Johnny, you can't walk down the hallway to the bathroom by yourself. No Susie, you can't run with the scissors. Yes, you have to wash your hands.* We protect students from so many things. Surely, we can protect our LGBTQ students from harm. But what would that protection look like?

Miller and Boggs have outlined a policy idea based on key First Amendment cases related to LGBTQ student sexual orientation expression and gender identity. Their chapter *Sexual Orientation and Gender Identity in Michigan's K–12 Educational System* begins by sharing the perspective that public educators see themselves as a form of public service more so than they see themselves as part of government. In addition to being novel, the utility in their framework lies in the fact that it is nestled within legal precedent. However, the utility in their framework is the fact that is nestles LGBTQ students in a protective cocoon of concern that treats them as if they were, well, human. We may not be able to prevent students from being unpleasant toward one another. But we can prevent schools from denying their freedom of expressing themselves and who they affiliate with.

The North Carolina Read to Achieve program was created to help every child in the state reach grade-level proficiency in reading by the end of third grade.

Dennis Davis, Chandra Alston, & Courtney Samuelson use the North Carolina Achievement initiative to recommend not one, but seven recommendations to make third grade reading levels achievable for every child in every state. Reading at grade level by third grade has been frequently suggested as a benchmark for educational achievement and a warning sign of doom for students that do not achieve it. Their chapter *What Will It Take to Help All Third Graders Learn to Read?: Recommendations for Improving policies on early literacy learning* significance is based on the fact that they suggest supporting schools with the resources teachers need to be successful agents in literacy reform by including a key factor in teacher quality, professional development. Many literacy instruction programs suggest including core literacy instruction, summer reading camps and supplemental programs. However, Dennis Davis, Chandra Alston, and Courtney Samuelson also include implementation of the support teachers need to achieve their goals in their recommendations. The implication that a policy recommendation can be wholistic in both its approach and design is timely.

Due to the promise of federal level education policy like the *Every Study Succeeds Act,* ESSA, Full-Service Community Schools FSCS, are becoming more and more common. Kathleen Provinzano's chapter *The Time is Now: Advocating for contextually responsive policy to support full-service community schools,* serves as a guide to understanding modern school reform issues like parental support and community resources. Education stakeholders which include teachers, principals, superintendents, and community leaders represent different forms of intelligence and supports to academic achievement. Different ways of looking at priorities often causes varying degrees of perspectives which in turn creates policy decisions that are in-equitable. Recommending policy changes that are distributed fairly is only possible if low-income students, students of color, students with disabilities, and English language learner's disparities are summarily addressed and not hidden. As Provinzano so accurately articulates, funding without accountability leaves far too many students behind.

Family engagement should include parental support in some format. After all, parents are the first teachers. But how often do policymakers consider parents, including fathers and grandparents, when making policy decisions? Or more pressing still, how often do we include parents, and grandparents when making decisions about how to allocate funding for student academic achievement? Eve Sullivan and Djamel Bekkai's chapter, *Make Parenting Education Universal* articulates how parents and other family members can contribute to positive school outcomes. Sullivan and Bekkai's premise are that parenting education is the key to civically engaged children. In short, supporting good parenting supports teachers in the classroom.

Parenting education policy recommendations are not far-fetched. For example, prenatal home visits have been known to increase education outcomes for students. Due to the impact of COVID 19 on parents, and educators, supporting parents is a heartfelt way to support all school children.

Theodore Ransaw's chapter Involved *Fathers: The missing link in education policy reform,* continues our theme of supporting family and communities by highlighting one of the most potent secret weapons teachers have in their fight for student achievement- Fathers! Ransaw reminds policy makers to remember that students who have an involved father or fathering figure in their lives have better outcomes than students who do not. Positive reading outcomes that are separate and independent of mothers, cultural competency, behavior, cognition and even empathy are all outcomes that can be supported by involved fathers and fathering figures. Ransaw not only articulates that father can make a positive difference in the lives of children when they feel welcomed, he also provides examples of successful fathering involvement school programs as part of his policy recommendations.

Career and technical education (CTE) have long been a hallmark of the American high school experience in most communities. Further, it has been a major point of policy discussion when it comes to funding and curricular needs related to this area. These programs availability and popularity have ebbed and flowed over the last five decades but continue to be a focal point of policy decisions. In Avery Newton's chapter *Advancing the Promise of Career Programming in High Schools: Critical components of driving key student outcomes*, she explores opportunities afforded by casual research in the CTE space. She concludes with three policy recommendations which include: (1) reconsider high school graduation requirements at the state level; (2) cultivating systems for college access and matriculation for students to earn college credit while in high school; and (3) creating a coalition of policymakers and influencers to strategize locally appropriate methods for embedding the critical components identified above at the school level.

Over the years, California has produced several key educational policy studies. In the K–12 arena, Susan Wilson's *California Dreaming* (2003) which covered the "math war" that focused on curricular reform, but provided valuable lessons for policymakers across the country. The same is true of Daisy Gonzales and Nadia Leal-Carrillo's chapter *Authentic Leadership: Lessons from workforce diversification efforts in California's community colleges*. In this chapter, the authors tackle the opportunity gaps that disproportionately impact African America, Latino, and Native American students in the California Community College system. In particular, only 48 percent of students who enter a community college complete a degree, certificate, or transfer to a four-year university within six years. To combat this, chancellor's Office (CO) examined the impact of faculty and staff diversity on student success and convened a Diversity, Equity, and Inclusion Task force (Task force), to develop a cultural change framework to increase faculty and staff diversity as an integral component of the system's Vision for Success (California Community Colleges Chancellor's Office, 2017). Specifically, the Task force theory of action asserted that faculty and staff diversity is a driver for the educational achievement and the social mobility of students, and that students who benefit from a diverse faculty are "better educated and better prepared for leadership, citizenship, and professional competitiveness" (Taylor et al., 2010). The result was a set of policy recommendations to implement and form existing faculty practices.

As we move into the next section of the book, we begin to look at the role of philanthropy and its engagement within the education and policy sphere. The first chapter that we look at is Christopher Shearer's chapter: A new north star: The role of progressive policy reform in re-envisioning more equitable educational goals, assessments, and accountability. This chapter, Shearer argues for the emergence of a domestic educational model for coherent systemic realignment, whether within a single influential state or across several. Ultimately, building the capacity and moment for large scale, progressive educational reform. He concludes that Progressive reformers are committed to widening the aperture of the K–12 education system for greater outcomes, to achieving equitable educational experiences and attainment, and to incorporating what is being learned about effective school leadership and teaching into student-centered instruction. The chapter makes several key recommendations to beginning the policy reform discussion.

Building from this push for large scale educational reform, we turn to the actual grantmaking process and the role of private foundations. Over the last several decades, the role of private philanthrope has greatly changed and has become less focused on local one-off changes and more focused on policy-level wide scale reform (Boggs, 2014). Based on these changes, philanthrope has ways of engaging in the policy arena that extremely powerful in shaping outcomes. Caitlan Cole's chapter: *Redistributing Power Through Grantmaking*, makes a case for private foundations to engage in community-led grantmaking. The key to this argument surrounds the role of equity and authenticity. The chapter looks at current trends and then turns to redistributing power in grantmaking to eliminate injustice. Cole concludes with a series of suggested policy redirections to begin the conversation of foundation reform.

The 1619 Project and Critical Race Theory, *CRT* have become one of the most hotly debated topics in recent education policy history. Theodore S. Ransaw, and Khalid Mumin have provided a much-needed history of the creation, controversy, and consternation surrounding the 1619 and the outcry to keep CRT out of schools. Arguments have become so heated that there does not seem to be any light at the end of the tunnel. Debates about the 1619 Project and CRT have become so heated that many school districts have asked for federal protection for its school board meetings. Ransaw and Mumin amplify what may be a glimmer of hope. Their policy recommendation is for school districts to model a novel initiative created and implemented by the Reading Pennsylvania School District in Reading Pennsylvania. The Reading Equity and Anti-Racism Resolution address systematic bias and institutional racism, historically underserved and marginalized groups and suggests equity teams to identify concrete actions to support diverse voices. The association of awareness and accountability in a school district policy has the potential to make school success a reality for all its students.

This next chapter departs from what has been a U.S. centered look at issues of policy and leadership, and turns to a larger global perspective. Kyle Chong and Devarajan's chapter: *Seeking Clarity and Justice: An analysis of India and the PRC's national education policies through a global lens of the UN sustainability development goals*, takes China and India to task on what the authors see as stepped up nationalistic and regionalist violence against minoritized religious and ethnic communities through their respective educational policies. Specifically, the authors state that India's New Education Policy *NEP*, (2020), and the PRC's *Outline of China's National Plan for Medium and Long-term Education Reform and Development, CNP,* (2010) claim to align and advance United Nations Sustainable Development Goal Four: Quality education (SDG4), which seeks to "ensure inclusive and equitable equality education and promote lifelong learning opportunities for all" (United Nations, 2015, p. 4) is not happening. As a result, the authors make several recommendations to overcome these inequities. Keeping within the intent of having readers interrogate and problematize education policy, our final chapter is a thought piece that begs the reader to question the philosophical and actual outcomes of Western education. Roger Duncan's chapter, *And Finally Delores, Do You Ever Question The Nature of Your Reality,* recommends that we return to traditional teaching and learning methods of education as well as value their wisdom. The method of this transformational policy recommendation is to include cultural Truths like rites of passage in schools. Including indigenous cultural Truth's with a capital T, eliminates the banking model of education where teachers are just merely depositors of irrelevant Western knowledge that does not help students of color thrive in the places where they live.

We hope that this volume offers the opportunity to read contributions from researchers who like to make a ruckus and policymakers that are not afraid to shake things up a bit. We also wanted to provide space for authors to take intellectual risks and to be on the cutting edge of policy reform. *Emerging Trends in Education Policy: Unapologetic progressive conversations,* was created to challenge established practices and form new pathways to solve today›s education problems. We feel that we have achieved that goal.

—*Theodore S. Ransaw and Brian Boggs*

SECTION I

ROLE OF EDUCATION SYSTEMS

Danielle, an emerging leader and policy consultant at Green & Associates, rushed up a towering set of steps to a striking university building. She wasn't running late; she was excited about her first-ever Education Policy Fellowship Program (EPFP) session. Forcing herself to stop and catch her breath, Danielle recalled how she got here. A few months ago, her boss, Dr. Murphey, recommended her for the experience. She remembered emphatically saying "yes" before he could finish explaining the program. Danielle's interest in education policy, which shaped her motivation to participate in her state's EPFP site, tracked back to when her sister, a middle school principal, begged her to get a substitute teaching license after one of the school's educators decided not to return following the COVID-19 pandemic. Teachers were scarce in the district, and Danielle's sister was looking for anyone qualified to help. As soon as she stepped into this substitute role, Danielle realized her love of the students and teaching. Although she was happy to go to whichever classroom she was assigned, Danielle's favorite class was adaptive physical education. The students were so appreciative of her presence after the previous year marred by teacher turnover that they cheered whenever she walked into the room. Moreover, they were glad to see her friendly face and felt cared for when she listened to them. The students' sentiments were reciprocated. Danielle loved seeing them too. Just as importantly, these pupils drove her interest in the EPFP experience. She cared for them, but she felt underqualified to understand and meet all the needs laid out in their Individualized Education Programs. Danielle felt similarly about other groups of students. She wanted to be a resource for LGBTQ students realizing their authentic identities, struggling readers at risk of falling behind, and a generation of kids traumatized by the pandemic. That said, she needed a peer network to support her, leadership skills to champion these students, and greater knowledge of their experiences. Hence, Dr. Murphey's recommendation of her for this year's cohort felt like a serendipitous godsend. Recalling her excitement to get to the session, Danielle raced up the remaining stairs, proceeded down a long, bustling hallway, and stepped into the meeting. She looked forward to learning more about the role of education systems in supporting the many students she valued and meeting like-minded education leaders that could help her realize her vision.

CHAPTER 1

AN INCLUSIVE SOCIETY FOR ALL THROUGH INCLUSIVE EDUCATION FOR STUDENTS WITH DISABILITIES

Rosanne Renauer

Michigan State University

INTRODUCTION

People with disabilities and notably students with disabilities (SWD) are often an overlooked marginalized population. While Individuals with Disabilities Education Act (IDEA) legislation has addressed the civil rights of all students to receive a free and appropriate public education, the educational standard for an inclusive education has yet to be reached (Rapp & Arndt, 2012). Education that excludes and segregates is education that perpetuates discrimination against marginalized populations.

Today, more than one billion people in the world live with some form of disability and nearly 200 million experience considerable difficulties in functioning (Bickenbach, J., 2011). In 2019, according to the Centers for Disease Control,

Emerging Trends in Education Policy: Unapologetic Progressive Conversations,
pages 3–15.
Copyright © 2023 by Information Age Publishing
www.infoagepub.com

about one in 4 or 26.7% of U.S. adults—61 million Americans—had a disability that impacted major life activities. Disability is an evolving and complex concept. In a somewhat groundbreaking effort in 2001, the World Health Organization developed the International Classification of Functioning, Disability and Health (ICF) defining disability as the interaction between persons with impairments and attitudinal and environmental barriers that hinder their full and effective participation in society on an equal basis with others (World Health Organization, 2001). This is in sharp contrast to the historical medical model focusing on internal deficits. Barriers to full social and economic inclusion of persons with disabilities include inaccessible physical environments and transportation, the unavailability of assistive devices and technologies, non-adapted means of communication, gaps in service delivery, and discriminatory prejudice and stigma in society. When education is inclusive, so are the concepts of civic participation, employment, and community life (OSF, 2019). Further development of key inclusive education related laws, policies, and strategies at the national level is essential to improve the life outcomes of marginalized groups.

OVERVIEW

This chapter identifies program considerations and recommends specific policies for building inclusive education systems that improve the adult life outcomes of *all* students. These policies are: (1) the required use of universal design (2) specialized teacher training in disability (3) development of scaffolded curriculum design emphasizing disability and (4) formalized networking systems that integrate vocational rehabilitation counselors into postsecondary systems to provide transition services to students with disabilities. The disability population has long been oppressed using a definition popularized by Young in her seminal work, Justice and the Politics of Difference. She describes the five faces of oppression as exploitation (occurs within the process of labor), marginalization (the inability or unwillingness of the system to incorporate the group into political, economic, and cultural life), powerlessness (lack of authority over one's own life), cultural imperialism (demeaning of the group by majority values), and violence (random or organized attacks on members of a group) (1990). Young adds, (1990, p. 8), "Marginals are people the system of labor cannot or will not use." While civil rights legislation such as the American with Disabilities Act (ADA) has attempted to address marginalization of people with disabilities, the long-term social, economic, cultural, and political realities continue to result in students and adults with disabilities who remain excluded. As evidenced by the Black Lives Matter demonstrations, raising awareness is one step, a major step, to changing the status quo of marginalized people (Lebron, C.J., 2017). A change in society requires a change in consciousness (Sukhow, 2020). Awareness -and action- are required if there is to be substantial change in the adult life outcomes of SWD who experience marginalization and continued poor quality of life in employment, postsecondary education, community participation and social activities. The usual vehicles of culture change are teaching and learning; the transformation of values and beliefs are conveyed through education. Once those values and beliefs are enculturated, actions become predicated on them and cultures change (Bornbaum, et al., 2015). Systems and institutions teach by example their deeply held values: inclusion, segregation, exclusion. The disproportionate representation of minority students, especially African American, American Indian and students in poverty in special education and segregated settings can be viewed as a reflection of the current social mores of our educational institutions (di Valenzuela, et al 2006). Acknowledging the likely contribution to institutionalized racism, the K–12 public education system has the potential to change the narrative, to vastly improve the adult lives of all marginalized groups, and specifically SWD. If we are to maximize the contributions of *all* citizens, education must raise awareness and assertively establish values of inclusion, access, opportunity, and social justice throughout a student's interaction with the system. Some may argue that inculcating democratic values in children is not the responsibility of schools, however, as Horace Mann, a 19nth century pioneer of American public schools opined, "Education, beyond all other devices of human origin is the great equalizer of the conditions of men, the balance-wheel of the social machinery." (Cahalan, 2013, p. 6)

The Benefits of Including Everyone

Why is inclusion, and ultimately access and opportunity, of students with disabilities such an important concept? Inclusion acknowledges the rights of every citizen in a democracy to belong, it establishes commitment to the value of diversity and emphasizes an egalitarian approach. It makes us better. It makes the life outcomes experienced by those who are engaged in inclusion better. Inclusive education as a belief must take hold of our collective psyche and be practiced fully without fail to realize the potential of all students. Inclusion encompasses policies to promote equality and nondiscrimination by improving the access of all people, including persons with disabilities, to services and benefits such as education, health, social protection, infrastructure, affordable energy, employment, financial services, and productive assets (World Bank, 2020).

The inclusion of students with disabilities in mainstream settings does not have a significant negative impact on students without disabilities (Farrell et al., 2007). In fact, findings demonstrate that inclusive education results in positive effects on social competence and social interactions for both students with and without disabilities (Nisbet, 1994). Students without disabilities demonstrate reduced fear of human differences accompanied by increased comfort and awareness, growth in social cognition, improvements in self-concept, development of personal principles and warm and caring friendships (Nisbet, p. 37, 1994,). For the student with a disability, the benefits are numerous. Students with disabilities will develop regular peer friendships, a positive self-concept, a positive attitude toward school and will be motivated to achieve academically (Gameros, 1995). Despite the passage of IDEA thirty years ago, equitable life outcomes for students with disabilities compared to their non-disabled peers, have not been achieved (Newman, et al., 2011). The 1990 IDEA, the legal foundation for inclusive education, mandates the right to a free and appropriate public education in the least restrictive environment for students with disabilities (20 U.S.C. 1415). While IDEA legislation has created substantial positive changes for SWD, progress at the secondary level is often mired in the immense special education bureaucracy. While the framework exists for achieving equitable life outcomes through inclusive education, much more needs to be done to reach this goal. Inclusive, quality education resulting in societal systems change can be optimized by implementing four strategies that taken together create a new policy framework for inclusion of STW: universal design for learning, teacher training, curriculum design and the innovative use of formal networking for effective transition services for SWD.

Critical Disability Theory: A Framework

These policy recommendations are grounded in critical disability theory (CDT) which refers to a diverse, interdisciplinary set of theoretical approaches. CDT reevaluates social, political, and intellectual explanatory paradigms used to understand the lived experience of people with disabilities and considers potential ways forward for social, political, and economic change. The task then of critical disability theory is to analyze disability as a cultural, historical, relative, social, and political phenomenon (Hall, 2019). CDT, constructed by disability scholars, borrows from the work of critical race theory, and offers a structural framework for social change acknowledging the complexities associated with disability, human rights, and equality. Moving from a medical model to a social model of disability supported the establishment of CDT principles, especially the major concept of disability as a social construction (Oliver, 1996) and the influence of ablism as a binary or us- them phenomena. Ableism is the belief that being without a disability, impairment, or chronic illness is the norm. Another grounding principle of CDT is the belief that people with disabilities have a unique voice and complex experience (Gleeson, 1999). This means that the complexity of disability cannot be reduced to a label or to the specific impairment that defines what the person can or cannot do. An important concept in CDT recognizes that disability should be viewed as part of a continuum of human variation (Asch, 2001). Instead of maintaining the dichotomy—disabled or not disabled—we should determine how to modify the environments so that they are not disabling and consider a continuum of abilities (Asch, 2001). CDT theorists are united by the belief that people with disabilities are undervalued and discriminated against and this cannot be changed simply through liberal or neo-liberal legislation and policy (Meekosha & Shuttleworth, 2009). Applying a framework of critical disability theory, the intent of this chapter is to identify, consider and recommend strategies constituting integrated policy that when implemented eliminate the marginalization of people with disabilities through social, political, and economic change. The elimination of marginalization relies on full inclusion and opportunity for everyone and requires analysis leading to action.

Policy Recommendations

Education policy recommendations to further inclusive education for students with disabilities that result in societal and systems change are: (1) the adoption of universal design for learning principles, (2) required teacher training on disability awareness and disability history, (3) curriculum design that introduces the concepts of disability to all students in a graduated manner throughout the K–12 experience and finally (4) the addition of vocational rehabilitation counselors to the current public school personnel contingency to assure effective transition of students into adult life. The consistent and integrated implementation of these policy changes will foster a societal appreciation of the value and worth of students with disabilities AND ultimately promote the value and worth of all citizens. This chapter recommends utilizing the identified four components to accomplish the goal of an inclusive and equitable education for students with disabilities that ultimately contributes to an inclusive and equitable society for everyone.

Universal Design for Learning

Universal Design for Learning (UDL) is a framework that can be used for inclusive education. (Rose, 2000). Learning through universal design and accessible technology is essential for students with disabilities. Without access, they would not gain the skills needed to complete their secondary or post-secondary degrees and obtain employment and a life of self-sufficiency. Mainstreaming and UDL principles can and should work harmoniously with technology to expand opportunities for access, participation, and progress.

The Higher Education Opportunities Act of 2008 is the first federal US legislation to define UDL. It is a scientifically valid framework for guiding educational practice that (A) provides flexibility in the ways information is presented, in the ways students respond or demonstrate knowledge and skills, and in the ways students are engaged; and (B) reduces challenges in instruction, provides appropriate accommodations, supports, and challenges, and maintains high achievement expectations for all students, including students with disabilities and students who are limited English proficient (Public Law 110-315). Simply put, UDL offers various strategies to differentiate instruction, integrate flexible options during instruction, and implement instructional strategies to engage and motivate all learners (CAST, 2021). UDL can inform effective, innovative uses of technology in the inclusive classroom at the secondary level and is growing in popularity. Overall, UDL-based instruction has the potential to increase engagement and access to general education curriculum for students with disabilities and improve students' academic and social outcomes. (Ok, et al., 2017). It is a relatively new model that encourages teachers to make their classes more accessible to students with disabilities by developing curricula that are flexible and customizable (Higbee, 2003).

While UDL is still a relatively new concept, it is time to expand its implementation in keeping with its definition. The value of physical universal design such as curb cuts has already been proven to be of benefit for all. If we are to succeed in designing educational spaces in a manner that takes into consideration the needs of all learners, then we must engage in a paradigm shift that places the inclusion of all students at the core of educational planning. Rather than an extension of a model for accommodation, UDL should be perceived as a means for actively engaging all students in the learning process, regardless of age, gender, race, religion, ethnic origin, language, social class, sexual orientation, or disability (Barajas & Higbee, 2003). True systems change relies on vision often tempered by fiscal constraints. The costs of inclusion are always significantly less or at least not more than special education (Biklen, 2020). Inclusive education incorporating UDL is now occurring in some US communities; Schools of Promise offer a successful, financially viable, whole school reform model that puts belonging at the center of its philosophy and operations (Biklen, 2020).

Teacher Training

Teachers' attitudes toward inclusion are often based on the practical implementation of inclusive education rather than a specific ideology and understanding of inclusiveness. A 2015 study found that four teacher attributes-age, gender, teaching self-efficacy and training collectively explained 42% of the variability in teachers' attitude toward including students with disabilities (Vaz, et al.). The 2011 World Report on Disability emphasizes the importance of appropriate training for mainstream teachers if they are to be confident and competent in teaching students with diverse educational needs. The report notes that teacher education should be about attitudes and values, not just knowledge and skills (Bickenbach, 2011).

In India, the inclusive education legislation passed in 2011 includes the following language: Develop and establish an inclusive undergraduate and postgraduate degree in education which trains all teachers to cater to the needs of a child with disability in an inclusive classroom; develop an inclusive curriculum based on the principles of non-discrimination and appreciation of diversity and tolerance; suggest measures for the adoption and integration of the inclusive curriculum in mainstream education; and monitor progress. According to Bhattacharya, additional language absolves the government of the need to provide teacher training due to feasibility and cost, but institutions of higher education continually offer a multiplicity of ways to build skills. He concludes that UDL as a practice is a subversive strategy to bring about a radical change in the way learning/teaching takes place and must become part of the curriculum. Although disabled students are the primary beneficiaries of such fundamental change, it is only through subverting the linear thinking and homogeneity that we can bring about a radical change in the general education system (Bhattacharya, 2017). In the US, there are comparable hurdles to overcome in conducting widespread teacher training in universal design, inclusion, diversity, and tolerance, however, if we are to generate widespread social change, this is exactly what must occur. Training teachers in inclusive education, disability awareness, disability history and the Americans with Disabilities Act provides a powerful context for mainstreaming and inclusion. The application of critical disability theory to teacher training offers a means to incorporate the recognition of disability as a social construct into the postsecondary teacher training curriculum. Sustained training and attention to developing general education teacher competencies in basic and advanced disability awareness can be expected to facilitate widespread systems change and eventual societal change.

Curriculum Design

Among the broad reasons for teaching a curriculum are to transmit the culture, to improve society or to realize the potential of individual students (Walker, 2002). Walker reminds us that identities and lives are shaped by what we study. Each nation teaches its own version of history. Surely this history must include key concepts of disability and a common foundation of disability knowledge. Imagine if every school year included a module that built progressively on the previous year to teach concepts of diversity, social justice, disability history. Critical disability theory might surmise based on Walker's statements that a disability curriculum can be expected to transmit the culture and improve society leading to greater awareness, less ableism and appreciation of an inclusive society. Attitudes towards persons with disabilities change but primarily depend on the type and the degree of disability, including physical, psychosocial disorders or intellectual disabilities. Researchers demonstrated that adolescents changed attitudes from negative to positive toward persons with intellectual disabilities after learning from a packaged curriculum, the "Join Us" Education Program for Special Olympics, (Wieczorek et al., 2019). A curriculum based on informed empathy and focused on the experiences of persons with disabilities can also result in more positive attitudes toward and advocacy for people with disabilities (Miller, 2013). The Special Olympics Unified Champion Schools program is an example of a curriculum promoting social inclusion by implementing inclusive sports, inclusive youth leadership opportunities and whole school engagement (Siperstein, et al., 2019).

Integration of academic curriculum design changes using grade specific modules focused on disability concepts, behaviors and impacts beginning in kindergarten and continuing each year is an exciting vision. Curriculum design or redesign is not an easy task as nearly everyone has a stake in it and therefore wants a voice in shaping it (Walker, 2002). Given the current challenges within our society and the dizzying changes in technology and education, curriculum design that incorporates the history of disability and diversity within a diverse and social justice context may be welcomed by today's educators. A transformation, or more realistically, a tweaking of the K–12 curriculum can benefit both teachers and students through building disability awareness, developing skills in facilitating inclusiveness and responding to calls for relevancy. Strong, progressive, collaborative leadership within general and special education and legislative advocacy is required to mandate social justice and disability rights history curricula as a policy requirement.

Innovative Networking

The nation's primary employment support program for people with a broad spectrum of disabilities is the $3 billion federal state partnership program known as the public Vocational Rehabilitation (VR) program. Originally established to assist returning veterans in the early 20th century, the program celebrated its 100-year anniversary in 2020 (Chamberlain, 2018). State VR agencies have evolved and seem well-positioned to assist people with disabilities in securing gainful employment (Stapleton and Martin, 2012). As a long-term educational partner and transition services provider, VR counselors within state agencies perform a critical role in delivering high quality transition services to youth with disabilities both during and after their exit from secondary school (Stodden, 2003). With the passage of the Workforce Innovation and Opportunity Act in 2014, the VR system is required to spend 15% of its funds in support of pre employment services for SWD. Pre-employment transition services are "required activities" specified in the Rehabilitation Act provided to SWD in need of such services. VR agencies are required to provide or arrange for the provision of pre-employment transition services for all SWD in need of such services, regardless of whether they have applied and been determined eligible for the VR program (Taylor, 2019, US DOE, 2019). This mandate offers an incredibly strong systemic opportunity to partner with education to address the skills needed to support quality employment life outcomes for SWD.

VR has a strong history of developing community networks and resources not readily available to educators. As workforce development professionals with the requisite transition and inclusion expertise, the VR counselor often fulfills a "bridge" role between the student, the community, and the employer (Kline & Kurtz, 2014). Through on site and now online presence, the VR counselor can develop greater familiarity and longer-term relationships with all students and will enhance the quality of transition and placement services provided. Within the school culture, the vocational rehabilitation counselor can exercise greater efficiencies and offer better access to address and support the adult life expectancies of SWD. The VR counselor is also in an excellent position to offer transition consultation to teachers regarding SWD.

Transition to adult roles is a complex process that *all* young people must negotiate, and a myriad of factors work together to influence students' lives after school completion (Benz et al., 2000; Kohler, 1993; Wehmeyer & Schwartz, 1997). In some cases, educational and service systems facilitate the preparation for post-school outcomes and in other cases leave it to chance or impede the process by establishing barriers, wasting instructional time, or limiting access (Kohler, Field, 2003). Devlieger and Trach (1999) found that interagency collaboration and support for individual students in transition and their families is a factor so important that when done well, it facilitates achievement of transition goals, and when done poorly, it limits or impedes those goals.

Given these findings and the policy expectations imposed by WIOA, it is timely and crucial to strengthen and embed the collaborative role of the vocational rehabilitation counselor in the school setting. Public education is strategically poised to embrace and include VR as a pivotal full partner in the transition of all SWD into adult life. This is beginning in some states as discussed in the Transition Guide to Postsecondary Education and Employment for Students and Youth with Disabilities (2020). The current federal VR program can loan staff to schools for the express purposes stated, continuing to cover VR counselor salaries, and creating seamless systems for SWD. Another option to build and strengthen the provision of pre employment and other transition services is the recruitment, acceptance and hiring of VR aka vocational counselors by the schools. While funding of positions is typically a concern, VR services may be added to the list of funded support services such as OT, speech, counseling usually provided in statute. Creative blending of funds and space sharing may also offer resources that support stronger partnerships. Strong visionary leadership at the state level is required in public education to investigate, collaborate, and implement these proposed linkages systemically.

CONCLUSIONS AND IMPLICATIONS

Education institutions support oppressive structures by separating and labeling disabled students from non-disabled students, through separate structures (entry points, classrooms) and specially designed curricula, and through "testing and evaluation biased toward the functional needs of the dominant culture" (Charlton, 1998, p. 33). A systematic and continuous approach to mainstreaming disability and enabling the effective participation of persons with disabilities is necessary if inclusion and full participation of SWD is to occur.

In the context of the US civil rights movement in the 50s and 60s, there emerged a parallel movement in the broader disability community for self-determination and equal treatment under the law. Inspired by black civil rights pioneers, the disability community came together to demand inclusion and freedom. Consisting of disability advocacy organizations, rehabilitation professionals, policy makers and academics, this community recognized principles which came to be known as independent living or rehabilitation philosophy. The principles include self-determination, societal contribution, holistic approach to rehabilitation, focus on residual assets and capabilities, the intrinsic value of each human being, environmental restructuring to fit people, dignity of risk, transdisciplinary team functioning, normalization, reality factors, criterion of ultimate functioning, and coping and adaptation (Maki, Riggar, 2003). Independent living philosophy is mirrored in the principles of creative disability theory acknowledging the individuality of the disability experience, the nature of disability as a social construct and notably the dignity and equality of the individual. The independent living principles became the basis for the Rehabilitation Act of 1973 known as the "billion-dollar program" that espoused greater consumer involvement and empowerment for people with disabilities. The disability rights movement activated at Berkeley in the 70s took decades of direct political action and lobbying to achieve remarkable gains in civil rights, transportation, public accommodations, housing and independent living, employment and education for people and students with disabilities. Disability rights and independent living philosophy set the stage for the Americans with Disabilities Act of 1990 (ADA, essentially a civil rights act mandating accessibility and the use of reasonable accommodations for otherwise qualified individuals (McMahon, 2016). IDEA, the landmark legislation passed in 1975 to provide education for students with disabilities was last authorized in 2004. Implementing the policy recommendations espoused within this chapter offer an integrated strategy for improving not only the outcomes of students with disabilities as they enter adult life but equally important building a 'critical mass' of citizens within our communities who support equity, inclusion and understand the civil rights and contributory value of everyone within society.

There is still much to be done to achieve a truly inclusive educational system that works for everyone. Booth (2003) notes: One of the greatest problems facing the world today is the growing number of persons who are excluded from meaningful participation in the economic, social, political, and cultural life of their communities. Such a society is neither efficient nor safe (p. 3). SWDs are being excluded from meaningful participation in the economic, social, political, and cultural life of their communities. The integrated policy recommendations are designed to remedy that by applying the principles of CDT and recognizing the universality and individuality of disability. Each tenet of the four recommendations contributes to that. Moving away from an ableist construction of normality to the use of universal design in learning affirms the value of learning for each learner regardless of disability. General education teacher training on disability awareness and history is supported by a CDT framework for positive social change that considers the individuality of the disability experience and does not diminish disability as anything other than a shared human experience. A graduated curriculum throughout the K–12 instructional experience of students offers a view of disability through the CDT lens that assures an integrated broader understanding of the individuality and complexity of disability. Finally, the role of the VR practitioner as a support to SWD will increase the likelihood that meaningful employment is obtained contributing to the economic, social, and political realities of SWD who become adults with disabilities. CDT envisions a rethinking of the current explanatory systems used with SWD and offers an expanded egalitarian perspective that incorporates the desire for change leading to systemic, economic, social, cultural, and political change. Meaningful participation of marginalized citizens, particularly students with disabilities, in the economic, social, political, and cultural life of their communities can be assured through the implementation of an integrated four pronged inclusive education policy designed to address and improve their life outcomes.

REFERENCES

Asch, A. (2001). Critical race theory, feminism, and disability: Reflections on social justice and personal identity. *Ohio State Law Journal, 62*(1), 391–423.

Barajas, H. L., & Higbee, J. L. (2003). Where do we go from here? Universal Design as a model for multicultural education. In J. L. Higbee (Ed.), *Curriculum transformation and disability: Implementing universal design in higher Education* (pp. 285–290). Center for Research in Developmental Education and Urban Literacy, General College, University of Minnesota.

Bhattacharya, T. (2017). Adoption of universal design for learning for meaningful inclusion. In D. Sonpal, S. Prasad, & S. Vaishnav (Eds.), *Child and disability* (pp. 404–424). Prabhat Publishing House.

Bickenbach, J. (2011). The world report on disability. *Disability & Society, 26*(5), 655–658.

Biklen, D. (2020). Presuming competence, belonging, and the promise of inclusion: The US experience. *PROSPECTS, 49*(3), 233–247.

Booth, T., Nes, K., & Strømstad, M. (Eds.). (2003). *Developing inclusive teacher education*. Routledge.

Bornbaum, C. C., Day, A. M., Izaryk, K., Morrison, S. J., Ravenek, M. J., Sleeth, L. E., & Skarakis-Doyle, E. (2015). Exploring use of the ICF in health education. *Disability and Rehabilitation, 37*(2), 179–186.

Benz, M. R., Lindstrom, L., & Yovanoff, P. (2000). Improving graduation and employment outcomes of students with disabilities: Predictive factors and student perspectives. *Exceptional Children, 66*(4), 509–529.

Cahalan, M. (2013). W*idening participation in higher education in the United States of America*. Institute for the Study of Opportunity in Higher Education, HEFCE and OFFA. https://www.voced.edu.au/content/ngv:59471

Center for Applied Special Technology. (2021). *About universal design for learning*. http://www.cast.org

Chamberlain, T. (2018). *Individual, agency, and state economic characteristics: a comparative analysis across state-federal vocational rehabilitation agencies*. The University of Iowa ProQuest Dissertations Publishing, 2018. 10838008. https://www.proquest.com/openview/b7116bdd59470ac1f6ca8093039657a7/1?pq-origsite=gscholar&cbl=18750

Devlieger, P., & Trach, J. (1999). Meditation as a transition process: The impact on post-school employment outcomes. *Exceptional Children, 65*, 507–523.

di Valenzuela, J. S., Copeland, S. R., Qi, C. H., & Park, M. (2006). Examining educational equity: Revisiting the disproportionate representation of minority students in special education. *Exceptional Children, 72*(4), 425–441.

Farell, P., Dyson, A., Polat, F., Hutcheson, G., & Gallannaugh, F. (2007). Inclusion and achievement in mainstreaming schools. *European Journal of Special Needs Education, 22*(2), 131–146.

Gameros, P. (1995). The visionary principal and inclusion of students with disabilities. *NASSP bulletin, 79*(568), 15–17.

Gleeson, B. (1999). *Geographies of disability.* Routledge.

Hall, M. C. (2019). *Critical disability theory.* Stanford Encyclopedia of Philosophy.

Higbee, J. L. (2003). *Curriculum transformation and disability: Implementing Universal Design in higher education.* University of Minnesota: Center for Research on Developmental Education and Urban Literacy.

Higher Education Opportunity Act of 2008: Pub L No 110-315, § 102 & §103(a) (24) (2008)

Kline, K. M., & Kurz, C. A. (2014). Collaboration between rehabilitation counselors and secondary educational institutions to optimize successful outcomes for high school students with disabilities. *Journal of Applied Rehabilitation Counseling, 45*(1), 18–24.

Kohler, P. D. (1993). Best practices in transition: Substantiated or implied? *Career Development for Exceptional Individuals, 16,* 107–121.

Kohler, P. D., & Field, S. (2003). Transition-focused education: Foundation for the future. *The Journal of Special Education, 37*(3), 174–183.

Lebron, C. J. (2017). *The making of Black Lives Matter: A brief history of an idea.* Oxford University Press.

Meekosha, H., & Shuttleworth, R. (2009). What's so 'critical' about critical disability studies?. *Australian Journal of Human Rights, 15*(1), 47–75.

Miller, S. R. (2013). A curriculum focused on informed empathy improves attitudes toward persons with disabilities. *Perspectives on Medical Education, 2*(3), 114–125.

Newman, L., Wagner, M., Knokey, A. M., Marder, C., Nagle, K., Shaver, D., & Wei, X. (2011). *The post-high school outcomes of young adults with disabilities up to 8 years after high school. A report from the National Longitudinal Transition Study-2* (NLTS2, NCSER 2011-3005). SRI International. http://nlts2.org/reports/

Nisbet, J. A., Jorgensen, C., & Power, S. (1994). Systems change directed at inclusive education. In V. J. Bradeley, J. W. Ashbaugh, & B. C. Blaney (Eds.), *Creating individual supports for people with developmental disabilities: A mandate for change at many levels* (pp. 213–236). Paul H. Brookes Publishing.

Ok, M. W., Rao, K., Bryant, B. R., & McDougall, D. (2017). Universal design for learning in pre-k to grade 12 classrooms: A systematic review of research. *Exceptionality, 25*(2), 116–138.

Oliver, M. (1996). *Understanding disability: From theory to practice.* St. Martin's Press.

Open Society Foundations. (May 2019). *The value of inclusive education* www.opensocietyfoundations.org/explainers/value-inclusive-education

Office of Special Education and Rehabilitative Services (OSERS), U.S. Department of Education. (2020). *A Transition Guide to Postsecondary Education and Employment for Students and Youth with Disabilities.* https://ncrtm.ed.gov/postsecondary-transition-guide-august-2020.pdf

Public Law 110-315 110th Congress, August 14, 2008, https://uscode.house.gov/statutes/pl/110/315.pdf

Rapp, W. H., & Arndt, K. L. (2012). *Teaching everyone: An introduction to inclusive education.* Brookes Publishing Company.

Rocco, T. S. (2005). *From disability studies to critical race theory: Working towards critical disability theory.* Adult Education Research Conference. https://newprairiepress.org/aerc/2005/papers/ 17

Rose, D. (2000). Universal design for learning. *Journal of Special Education Technology, 15*(3), 45–49.

Siperstein, G. N., McDowell, E. D., Jacobs, H. E., Stokes, J. E., & Cahn, A. L. (2019). Unified extracurricular activities as a pathway to social inclusion in high schools: AJMR. *American Journal on Intellectual and Developmental Disabilities, 124*(6), 568–582. doi:http://dx.doi.org.proxy2.cl.msu.edu/10.1352/1944-7558-124.6.568

Stapleton, D. C., & Martin, F. (2012). *Vocational rehabilitation on the road to Social Security Disability: Longitudinal statistics from matched administrative data.* Michigan Retirement Research Center Research Paper. Paper No. 2012-269. https://papers.ssrn.com/sol3/papers.cfm?abstract_id=2206359

Stodden, R. A., Conway, M. A., & Chang, K. B. (2003). Findings from the study of transition, technology, and postsecondary supports for youth with disabilities: Implications for secondary school educators. *Journal of Special Education Technology, 18*(4), 29–44.

Sukhov, M. J. (2020). Herbert Marcuse on radical subjectivity and the "new activism": Today's climate and Black Lives Matter movements. *Radical Philosophy Review, 23*(2), 361–388.

Taylor, J. P., Whittenburg, H. N., Thoma, C. A., Gokita, T., & Pickover, G. S. (2019). Collaboration to Improve Employment Outcomes for Youth with Disabilities: Implications of the Pre-ETS Components of WIOA on IDEA Transition Requirements. *DADD Online, 6*(1), 38.

US Department of Education. (2019). *Increasing postsecondary opportunities and success for students and youth with disabilities.* https://www2.ed.gov/policy/speced/guid/increasing-postsecondary-opportunities-and-success-09-17-2019.pdf

Vaz, S., Wilson, N., Falkmer, M., Sim, A., Scott, M., Cordier, R., & Falkmer, T. (2015). Factors associated with primary school teachers' attitudes towards the inclusion of students with disabilities. *PloS one, 10*(8), e0137002.

Walker, D. F. (2002). *Fundamentals of curriculum: Passion and professionalism.* Routledge.

Wehmeyer, M., & Schwanz, M. (1997). Self-determination and positive adult outcomes: A follow-up study of youth with mental retardation or learning disabilities. *Exceptional Children, 63*, 245–255.

Wieczorek, M., Sadziak, A., & Matczak, D. (2019). Attitudes towards persons with intellectual disabilities in adolescents. *Journal of Education, Health and Sport, 9*(1), 106–123.

World Bank. (2020). *"Pivoting to inclusion : Leveraging lessons from the COVID-19 crisis for learners with disabilities.* Author. https://openknowledge.worldbank.org/handle/10986/34237

World Health Organization. (2001). *International classification of functioning, disability and health (ICF).* Geneva: World Health Organization.

Young, I. M. (1990). *Justice and the politics of difference.* Princeton University Press.

CHAPTER 2

EXPRESSION OF STUDENT LGBTQ FREE SPEECH FRAMEWORK

Amanda Miller and Brian Boggs

Michigan State University and University of Michigan-Dearborn

INTRODUCTION

We live in a society that challenges, insults, and oppresses the seemingly "different" of the herd. In particular, the LGBTQ community has experienced societal mistreatment, which is difficult enough for adults, but the forces of societal judgment can feel insurmountable for students who generally are minors and not completely aware of their rights in the adult-run educational establishment. It can be difficult to prevent students from acting unpleasant toward one another, but it is unjust for adults and the educational system to treat LGBTQ students differently because they are LGBTQ.

To understand the current First Amendment protections afforded to LGBTQ students who wish to express their sexual orientation or gender identity in K–12 public schools, we must explore key First Amendment cases in education. Specifically, there has been a series of First Amendment cases that have applied to K–12

Emerging Trends in Education Policy: Unapologetic Progressive Conversations,
pages 17–25.

17

schools. Based on the analysis of these cases, a general theory can be synthesized about when, how, and why LGBTQ student expression of gender identities or sexual orientation is a form of protected speech.

Free Speech and Schools—Foundational Cases

One of the most often quoted, but perhaps the least understood, phrases in educational law is: "It can hardly be argued that neither students or teachers shed their constitutional rights to freedom of speech or expression at the schoolhouse gate." Just because students enter a public school building does not mean they are without rights they would have outside of the school (*Tinker v. Des Moines Independent Community School District*, 1969). Educators are not lawyers and often inadvertently abrogate students' constitutional rights—maybe without even knowing it—in an effort to maintain the educational environment in the name of order. However, before getting into the elements specifically of how the First Amendment applies to schools, we must first look at what freedom of speech truly is.

The First Amendment states, "Congress shall make no law respecting an establishment of religion, or prohibiting the free exercise thereof; or abridging the freedom of speech, or of the press; or the right of the people peaceably to assemble, and to petition the government for a redress of grievances" (U.S. Const. amend. II). For our purposes, the key here is the freedom of speech clause. This has generally been interpreted to mean the right to express opinions or facts without restriction or censorship by the government (Black, 1951, p. 1065). As Alexander and Alexander (2012) argue, "even though the First Amendment does not actually use the word 'expression,' the Supreme Court has treated it as interchangeable with 'speech.'" However, the Constitution is silent on its application to schools or students, particularly those under 18 years of age or those who have not graduated from a public K–12 school.

This requires us to consider what a school is. Often, educators do not see themselves as part of government, but rather as some form of public service (Boggs, 2014). However, public schools are special purpose forms of government by legal definition and as such, fall under a category of government speech and are a type of public forum (Choper et al., 2019, p. 1047). Public schools are governmental property and carry out a government function, and thus have all the additional embedded rights that any public institution or public forum has including the application of the Bill of Rights. However, affording students their rights while in school has not always been seen as necessary or even required.

Schools have often had a great deal of latitude in the education and the care of students when in school. Part of this reason, highlighted by Essex (2016) is a concept called *in loco parentis,* which means 'in place of parents.' This concept stands for the principle that the school, and thus its personnel, stand in for the parent when the student is in school. However, they do not replace the parent and as such, the power the school wields in place of the parent is also not absolute. So, ultimately, while the school has considerable authority over the student, it is not unconditional—it is still government, and government still has to allow the students an expression of their rights, albeit limited. To fully understand this, we must turn to the landmark case of *Tinker* (1969) and consider the forums that the case creates.

The Tyranny of Tinker *and Restricted Forums*

Tinker is a bedrock case upon which all the other educational freedom of speech cases are built and has particular significance to the LGBTQ community. For, under this case, expression of sexual orientation—without heightened additional factors—cannot be seen as a disturbance of the educational environment.

In 1965, a group of students planned a public showing of their view on the Vietnam War—in particular, their desire for the war to come to an end. Students planned to wear black arm bands to school beginning in December and continuing for the remainder of the year. When the school principals of the school district learned of the plans, they adopted a policy prohibiting this display. Needless to say, all three students wore their arm bands and were suspended. While the lower courts ruled in favor of the school and upheld the constitutionality of the school authorities' action on the ground that it was reasonable to prevent a disturbance which might result from the wearing of the armbands, the United States Supreme Court saw this very differently (*Tinker*).

The Supreme Court stated that what the students were doing was really "closely akin to 'pure speech'" and was divorced from any conduct associated with it (*Tinker 505*). If a particular act does not substantially interfere with the educational environment, then it must be allowed, stating, "in our system, undifferentiated fear or apprehension of disturbance is not enough to overcome the right to freedom of expression" (*Tinker 508*). Further, "Any word spoken, in class, in the lunchroom, or on the campus, that deviates from the views of another person may start an argument or cause a disturbance" (Tinker 508). The Court concluded, and principals should consider in their leadership, that school officials are acting in the person of the state, or government—an often-forgotten perspective of the school official. Second, they have a duty to allow students to express themselves. Finally, that just because an idea or expression will be unpleasant and may cause discomfort and the expression of that discomfort by others, it does not rise to the level of substantially disrupting the educational environment.

Bethel School District *and Heightened Factors*

Bethel School District v. Fraser adds an additional dimension that was not present in the first. In 1986, a student, Matthew Fraser delivered a speech to his fellow classmates as part of a student rally related to student government (*Bethel* 675). During a nominating speech, Fraser referred to "his candidate in terms of elaborate, graphic, and explicit sexual metaphor" (*Bethel 678*). This speech, at best was a series of campy double entendres, was considered inappropriate by school administrators and a violation of the school rule prohibiting the use of obscene language. As a result, he was suspended for three days, and he sued the school.

The Court makes a sound distinction between expression and speech, but it goes a step further to define the role of public education as to "prepare pupils for citizenship in the Republic" (p. 681). Included in this must be "tolerance of divergent political and religious views, even when the views expressed may be unpopular ... but these 'fundamental values' must also take into account consideration of the sensibilities of others, and, in the case of a school, the sensibilities of fellow students" (p. 681). The Court holds that the student's use of language was sexually offensive to the teachers and the students, and they go on to say that it would be to anyone. Thus, this case puts limits on expression that may be offensive or vulgar to an objective legal standard.

Morse *and the Promotion of Illegal Acts*

In *Morse v. Frederick,* Joseph Frederick sued the principal for a violation of his First Amendment rights, when the principal allowed the students to cross the street to non-school property to watch the Olympic torch pass by on its way to Salt Lake. Joseph Frederick, a high school senior, unrolled a 14-foot banner that read "BONG HITS 4 JESUS." The principal confiscated the sign and suspended him for ten days, stating that the sign encouraged illegal drug use and was a violation of school policy. Frederick appealed to the superintendent who upheld the suspension. The superintendent stated Frederick "was not disciplined because the principal of the school 'disagreed' with the message, but because his speech appeared to advocate the use of illegal drugs." Further, the superintendent argued this kind of action in front of the student body interfered with the work of the school.

The Supreme Court found the banner to be "cryptic," with multiple, unclear meanings. However, "Principal Morse thought the banner would be interpreted by those viewing it as promoting illegal drug use, and that interpretation is plainly a reasonable one." There is a tension that educators must sort through in their engagement with students on expressing their freedom of speech rights. While students, and presumably teachers, do not shed their rights when they enter the school environment, these rights are not the same as an adult in a non-school public venue. Schools are a limited public forum. If Frederick had been an adult in a public, non-school forum, then his speech would have been protected.

Hazelwood School District *and Written Student Speech*

The last of the bedrock school law cases that we must examine to have a firm foundation on First Amendment rights and their application to LGBTQ students is *Hazelwood School District v. Kuhlmeier*. This case looks at what level of control a school district has in "exercis[ing] editorial control over the contents of a high school newspaper produced as part of the school's journalism curriculum" (p. 262).

Three students sued the school for deleting two pages of articles from an issue of the school newspaper (p. 262). The principal reviewed the newspaper before every publication, and in this issue took umbrage with articles discussing teenage pregnancy and the impacts of divorce on students. The Court states that schools are a closed forum, in many regards, unless the school purposefully opens itself up to a public (meaning outside of the school in this case) function. As a result, there are limits on student First Amendment speech and expression that would not normally be placed on adults in a non-school public forum.

The Court makes one last distinction in this case that is important for LGBTQ considerations of First Amendment rights: Schools cannot silence a student's personal expression that occurs on school grounds, so long as it is not disruptive (p. 261).

Asserting LGBTQ Identity in Education

The previous cases, all except the last one, were U.S. Supreme Court cases and have set the tone for almost everything that has followed involving school law and the First Amendment. As of the time of this writing, there has not a been a particular case before the U.S. Supreme Court that has dealt with K–12 LGBTQ student expression and speech that has provided a decisive set of tests or rules to apply. What follows are lower court decisions that apply these previous fundamental cases to issues raised by LGBTQ students. The previous case in conjunction with the cases presented below will provide more elements to incorporate into the overall framework presented in this paper, but may not be how the U.S. Supreme Court will rule when they do eventually take up a case on this narrow combination of K–12 schools and LGBTQ rights.

Fricke and Going to a Dance

This first case, *Fricke v. Lynch*, takes place at Cumberland High School in Rhode Island in 1980. A senior, Aaron Fricke, decided that he would like to ask another male student to be his date to the senior prom. In a previous year, another student wanted to bring a male student to the same event and was denied by the principal because the principal "fear[ed] that student reaction could lead to a disruption at the dance and possibly to physical harm" (p. 778). The Court stated that going to the dance, as a social event, has expressive content in and of itself and there is an "exchange of ideas [that] takes place at informal social functions" such as these (p. 780). Fricke testified during his injunction request that his attendance "would have a certain political element and would be a statement for equal rights and human rights" (p. 780).

The Court states that, "the school unquestionably has an important interest in student safety and has the power to regulate students' conduct to ensure safety," but the Court does not feel the school made any effort to increase security or take other precautions before outright denying Fricke the ability to attend (p. 781). The Court ultimately held, "a legitimate interest in school discipline does not outweigh student's right to peacefully express his views in appropriate time, place, and manner" (p. 782). Going back to the tyranny of *Tinker*, threshold for disturbance is much higher than most educators realize when implementing discipline when counterbalancing it with First Amendment rights.

McMillen *and the Second Dance*

A similar case is *McMillen v. Itawamba County School District*. In this case, Constance McMillen wishes to take another woman to the senior prom to which she was denied. When she met with the principal, the principal said the two could attend the dance, but had to go separately and not as a couple and would not be allowed to slow dance together. Further, if they made anyone uncomfortable, they would be "kicked out."

The Court seems sympathetic to her cause and begins its analysis by stating, "vigilant protection of constitutional freedoms is nowhere more vital than in the community of American schools" (p. 786). It continues, "The Fifth Circuit has established that the 'expression of one's identity and affiliation to unique social groups' may constitute 'speech' as envisioned by the First Amendment" and that "the United States Supreme Court has also held that 'states and their agencies, such as the defendant, cannot sit out homosexuals for special treatment, neither inclusive or [sic] exclusive'" (p. 787). The Court concludes on this element that the school district, "violated her First Amendment right by denying Constance's request to bring her girlfriend as her date to the prom" (p. 787).

The Court also addressed the issue of dressing in non-gender-conforming attire as a form of freedom of expression. The Court uses the same test that was used in *Blau v. Fort Thomas Public School District*. Specifically, the court identifies two key elements: (1) "An intent to convey a particularized message was present," and (2) that "the likelihood was great that the message would be understood by those who viewed it" (*McMillen*, p. 788). The Court concludes that her being allowed to wear a tuxedo as a silent "expression and communication of her viewpoint is the type of speech that falls squarely within the purview of the First Amendment" (p. 788). And, thus her rights were violated.

Doe and the Expression of Gender Identity

The last case that we will look at is from the Superior Court of Massachusetts in 2000, *Doe v. Yunits*. In this case, the plaintiff was excluded from South Junior High School over an expression of her gender identity and sought to be allowed to return to school. The suit was brought on the "basis of the plaintiff's sex, disability, or gender identity and expression" (*Doe* p. 789). According to the Court, the plaintiff has a medical diagnosis of gender identity disorder and should be allowed to wear the clothing conforming to her gender identity. However, the school contended it had "not barred the plaintiff from school but merely provided limits on the type of dress the plaintiff may wear" (p. 791).

The dress, as a form of expression, is separate from the actions of the student. The school district contended that they would discipline other students who dressed in this manner and are not singling her out. However, the Court points out that it is about the gender orientation of the clothing selection and that considering a girl wearing the same thing as the plaintiff would go unnoticed and therefore should not be a distraction here either. Thus, it fails the substantial disruption test of *Tinker*.

FREE SPEECH FRAMEWORK AND
PROTECTIONS FOR LGBTQ STUDENTS

Based on the above key cases, there are several concepts that can be blended together and synthesized into a theory of what constitutes protected speech under the First Amendment for LGBTQ students and the steps that a court would conduct in its analysis.

First, the Court would need to make a determination related to what was conveyed. If it is expressive conduct, we begin with *Spence* and *O'Brien*, and if it is pure speech, we move past these two tests and go right to *Bethel* and *Morse*. Specifically, *Spence v. Washington* (and as applied in *Texas v. Johnson*) has two components: (1) "An intent to convey a particularized message was present," and (2) that "the likelihood was great that the message would be understood by those who viewed it.

Next, as *Fricke* and *Hazelwood* demonstrate, a First Amendment case should continue its analysis with the O'Brien test and the issues that surround education will most likely revolve around the third prong of the test—was the governmental interest unrelated to the suppression of free expression? In this case, we must consider what actions the school engaged in that curtailed the speech and if the school claimed a substantial government interest in regulating the plaintiff's speech.

Once the analysis moves through these traditional First Amendment tests, it must look at the special legal characteristics of a school. In doing so, the school must look at the form of expression and separate it from any conduct of the student under *Tinker*. The Court may then look to apply the substantial disruption test. When determining if a substantial disruption has occurred, there must be more than fear of one or slight outbursts from students that result from a difference of view or opinion. It is a much higher bar to constitute substantial disruption to curtail First Amendment rights than educators have been trained to realize.

Most educators only think of disruption in the case of their educational training which could be anything from talking in class and passing notes to violence. Their training has not been within the scope of a legal framework. Schools can limit the delivery of speech to socially appropriate words, it cannot limit the conveyance of controversial ideas *(Bethel)*. The "light of the special characteristics of the school environment" curb certain speech that would be protected of adults in public and because of the nature of the school creates a limited forum for minors that has 'bumper lanes' for their expression (*Bethel*).

Finally, we must divide the educational environment additionally. The Court concludes that because a school can be seen as a closed forum, it can also divide the student speech and expression into further categories. Specifically, while the school cannot limit individual student speech unless it is disruptive, it can limit student speech that uses the school's educational resources or research as an audience where (1) it looks like a school endorsed or supported message; and (2) where the audience is supposed to learn a specific concept, it can control that educational message (*Hazelwood*).

CONCLUSION

Through careful analysis of judicial decisions of key First Amendment cases, a framework can be created that outlines protected forms of LGBTQ student sexual orientation expression and gender identity in K–12 schools. The main elements to consider when conducting an analysis of LGBTQ First Amendment rights in the educational environment include: (1) Do the symbolic acts constitute expressive speech which is protected, such as political speech—*Spence v. Washington*; (2) was the school district's conduct impermissible because it was meant to suppress that speech; (3) does the school district's action further substantial governmental interests—*O'Brien* test; (4) did the action of the student interfere with the educational environment or is a silent expression—*Tinker* sustainably disruptive test; (5) was it vulgar or profane—*Bethel* standard; (6) did it promote illegal activities—*Morse* standard; and (7) was it part of school-sponsored expressive activities—such as a student newspaper—*Hazelwood* standard?

Returning to the EPFP policy pillar, these cases provide a way for policy advocates to legally protect student rights through court action. It is important to remember that court actions are examples of policy histories and reflect the issues of the day. In other words, they build upon each other serving as the bedrock for the current issues of LGBTQ rights. There is an intersection of this legal framework with school policy, particularly at the district-level and importance of student rights in today's context. It is important to note again that these are the bedrock cases at the time of this writing's completion. As time progresses, the Courts are likely to continue the evaluation of LGBTQIA+ issues across the Country, and therefore, the cases and precedent are likely to evolve.

REFERENCES

Alexander, K., & Alexander, M. D. (2012). *American public school law*. Wadsworth Cengage Learning.

Bethel Sch. Dist. v. Fraser, 478 U.S. 675 (1986).

Black, H. C. (1951). *Black's law dictionary* (4th ed.) Thomson/West.

Blau v. Fort Thomas Public School District, 401 F.3d 381 (6th Cir. 2005)

Choper, J., Dorf, M., Fallon, R., & Schauer, F. (2019). *Constitutional Law: Cases, Comments and Questions* (p. 1047). West Academic Publishing.

Essex, N. (2016). *School law and the public schools.* Pearson.

Fricke v. Lynch, 491 F. Supp. 381 (1980)

Hazelwood Sch. Dist. v. Kuhlmeier, 484 U.S. 260 (1988)

Morse v. Frederick, 551 U.S. 393 (2007)

Texas v. Johnson, 491 U.S. 397 (1989)

Tinker v. Des Moines Independent Community School District, 393 U.S. 503 (1969)

U.S. Const. amend. XIX.

CHAPTER 3

WHAT WILL IT TAKE TO HELP ALL THIRD GRADERS LEARN TO READ?

Recommendations for Improving Policies on Early Literacy Learning

Dennis Davis, Chandra Alston, and Courtney Samuelson

NC State University

INTRODUCTION

The North Carolina Read to Achieve program (abbreviated here as RtA), established by the state legislature in 2012, was an ambitious investment in the early literacy achievement of children across the state. North Carolina is one of several US states that have adopted so-called "third-grade reading laws" in response to persistent concerns about reading achievement of students. As of the 2019–2020 school year, similar policies were in place in over half of US states. These policies are called third-grade reading laws because they either require or allow grade retention for third-grade students based on reading proficiency (Weyer, 2018).

Emerging Trends in Education Policy: Unapologetic Progressive Conversations,
pages 27–40.
Copyright © 2023 by Information Age Publishing
www.infoagepub.com
27

These policies are multifaceted, but they center primarily on retention/promotion as the main mechanism for improving reading achievement.

There is no doubt that improvements in educational opportunity to support reading achievement in the early elementary years are needed in North Carolina. In 2019, only 36 percent of the state's fourth graders were reading at a proficient level according to the National Assessment of Educational Progress (NAEP, 2019). However, the mechanisms used in the RtA policy to improve reading performance should be approached with skepticism. What would it take to really accomplish the goal of ensuring reading proficiency for all third-grade children? In the sections that follow, we draw on our expertise as literacy researchers and teacher educators to propose an answer to this question. Our answer takes the form of seven policy recommendations that can inform policy makers not only in North Carolina but in other states engaged in similar legislative efforts.

POLICY OVERVIEW

Like other third-grade reading laws, Read to Achieve (RtA) is often described as an end to social promotion, that is, promoting children to the next grade level based on age and completion of a grade, rather than on demonstrated achievement. RtA set into motion a complicated promotion process for third-grade students (see NC Read to Achieve Guidebook, NCDPI, 2018). Under the law, before students can be promoted to fourth grade, they have to show proficiency by passing the North Carolina End of Grade (EOG) reading test. Students who do not meet this criterion are given alternative ways to demonstrate proficiency. These alternatives include reaching a specific cut-score on one of several alternative reading assessments approved by the State Board of Education, retaking the EOG, or completing an extensive reading portfolio that shows mastery of state standards across multiple reading passages. Children who do not meet any of these proficiency standards are invited to attend a 72-hour summer reading camp to receive supplemental reading instruction. At the end of camp, they are re-assessed to determine if they can be promoted. Those who are not promoted are placed in an accelerated third-grade class or a transitional fourth-grade class, where they receive extra reading intervention during the year.

Ending social promotion is only one of the stated components of the RtA policy. The law also required the development of a comprehensive plan for reading achievement in the state, established procedures for early identification and intervention for students in K–3 who are not developing as expected in reading (including retained students), and mandated frequent parental notification of students' reading progress (NC Excellent Public Schools Act, 2012). Collectively, these components have had a profound impact on the experiences of teachers and students, not only in third grade, but in earlier grades as well (Aiken, 2020; Smith et al., 2018), without having much observable impact on reading achievement.

As much as we applaud the huge investment of money and other resources to address challenges associated with reading proficiency, we worry that policies focused on third-grade testing and retention will have few rewards in the end. The Read to Achieve legislation places many demands on North Carolina schools and local education agencies (LEAs), either explicitly (in the requirements of the policy) or implicitly (in the form of resources and expertise that are necessary for the legislation to be fulfilled). There is increasing concern that the capacity to successfully implement the requirements of the policy—in every classroom, for every child, every day—is not equitably distributed across the hundreds of LEAs and charter schools in our state (WestEd et al., 2019).

There is also concern that the policy's emphasis on screening, assessment, summer intervention, and student retention does not adequately address the issues that are preventing children from reaching proficiency in reading. A recent evaluation found that the initial cohorts of third graders affected by the legislation did not benefit in reading achievement (Weiss et al., 2018). In fact, trends on the state EOG for third and fourth graders have not improved since the initial implementation of the policy (North Carolina Department of Public Instruction, 2019), nor have trends for North Carolina fourth graders on the National Assessment of Educational Progress (NAEP, 2019).

FRAMEWORK AND METHODOLOGY

To ground the development of the guidance that we provide in this chapter, we employ a critical sociocultural framework (Moje & Lewis, 2007). This framework is commonly used in literacy research to examine issues of equity and power in school-based literacy instruction and policies. A strength of this framework is that it emphasizes the fact even when constrained by "power relationships and social structures, … people may exercise agency to impact practices and identities, potentially shifting power relationships even if in small ways" (Handsfield, 2016, p. 91). The authors of this chapter are literacy researchers and teacher educators who are deeply engaged in the evidence base on the causes of reading challenges in schools and how teachers and other members of the school community can collectively work to improve educational opportunities for children. The guidance we provide in this chapter is based on research and theory in early literacy instruction and intervention, reading comprehension, teacher development, and educational assessment. We identified these areas as crucial for understanding large-scale reform efforts in early reading instruction.

Using the literature in these areas as a resource, we engaged in a policy analysis in which we carefully read the goals and mechanisms of the Read to Achieve policy, with this question in mind: What would it really take for a statewide policy like this to substantially move the needle on reading proficiency? Our proposed answer to this question provides theoretically and empirically driven recommendations that can inform future versions of Read to Achieve or similar legislative actions. Our hope is that these recommendations can help policy makers address the challenges that have prevented the current legislation from making a stronger impact on reading proficiency.

MAIN POINT

This chapter briefly describes what it might take for the goals of third-grade reading policies to be fully met at scale. As detailed below, the main point of our argument is that it will take a much more intensive focus on teacher professional development, allocation of resources, and increased access to high-quality school-day and supplemental instruction for the state's most vulnerable readers. The recommendations explained in this chapter are as follows.

1. Recognize that no amount of tinkering with literacy policy will be sufficient, by itself, to overcome the systemic historical conditions that give rise to differences in educational achievement.
2. Improve core literacy instruction through radical new levels of investment in high-quality professional development for teachers and school leaders.
3. Re-design summer reading camps to reflect realistic expectations and to offer diagnostic instruction in specific areas that can, over the long term, improve overall reading performance.
4. Develop coherent school-day intervention strategies and ensure that every LEA has access to materials, training, and resources necessary to implement them well.
5. Provide and incentivize specialized professional development for teachers who take on interventionist roles in summer camps and who work with retained students in their third and fourth grade classrooms.
6. Build assessment expertise across the state so educators and school leaders can more effectively use diagnostic and formative assessments.
7. Do not forget about the children in grades 4–12 who still need continued support in literacy development.

RECOMMENDATIONS AND EVIDENCE

In the sections below, we explain each of the policy recommendations we have developed using current research evidence. Although our recommendations refer directly to North Carolina policy, they also apply more broadly to any district or statewide policy that seeks to improve reading outcomes by targeting third grade as a key pivot point in children's development.

Considering the Broader Context and Historical Conditions That Give Rise to Differences in Educational Achievement

The potential impact of third-grade reading laws must be understood within the broader context affecting educational achievement in the United States. A narrow focus on reading, without considering the historical and systemic factors that lead to the current gaps in literacy achievement, will not ameliorate inequities and improve reading outcomes for children in under resourced schools and those historically marginalized and living in poverty. Research has shown that children attending under resourced schools receive an unequal education, with fewer resources and less qualified teachers (Darling-Hammond, 2000). This has been clearly documented across the LEAs in North Carolina, many of which have tremendous unmet financial, and personnel needs due to huge discrepancies in funding and hiring availability (WestEd et al., 2019). Often these inequities are rooted in larger systemic inequalities related to race, ethnicity, class, and language (Leonardo, 2009). Rather than a focus on testing and remediation, a consideration of both the wraparound services needed to support the whole child as well as attention to improved resources, including qualified teachers, is necessary to improve reading outcomes for all children.

Poverty in particular should be a more central focus if our goal is to improve both student literacy and high school graduation rates. An influential report from the Annie E. Casey Foundation (Hernandez, 2011) is often cited as an impetus for literacy policies such as RtA. However, the findings of this study related to the strong influence of poverty on educational attainment are often selectively missing from the conversation. The Hernandez study found that 26 percent of children in the study who were living in poverty for at least a year and were not reading proficiently in third grade did not graduate high school. The study also found that 11 percent of children living in poverty who were proficient readers in third grade still did not finish high school. Hence, policy must include a sustained focus on mitigating the ways poverty impacts children and families as well as working to improve literacy outcomes for children.

Investing in Improvements in Core Classroom Literacy Instruction

By emphasizing intervention supports for retained or nearly retained students, the Read to Achieve initiative underemphasizes the importance of ensuring that every child in every classroom receives high-quality instruction in literacy, using evidence-based methods that can reduce children's vulnerability to reading difficulties. No amount of screening or supplemental intervention can replace the need for excellent core instruction, implemented effectively and consistently by all K–3 teachers and supported by highly knowledgeable administrators. The empirical research provides clear directions for the foundational practices that support early reading development in foundational code-based skills (Foorman et al., 2016) and in comprehension (Shanahan et al., 2010). The challenge is to ensure that these practices are implemented effectively across the entire state, particularly in schools and districts that have historically had a harder time attracting and retaining qualified educators.

Improving the quality of evidence-based reading instruction in the early years will be essential for policies like RtA to meet their goals. Improvements in instruction will require a systematic and coherent statewide effort to enhance professional learning opportunities to ensure that early reading expertise is widely available in every school. Third-grade reading policies should support all educator preparation programs in the state to meet their commitments to cultivate teacher expertise. Even with excellent initial preparation, educators and school leaders will need ongoing sustained professional learning opportunities to strengthen expertise in effective classroom literacy instruction and in implementation of intervention practices.

Through a critical sociocultural framework, it becomes clear that the RtA policy requires much more of educators than simply identifying and providing effective instruction. Given that differences in literacy attainment are often linked to historical inequities, it is imperative that professional development for teachers helps them find ways to disrupt inequities and advocate for transformative practices in reading. Efforts to promote teacher capacity must be grounded in the evidence base for effective professional development. A recent review of this literature identified important elements that must be in place to foster teacher learning (Darling-Hammond et al., 2017). Effective professional development includes opportunities to practice new teaching strategies, includes models of expert practice along with coaching and feedback, and importantly, lasts long enough for all these elements to be effectively implemented.

Re-Conceptualizing the Role of Summer Reading Camps

Summer reading camp is one of the most prominent aspects of the Read to Achieve legislation. The logic underlying this strategy is that summer camps can provide extra instructional time for children who need additional support. Given concerns about summer reading loss and the possible benefits of adding additional instructional time to the year for the state's most vulnerable readers, the excitement around the summer camps is understandable. But this excitement should be tempered. Supplemental summer instruction is an important learning opportunity, but it is not sufficient as the main intervention support for third-grade readers at risk of retention. A recent evaluation of Read to Achieve found no differences between children who attended camp and those who were eligible but did not attend (Weiss et al., 2018). Historical trends since 2014 show that just under 30% of camp attendees achieve proficiency and avoid retention during camp (North Carolina State Board of Education, 2019). These findings have prompted many conversations about how to improve the efficacy of these camps. Although improvements are possible and warranted, there is a risk that focusing on optimizing the effectiveness of summer camps will allow schools, districts, and state leaders to tinker around the edges of the problem without addressing the more pressing systemic issues affecting the learning opportunities provided during the school day.

Summer reading intervention can only do so much. When implemented at their minimum legislated level, summer camps amount to around a 30% increase in instructional time for those who attend (72 hours as a percentage of the total reading/literacy time in a school year, estimated conservatively at 14,400 minutes, or 90 minutes x 160 days). This sounds like a lot of time, but the potential of the summer intervention has to be examined in the context of what is known about what it takes to produce meaningful growth among elementary children on standardized measures of reading.

Researchers estimate that typical growth in reading on nationally normed tests across the third-grade year is around 0.60 standard deviations, on average (Lipsey et al., 2012). If summer camp is the equivalent of the addition of around 0.30 school years, then its average effect would be about one-third of this yearly estimate, or an effect size of around 0.20. The standard deviation (SD) for the 3rd grade EOG in 2018 and 2019 was 10.7 and 11.4, respectively (NCDPI, 2019). An effect size of 0.20 with respect to this SD would be around two raw scale score points (11 x .20). In short, it is not plausible to expect a 72-hour summer camp to produce drastic changes in the percentage of children who reach the EOG proficiency level. Only children who begin the camp within a few points of the proficiency cut-off are likely to reach this goal.

The above illustration is a rough, back-of-the-envelope calculation. Evaluations of the actual score gains associated with reading camp attendance can yield more precise estimates. The point here is that the expectations placed on the summer reading camp are unreasonable given what is already known about reading comprehension development and assessment. Our small estimate of summer camp impact, although hypothetical, aligns closely with previous literature on the impact of summer reading programs (Kim & Quinn, 2013), and with typical achievement gains observed in rigorous studies of reading comprehension instruction (e.g., see effect sizes reported in Shanahan et al., 2010).

These cautions do not mean that summer camps cannot be a useful intervention strategy. Young readers can improve during summer reading camps, but they are more likely to grow in specific skill areas than in broad reading comprehension proficiency, and only with highly intensive instruction. States that use summer camps as an important piece of their reading policies will need to take measures to ensure that high-quality camps (and other out-of-school options) are available in every district, particularly those with limited capacity to hire exemplary teachers and to design and implement evidence-based practices consistently. The supplemental instruction offered during camps should be built on a comprehensive and theoretically valid model of the component skills needed for reading comprehension development. The camps should focus on helping students develop important language and literacy skills in a logical sequence, with enough practice to ensure mastery. They should also be engaging so that children are motivated to accelerate their literacy learning.

The metrics for judging the success of reading camps should be more granular. They should include attention to readers' growth in carefully selected skill areas. This will require using and reporting diagnostic assessment data beyond EOG proficiency attainment. It takes an intense intervention to make meaningful changes in reading performance as measured on standardized tests like the EOG. Furthermore, instruction that focuses exclusively on improving performance on such tests, by practicing test items and test-taking strategies, is unlikely to produce genuine improvements in the underlying skills of reading those children need (Davis & Vehabovic, 2018; Shanahan, 2014).

The benefits of the summer camp strategy will also depend on attendance. Many students who are eligible for reading camp do not attend. For instance, in 2019, only 48.3% of third-grade students eligible for priority enrollment attended summer camps (NCSBE, 2019). Increasing camp enrollment will not be easy. It will require gaining a fuller understanding of why parents choose not to enroll their children in camp so that the specific challenges/reasons can be systematically addressed by LEAs. If summer is found to be a difficult time for families, flexibility should be offered to allow camp-like supplemental programs to be held after school as well. Summer camps should be seen as one part of a larger system of school-day and beyond-the-school-day supplemental instruction.

Fostering Coherent School-day Intervention Strategies

Readers who do not meet grade-level expectations are a heterogenous group with difficulties in many different areas of reading (Wixson, 2017). Districts and schools will not be able to properly support the reading development of these students unless they have access to evidence-based supplemental interventions addressing all the areas in which children might have difficulties. Every school in the state will need a robust menu of interventions covering foundational reading skills related to the alphabetic code and skills related to language and text comprehension. Both clusters of skills are important for reading development in early elementary grades (Kendeou et al., 2009). Schools will also need access to materials, training, and resources necessary to fully implement these interventions.

The literature on effective instruction within the Response to Intervention (RTI) or Multi-Tiered Systems of Support (MTSS) approach makes it clear that some students will need intensive instruction beyond their core classroom time. This instruction is best when provided in a tiered framework, during protected blocks of time in the school-day schedule, and should supplement, not replace, their core (Tier 1) literacy instruction. Tier 2 instruction should focus on a few carefully identified skills, taught 3–5 times a week for at least 20–40 minutes. When students do not respond to this level of support, they may need Tier 3 instruction. Tier 3 instruction is intensified by reducing the number of focus skills, reducing the group size, and increasing the amount of supplemental instructional time (Gersten et al., 2008). One of the main benefits of tiered intervention is that it can be tailored to a student's specific needs. High-quality, individualized instruction can catalyze improvements in literacy by providing more time to practice essential skills with guidance and mentorship from a supportive educator.

To fulfill the promise of intervention, districts will need a coherent strategy for matching interventions to readers. The list of interventions reported by North Carolina school districts in recent years (required as part of the legislation, see NCSBE, 2019) includes a wide array of intervention approaches. The reports list commercial products, websites, general teaching strategies, small group reading approaches, computerized interventions, afterschool tutoring, and many other methods. It makes sense that a variety of intervention supports are in use across the state. However, districts will need support to ensure that their intervention strategies are part of a coherent framework, implemented consistently and systematically by educators with the appropriate expertise.

The difficulties associated with effectively implementing coherently designed tiered intervention should not be underestimated. Adoption of a tiered intervention structure that includes general guidelines and lists of possible interventions does not guarantee that the interventions will be implemented consistently or that they will result in positive student outcomes (Balu et al., 2015). Effective implementation of intervention services requires strong campus leadership, teacher collaboration, schedules that support adequate time for intervention, and expertise in data use to ensure proper alignment of interventions to students' needs (Coyne et al., 2016).

Providing and Incentivizing Specialized Professional Development for Teachers

The Read to Achieve legislation stipulates that teachers who work with students who are not reading proficiently must be selected based on demonstrated outcomes in reading. This applies to teachers in summer reading camps and 3rd/4th grade accelerated and transitional classes. This requirement assumes that all LEAs and charter schools have sufficient concentrations of teachers who meet these criteria, which may not be the case. Even in districts where there are large numbers of teachers with demonstrated success in reading outcomes, teachers selected for these roles will need to have specialized expertise in evidence-based intervention methods.

Professional standards for literacy specialists call for expertise in selecting, adapting, and implementing interventions that are explicit and carefully scaffolded for readers (International Literacy Association, 2018). Teachers in the reading camps are asked to take on these complex practices. To do so, they will need specialized knowledge of language and literacy development and opportunities to build this knowledge through intensive professional development, advanced university coursework, and professional coaching. It is not sufficient for teachers to be familiar with general principles of effective reading instruction. Teachers also need structured opportunities to deliberately practice implementing specific tools and resources found in research to be promising for accelerating literacy learning (Hindman et al., 2020).

Teachers assigned to accelerated/transitional classrooms are expected to fulfill an even more daunting professional role. They are tasked with leading hyper-differentiated, multi-grade classrooms. Even the most skilled teachers will need specialized training in how to organize instruction in this context. Many of the most qualified teachers may not want to take on this role without proper support and incentives. The challenges associated with these complex instructional arrangements, for both students and teachers, should be examined more fully to understand how and if they impact student achievement.

Building Assessment Expertise

In addition to professional learning opportunities related to evidence-based early literacy instruction, successful implementation of RtA will require a more concentrated effort on building assessment expertise across the state. The policy demands effective use of formative and diagnostic assessment data to precisely pinpoint students' difficulties and to make sound instructional decisions. The expertise needed for using data in this way is often called assessment literacy (Xu & Brown, 2016). The need for robust assessment literacy among teachers, school leaders, and district personnel is distributed across multiple aspects of the RtA policy, including the comprehensive reading plan, the screening and assessment mandates across grades K–3, the design of the reading camps, and the provision of supplemental instruction for retained students.

Assessment of reading is not straightforward. Reading is a multidimensional construct that is challenging to measure (Fletcher, 2006). Different assessments reflect different conceptualizations of reading. Assessments also differ in their predictive relationships with other language and literacy skills that are measured for formative or diagnostic purposes (Cutting & Scarborough, 2006).

As an example of how this complexity plays out within the RtA context, consider the scenario faced by summer reading camp teachers who, at best, are provided with their students' end-of-year assessment profile from a mandated diagnostic assessment and EOG reports. It takes specialized expertise in reading to use these data sources to pinpoint the source of students' reading difficulties. Students reading at a non-proficient level according to either measure might have word reading difficulties, language comprehension difficulties, or both (Spear-Swerling, 2016). If they have word reading difficulties, they might lack the level of phonemic mastery required for efficient word learning, they might have gaps in their knowledge of specific letter-sound patterns, or they might need help with more complex multisyllabic words. If they have a specific comprehension difficulty, they might need support with vocabulary, making causal inferences across non-adjacent ideas in the text, monitoring and fixing-up their understanding, or understanding text structure (Oakhill et al., 2015). Chances are that most students in these contexts will need to build new content knowledge so that they can understand a more versatile range of grade-level texts.

These detailed areas of difficulty are not always evident in the typical assessment profiles that teachers have access to. To properly intervene, teachers will need to leverage their assessment expertise to gather additional diagnostic assessment data to inform their instruction. It is not easy to administer, score, interpret, and appropriately act on assessment data. According to the literature, educators vary tremendously in their knowledge and skills related to assessment. The good news is that assessment literacy can be developed through high-quality professional development (DeLuca et al., 2015). As detailed above, effective professional development in this area will need to be intensive, long-term, and applicable to teachers' daily practices.

Maintaining a Commitment to Children in Grades 4–12

The current emphasis on ensuring that children develop reading proficiency in the early grades makes a lot of sense. It is incredibly important that children are prepared in grades K–3 for the shifting literacy demands they will encounter as they move into upper elementary and middle school. But what about the children who make it past the third-grade gateway and need continued support? States should not let their huge investments in early reading have a negative impact on the opportunities provided to students in grades 4–12. In 2019, as in previous years, less than half of fourth graders in North Carolina reached level four (defined as solid command of knowledge and skills) on the state end-of-grade assessment in reading (NCDPI, 2019). This means most students entering fifth grade will need some level of support to meet grade-level expectations.

Research continues to show that literacy instruction shifts in focus and quantity from 4th to 8th grade, signaling a critical need to consider the instructional supports in place beyond third grade (Mihaly & McCaffrey, 2014). Many secondary language arts teachers are primarily prepared to teach literature (Pasternak et al. 2017), while the many of the texts that readers must learn to access are nonnarrative and informational. Although we see an increase in the use of informational texts in middle and high schools due in part to the Common Core State Standards, the literacy instruction accompanying those texts often does not support critical literacy development and instead focuses on basic comprehension (Alston, under review; Fisher & Frey, 2014). Given these findings in relation to grades 4–12, policy must consider the long-term literacy development of children and their instructional needs beyond third grade.

CONCLUSION AND IMPLICATIONS

When lawmakers across the US enact third-grade reading policies, they rightfully make early literacy achievement a top priority. These policies would be more effective, however, if they aligned more closely with what is known from educational research about how to achieve genuine transformations in the teaching and learning of reading. The recommendations we have provided in this chapter, grounded in current evidence, and aligned to a critical sociocultural framework in literacy, can help re-focus these policies on the important goal of ensuring that the proper expertise and resources are in place to support literacy development in every school and LEA, rather than on testing and grade retention.

As detailed above, we recommend that schools re-configure the intervention supports that are offered, not just for retained or nearly retained students, but for all vulnerable readers in grades K–3. This will require developing more coherent school-day intervention strategies, ensuring that every LEA has access to materials, training, and resources necessary to intervene in evidence-based ways, and increasing access to intensive out-of-school programs, including summer camps. Summer reading camps should be re-designed to reflect more realistic expectations and to offer more intensively diagnostic instruction in specific areas that can, over the long term, improve overall reading performance.

In addition, the goals of third-grade reading policies depend on the availability of high-quality core classroom literacy instruction for every child. This will require an unprecedented statewide effort to support the professional development of teachers and campus leaders through evidence-based methods that promote deep changes to educators' knowledge and practices, including coaching and collaborative, job-embedded training. Educators will need learning opportunities to enhance their implementation of evidence-based K–3 literacy instruction. They will also need to hone their assessment expertise to effectively use the diagnostic and formative assessments required in the policy.

All these improvements must be done with a clear recognition that ambitious policies related to elementary reading instruction will be necessary but not sufficient to make the kinds of changes needed for children's literacy success. Such policies will have to be situated within even broader—even more radical—investments in disrupting systems of power that create differential opportunities for literacy learning across communities.

REFERENCES

Aiken, H. (2020). *Assessing for accountability: How reading assessments shape early literacy instruction in North Carolina schools* [Doctoral Dissertation]. The University of North Carolina at Chapel Hill.

Alston, C. L. (under review). *Informational text use in upper elementary and middle grades English Language Arts classrooms.*

Balu, R., Zhu, P., Doolittle, F., Schiller, E., Jenkins, J., & Gersten, R. (2015). *Evaluation of response to intervention practices for elementary school reading* (NCEE 2016-4000). National Center for Education Evaluation and Regional Assistance, Institute of Education Sciences, U.S. Department of Education.

Coyne, M. D., Oldham, A., Leonard, K., Burns, D., & Gage, N. (2016). Delving into the details: Implementing multitiered K–3 reading supports in high-priority schools. *New Directions for Child and Adolescent Development, 154,* 67–85.

Cutting, L. E., & Scarborough, H. S. (2006). Prediction of reading comprehension: Relative contributions of word recognition, language proficiency, and other cognitive skills can depend on how comprehension is measured. *Scientific Studies of Reading, 10*(3), 277–299.

Darling-Hammond, L. (2000). New standards and old inequalities: School reform and the education of African American students. *Journal of Negro Education, 69*(4), 263–287.

Darling-Hammond, L., Hyler, M. E., & Gardner, M. (2017). *Effective teacher professional development.* Learning Policy Institute.

Davis, D. S., & Vehabovic, N. (2018). The dangers of test preparation: What students learn (and don't learn) about reading comprehension from test-centric literacy instruction. *The Reading Teacher, 71*(5), 579–588.

DeLuca, C., Klingner, D., Pyper, J., & Woods, J. (2015). Instructional rounds as a professional learning model for systemic implementation of assessment for learning. *Assessment in Education: Principles, Policy & Practice, 22*(1), 122–139.

Excellent Public Schools Act. (2012). https://www.ncleg.gov/Sessions/2011/Bills/Senate/PDF/S795v4.pdf.

Fisher, D., & Frey, N. (2014). Scaffolded reading instruction of content-area texts. *The Reading Teacher, 67*(5), 347–351.

Fletcher, J. M. (2006). Measuring reading comprehension. *Scientific Studies of Reading, 10*(3), 323–330.

Foorman, B., Beyler, N., Borradaile, K., Coyne, M., Denton, C. A., Dimino, J., Furgeson, J., Hayes, L., Henke, J., Justice, L., Keating, B., Lewis, W., Sattar, S., Streke, A., Wagner, R., & Wissel, S. (2016). *Foundational skills to support reading for understanding in kindergarten through 3rd grade* (NCEE 2016-4008). National Center for Education Evaluation and Regional Assistance (NCEE), Institute of Education Sciences, U.S. Department of Education.

Gersten, R., Compton, D., Connor, C. M., Dimino, J., Santoro, L., Linan-Thompson, S., & Tilly, W. D. (2008). *Assisting students struggling with reading: Response to Intervention and multi-tier intervention for reading in the primary grades. A practice guide.* (NCEE 2009-4045). National Center for Education Evaluation and Regional Assistance, Institute of Education Sciences, U.S. Department of Education. http://ies.ed.gov/ncee/wwc/publications/practiceguides/.

Handsfield, L. J. (2016). *Literacy theory as practice: Connecting theory and instruction in K–12 classrooms.* Teachers College Press.

Hernandez, D. J. (2011). *Double jeopardy: How third-grade reading skills and poverty influence high school graduation.* Annie E. Casey Foundation.

Hindman, A. H., Morrison, F. J., Connor, C. M., & Connor, J. A. (2020). Bringing the science of reading to preservice elementary teachers: Tools that bridge research and practice. *Reading Research Quarterly, 55*(S1), S197–S206.

International Literacy Association. (2018). *Standards for the preparation of literacy professionals 2017.* International Literacy Association.

Kendeou, P., van den Broek, P., White, M. J., & Lynch, J. S. (2009). Predicting reading comprehension in early elementary school: The independent contributions of oral language. *Journal of Educational Psychology, 101*(4), 765.

Kim, J. S., & Quinn, D. M. (2013). The effects of summer reading on low-income children's literacy achievement from kindergarten to grade 8: A meta-analysis of classroom and home interventions. *Review of Educational Research, 83*(3), 386–431.

Leonardo, Z. (2009). *Race, whiteness, and education.* Routledge.

Lipsey, M. W., Puzio, K., Yun, C., Hebert, M. A., Steinka-Fry, K., Cole, M. W., Roberts, M., Anthony, K. S., & Busick, M. D. (2012). *Translating the statistical representation of the effects of education interventions into more readily interpretable forms.* (NCSER 2013-3000). National Center for Special Education Research, Institute of Education Sciences. U.S. Department of Education. http://ies.ed.gov/ncser/

Mihaly, K., & McCaffrey, D. (2014). Grade level variation in observational measures of teacher effectiveness. In T. Kane, K. Kerr, & R. Pianta (Eds.), *Designing teacher evaluation systems: New guidance from the measures of effective teaching project* (pp. 9–49). Jossey-Bass.

Moje, E. B., & Lewis, C. (2007). Examining opportunities to learn literacy: The role of critical sociocultural literacy research. In C. Lewis, P. E. Enciso, & E. B. Moje (Eds.), *Reframing sociocultural research on literacy: Identity, agency, and power* (pp. 15–48). Lawrence Erlbaum.

National Assessment of Educational Progress (NAEP). (2019). *NAEP Report Card: 2019. NAEP Reading Assessment.* https://www.nationsreportcard.gov/reading/states/scores/?grade=4.

North Carolina Department of Public Instruction (NCDPI). (2018). *North Carolina read to achieve guidebook.* https://www.dpi.nc.gov/documents/k-3literacy/resources/read-to-achieve-guidebook.

North Carolina Department of Public Instruction (NCDPI). (2019). *2018–19 North Carolina state testing results green book.* https://www.dpi.nc.gov/districts-schools/test-ing-and-school-accountability/school-accountability-and-reporting/testing-results-green-book.

North Carolina State Board of Education (NCSBE). (2019). *Report to the North Carolina General Assembly: Read to Achieve data—state level summary.* https://legislative.ncpublicschools.gov/legislative-reports/report-rtadata-statelevelsummary2020.pdf

Oakhill, J., Cain, K., & Elbro, C. (2015). *Understanding and teaching reading comprehension: A handbook.* Routledge.

Pasternak, D. L., Caughlan, S., Hallman, H. L., Renzi, L., & Rush, L. S. (2017). *Secondary English teacher education in the United States.* Bloomsbury Publishing.

Shanahan, T. (2014). How and how not to prepare students for the new tests. *The Reading Teacher, 68*(3), 184–188.

Shanahan, T., Callison, K., Carriere, C., Duke, N. K., Pearson, P. D., Schatschneider, C., & Torgesen, J. (2010). *Improving reading comprehension in kindergarten through 3rd grade: A practice guide* (NCEE 2010-4038). U.S. Department of Education.

Smith, R. W., Imig, S., Walker, B., & Evans, S. (2018). Where intention meets implementation: The challenges and concerns of high-stakes literacy policy. *International Journal of Education and Human Developments, 4*(1), 13–21.

Spear-Swerling, L. (2016). Common types of reading problems and how to help children who have them. *The Reading Teacher, 69*(5), 513–522.

Weiss, S., Stallings, D. T., & Porter, S. (October 2018). *Is Read to Achieve making the grade?: An assessment of North Carolina's elementary reading proficiency initiative.* North Carolina State University College of Education. https://www.fi.ncsu.edu/projects/rta/

WestEd, Learning Policy Institute, & Friday Institute for Educational Innovation. (2019). *Sound basic education for all: An action plan for North Carolina.* WestEd.

Weyer, M. (2018). *A look at third-grade reading retention policies.* National Conference of State Legislatures. http://www.ncsl.org/documents/legisbriefs/2018/june/LBJune2018_A_Look_at_Third_Grade_Reading_Retention_Policies_goID32459.pdf

Wixson, K. K. (2017). An interactive view of reading comprehension: Implications for assessment. *Language, Speech, and Hearing Services in Schools, 48,* 77–83.

Xu, Y., & Brown, G. T. L. (2016). Teacher assessment literacy in practice: A reconceptualization. *Teaching and Teacher Education, 58,* 149–162.

SECTION II

ROLE OF FAMILIES AND COMMUNITIES

Listening to the panel of experts at her monthly EPFP session, Danielle felt herself becoming increasingly overwhelmed with the complexities of advanced education policy and the political barriers to enacting significant reform. She surveyed the room, observing a cohort filled with former teachers, a professor of education administration, someone from a policy office like hers, a few school leaders, and a collection of representatives from the state's Department of Education. Over networking lunches and breaks, they got along well, but Danielle felt like the group hardly ever agreed on solutions. This realization troubled her because she sensed that the students, teachers, community, and parents in her life needed to see changes in education if schools were going to meet their needs. She also knew that these desired reforms demanded coalitions and consensus-building. Danielle's attention snapped back to the guest speaker that explained the influence of Parent-Teacher Associations (PTAs) on school policies. She heard about how parents from certain neighborhoods adopted a duty of being involved in every school decision and each policy recommendation to district leaders. She heard about their vocal opinions and perfect attendance at all school board meetings. She contrasted these actions with those of parents she knew from other neighborhoods that seemed frustrated with their decision-makers, appeared distrustful of the instruction that their children received, and were consequentially absent from their district's meetings. As she worked to unite her thoughts, the presenter shared research showing a positive link between PTA membership and student achievement. The point made her think of her mom saying, "It takes a village to raise a child." Through the presentation and her reflections, Danielle realized that she did not need to fight for the students she cared about on her own. She could leverage the strengths of her education allies and work with them to overcome her sense of being overwhelmed. Along the way, Danielle knew that she would need to answer questions like "What do you do when parents from one neighborhood have friends on the school board and other neighborhoods don't even speak the same language as the people on their schoolboard?" She also knew she would have to overcome the policy complexities and political realities vexing her on other topics. That said, the EPFP session's discussion of the issues and the opportunity to consider things from another person's point of view facilitated her learning. Danielle knew she was up for the challenge of uniting schools, families, and communities in the service of youth.

CHAPTER 4

THE TIME IS NOW

Advocating for Contextually Responsive Policy to Support Full Service Community Schools

Kathleen Provinzano
Drexel University

OVERVIEW

Education achievement gaps between subgroups of students (i.e., race and/or ethnicity, gender, economic standing, special education status) have long been a subject of interest for educational researchers and policymakers looking to remedy academic inequalities (Hung et al., 2020). Specifically, the Black-white and Hispanic-white achievement gaps, which literature defines as differences in standardized test scores across racial/ethnic groups (Gopalan, 2019), has for the most part persisted in spite of school improvement efforts aimed at closing these gaps (Hemelt & Jacob, 2020). Carey (2014) emphasized that the achievement gap has arguably, "become the single most pervasive and widely discussed educational issue of our current time" (p. 441). Education reform agendas, however, have responded in ways that discount the "substantial racial and socioeconomic segregation across schools, and the wide variance of achievement within observably

Emerging Trends in Education Policy: Unapologetic Progressive Conversations,
pages 43–54.

homogeneous schools" (Hemelt & Jacob, 2020), and thus have failed to systemi-cally address inequality associated with access and opportunity as it relates to these gaps.

Education stakeholders (e.g., school leaders, teachers, policymakers, families/caregivers) often apply an "achievement gap discourse" when thinking and talk-ing about education reform (Carey, 2014, p. 443). Assumptions associated with school improvement and student achievement emanate from overly vague and individualized language that is commonplace in the achievement gap literature and "inform a discourse where what is valued, discussed, and labeled comes through commonly employed school reform language" (Carey, 2014, p. 443). The result is a vernacular that includes words and phrases routinely used during the era of No Child Left Behind (NCLB), including adequate yearly progress (AYP), highly qualified teachers, basic, and below basic. Blame for gaps in learning are implicitly, and in many cases explicitly, placed on individual students, teachers, and schools. This frame exacerbates a deficit lens (Ladson-Billings, 2006), while simultaneously overlooking structural inequalities that do perpetuate differences. Consequently, "technical and quick-fix interventions as solutions to problems that require far more complex understandings" (Carey, 2014, p. 443) end up dominat-ing what should be larger conversations around uprooting education systems that reproduce inequalities.

Policymakers interested in providing equitable teaching and learning oppor-tunities to students across all zip codes must be willing to move away from con-temporary thinking around the individualized achievement gap and concentrate on in and out-of-school disparities that result in differences in student outcomes. Federal education policy, however rarely addresses the impact of external forces (i.e., poverty, inequitable resources) on student learning and school performance (Green & Gooden, 2014). The majority of school-based reform initiatives over the past two decades have been unwilling and unable to adapt to the changing social and economic conditions of children, families, and communities; and resultantly, have produced less than stellar results (Lawson & van Veen, 2016). In fact, re-forms have done little to transform schools and their surrounding communities (Green & Gooden, 2014), largely because of their lack of focus on out-of-school challenges experienced by students and families, particularly those living in con-centrated poverty (Milner, 2013). The trilogy of poverty, social exclusion, and isolation "make it difficult for educators working in stand-alone schools focused exclusively on student academic achievement to succeed sustainably and at scale" (Lawson & van Veen, 2016, p. 4).

The Every Student Succeeds Act (ESSA) includes specific requirements relat-ed to equity (Fusarelli & Ayscue, 2019), thereby positioning states to implement and be held accountable to state plans that advance equitable reform. Instrumental to this work are alternatives to conventional models of schools that are centered around health services, social services, parent and family engagement, positive youth development, and out-of-school learning (Lawson & van Veen, 2016). Full-service community schools (FSCS) by design meet this call by offering an innovative solution to the complex problem of school reform (Provinzano et al., 2020a). Defined as "public schools that partner with families and community organizations to provide well-rounded educational opportunities and supports for students' school success," FSCS create space for school and neighborhood stakeholders to "come together to support innovative learning and to address the impact of out-of-school factors, such as poverty, racism, and violence, which can undermine the effectiveness of in-school opportunities" (Community Schools Playbook, n.d., pp. 3–4). Given this conceptualization, it is not surprising FSCS are gaining traction in school reform discourse (Anderson et al., 2019).

To date, there are approximately 5,000 FSCS in the United States (U.S.) and numbers are increasing nationally with increased fiscal and political support from the Biden administration (Mohler, 2021). At the time of this writing, President Biden's budget request for the U.S. Department of Education investment in FSCS is $443 million, nearly 10 times more than the amount invested in 2021 (Pierce, 2021). This increase can be attributed in part to FSCS demonstrated promise for improving educational outcomes for underserved students (Anderson et al., 2019; Galindo & Sanders, 2021; Provinzano et al., 2020b; Sondergeld et al., 2020), coupled with efforts to keep supports and services (e.g., medical and mental health, extended learning time, family and community engagement, and collaborative leadership) in place during a time when most schools were forced to close their doors as a result of the COVID-19 global pandemic (Oakes et al., 2020). Consequently, as schools reemerge post-COVID, it is critical for policymakers to shift the school reform narrative to more prominently center FSCS, as "they are viewed as part of a broader movement to redefine and restructure schools to be more responsive to the needs of underserved students, families, and communities" (Galindo & Sanders, 2021, p. 3).

Following a discussion on the relationship between equity, FSCS, and ESSA, this chapter presents the argument that the federal government can and must do more under ESSA to strengthen the place-based, contextual nature of FSCS by funding schools adequately and equitably.

CONTEXT

The impetus for the unapologetic progressive FSCS policy position and recommendation that follows draws from literature related to the widespread inequitable funding of public schools in the U.S., which stems from antiquated formulas largely reliant on local property tax bases (Learning Policy Institute, 2020; Raikes & Darling-Hammond, 2019). Neighborhoods with high property taxes are able to fund schools in ways that schools residing in areas of concentrated poverty cannot, yet states' K–12 funding allocations have persistently remained below pre-Great Recession (2008) levels (Lays, 2019).

The majority of the fifty states have unfair funding systems that do not prioritize or allocate additional funding streams to school districts in areas with high levels of concentrated poverty (Baker et al., 2018). To be sure, in their analysis of school funding equity across the U.S. and within each state, Morgan and Amerikaner (2018) explained students attending high-poverty schools lack equitable access to resources commonplace in wealthier districts such as high-quality teachers, early education programs, career and college readiness programming, and other out-of-school resources that support students' academic progress. Clearly, there is a need to shift the funding narrative to one that accounts for neighborhood differentials, as "…differences among local contexts help to explain variability in child, family, school, and community outcomes. Contexts thus are consequential, not incidental, to educational policy and practice, demonstrating that place-based uniqueness needs to become a priority in school designs and operations" (Lawson, 2016, p. 2). Further emphasis on gaps in opportunity (Milner, 2012) and disparate access to high-quality schools is also warranted, especially as public schools become increasingly segregated by both race and class in the U.S. (Darling-Hammond, 2018).

INTRODUCTION

Across different educational settings, students' life chances are strongly influenced by the quality of education they receive. While educational equity should be a foremost goal of policy, governmental systems often fall short in actualizing justice-centered reforms. In the U.S. specifically, schools across high-poverty, racially, and ethnically diverse communities are affected by limited financial and human resources. In this way, "not unlike society itself, students' gender, race, and class identities give them access to opportunities or serve as barriers to academic success" (Gadsden, 2017, pp. 12–13). Edley and Darling-Hammond (2018) explained that "the persistence of multigenerational poverty is the most villainous explanation for these continuing disparities, with structural racism as its regular sidekick" (¶ 5). Accordingly, when planning for and enacting reform across education systems it is imperative that a community-wide approach be implemented, where emphasis on achievement gaps and deficits is replaced with discourse around the broader sociopolitical, historical, and economic conditions that have excluded underserved students for generations (Ladson-Billings, 2006).

The FSCS approach is designed to target and reduce systemic, educational inequality for marginalized youth and communities by providing "services that address students' complex and multifaceted needs while also empowering their families to generate lasting and consequential changes in educational opportunities and communities" (Galindo et al., 2017, p. 141S). Partnerships between the school and families, local businesses, community-based organizations, and faith-based institutions are employed and coordinated by full-time coordinators who can read the communal pulse of residents. FSCS context acknowledges schools and communities are not mutually exclusive and that they must work together to create conditions for students and families to thrive. These schools rely on relationships and partnerships, and serve as an important example of an equitable, place-based strategy that supports community activity and transformation (Jacobson, 2016).

Given the localized nature of FSCS, implementation looks different across varying contexts. These schools are intentionally designed to reduce risk and increase opportunity for students experiencing poverty (Daniel & Snyder, 2015), which in the U.S. is approximately one in five children, with Latinx, African American or Black, and American Indian children disproportionately represented (KIDS COUNT, 2020). Partnerships and services center around four core pillars that "provide an infrastructure to embed the characteristics of more advantaged schools in community schools' structures and practices" (Oakes et al., 2017, p. 4). These pillars are evidence-based as contributing to school improvement and include: 1.) integrated student supports, 2.) expanded learning time and opportunities, 3.) family and community engagement, and 4.) collaborative leadership and practices (Maier et al., 2017).

Research suggests that community-focused schooling, coupled with integrated services, positively correlates with increased student outcomes (Abrams & Gibbs, 2000). A developing body of literature specifically focused on the impact of the FSCS approach on students' academic and non-academic outcomes is promising (see Daniel & Snyder, 2015; Maier et al., 2017; Provinzano et al., 2020a, 2020b; Sondergeld et al., 2020). In their systematic review of 57 studies on community schools operating in varying contexts within and outside the U.S., Heers et al. (2016) summarized the impact of FSCS, underscoring their potential benefits. The authors, while noting much of the evidence was mainly correlational and not causal, concluded parental engagement, student participation in extracurricular activities, and engagement with partners were associated with increased academic performance, decreased dropout rates, and decreased risky behavior such as school violence, substance use, and delinquency rates overall.

Although research on the effectiveness of the FSCS strategy is in the emergent stage, the approach passed muster when the FSCS grant program was included under Title IV, Part F of ESSA. The program provides "support for the planning, implementation, and operation of FSCS that improve the coordination and integration, accessibility, and effectiveness of services for children and families, particularly for children enrolled in high-poverty schools" (Congressional Research Service, 2019, p. 2).

ESSA also includes a number of roundabout funding opportunities that would permit communities to start or scale strategies associated with the FSCS strategy. They include Title I, Part A school improvement funds in the lowest-performing schools, and Title IV programming under the 21st Century Community Learning Centers and Student Support and Academic Enrichment (Community Schools Playbook, n.d.; Frankl, 2016). Funding amounts from these programs remains uncertain and a significant portion of funding for FSCS comes from a combination of district/local, state, and federal sources (Galindo & Sanders, 2019).

BACKGROUND AND MAIN POINT

As discussed, equity, ESSA, and FSCS are inextricably related. ESSA emphasizes evidence-based practices for school improvement, and community schools have demonstrated to meet that criteria (Oakes et al., 2017). By placing power over education back into the hands of the states, the law is said to advance equity in the following ways:

> (1) Within the ESSA plans they submit to the U.S. Department of Education (DOE), States must explicitly describe how they intend to address equity concerns, (2) States must report school-level per-pupil spending when they issue school report cards, (3) States have to identify and address any inequities in resources for schools that need support and improvement, and (4) districts are incentivized to implement strategies for funding schools based on student need and to expand opportunities for traditionally underserved students. (Fusarelli & Ayscue, 2019, p. 33)

The degree to which states are using the flexibility afforded them by ESSA in the most equity-minded ways remains suspect. Ushomirsky et al. (2017) were not encouraged by some state ESSA plans that intentionally sought to hide disparities in achievement and opportunity for low-income students, Students of Color, students with disabilities, and English Language Learners by ignoring results of individual subgroups or setting standards too low. Further, independent reviews of state ESSA plans demonstrate that in some states, schools "are not sufficiently being: held accountable for the performance of each student subgroup; identified when subgroups consistently underperform; or required to participate in federal annual testing requirements—all central tenets of the law" (Jimenez & Flores, 2019, p. 5).

Fortunately, the outlook is not entirely bleak. Twelve states to date have included FSCS as a strategy to support school improvement in their initial ESSA plans (Community Schools Playbook, n.d.), signifying there is a commitment in some spaces to use federal education dollars to support equitable, place-based school reform initiatives. Therein lies the main point of this chapter. Given that accountability for equity and school improvement has been handed back to the states and some states are more invested in this work, there should be opportunities embedded within ESSA that extend beyond the aforementioned funding sources to support organic, on-the-ground, community-initiated, well-designed FSCS. Education is a local endeavor and federal oversight, albeit important in many ways, should not replace trust in communities to advance local policies and practices designed to serve disadvantaged students.

RECOMMENDATIONS AND EVIDENCE

ESSA provides more funding than NCLB for programs that support FSCS (Oakes et al., 2017), yet there is still work to be done from a policy perspective. If we have learned anything in 2020 (global pandemic, national reckoning on race and structural racism etc.), it is that we need more funding for place-based school reform initiatives like FSCS. In many communities, the FSCS is a hub of activity for families and residents and a space for cross-sector leadership to work in partnership to develop policies, supports, and plans for resources that are responsive to the needs of the community (Jacobson, 2016). Consistent, reliable funding remains a primary challenge for sustaining and scaling FSCS (Galindo & Sanders, 2019; Jacobson, 2019), especially those operating outside the realm of large-scale projects that have the backing of state legislatures and mayors (i.e., Philadelphia, New York City, Oakland, Chicago). It is only fair to ask, how can what the federal government envisioned as equity under ESSA be enacted at the local level? Including a funding stream in Title 1, Part A might be the answer.

This chapter recommends that Congress modify the Title I funding formula to allocate spending for local districts to boost the planning, implementation, scaling, and evaluation of placed-based, FSCS initiatives. The recommendation is being offered in lieu of the competitive Full-Service Community School grant program authorized under Title IV and is intended to alleviate the necessity for districts supporting FSCS to have to smatter together sections of Title I, Part A to fund various elements of the FSCS approach. The following evidence supports this recommendation.

When ESSA was signed into law significant control over accountability was placed back into the hands of states. What did not change was Title I, Part A funding formulas. Title I is the largest funding allocation and monies are specifically earmarked to improve education for low-income students (Michelman, 2016). ESSA affirms the purpose of Title I is "to provide all children significant opportunity to receive a fair, equitable, and high-quality education, and to close educational achievement gaps" (ESSA: A Comprehensive Guide, n.d.). Thus, aligned with principles of FSCS, education aid under Title I is directed toward resources that are centered around opportunity, access, and equity.

Gordon (2017) explained that Title I, Part A has four formulas that disperse different levels of funding per each Title-I eligible child: 1.) Basic Grants, 2.) Concentration Grants, 3.) Targeted Grants, and 4.) Education Finance Incentive Grants. Funds are allocated to states via a complex Title I formula. In turn, states then allocate funds to districts using the same formula. Once districts are in possession of Title I funding, they have substantial flexibility to disperse to individual schools, beginning with those that have the highest level of child poverty (Michelman, 2016). The open-ended nature of how districts choose to use their Title I allocations seems ideal on its face, however, "approximately 75 percent of Title I allocations are spent on teacher and paraprofessional salaries" (Michelman, 2016, ¶ 40). While important, states should not be in a position to have to choose between employing the appropriate number of qualified staff and investing in others systemic educational opportunities for students from low-income backgrounds. Unless Title I receives significant increases in its funding, or formulas that have been in place for over 15 years are modified, the community-focused approach to schooling may remain nothing but a pipe dream for some of the neediest communities.

Title I funding investments play a major role in how schools operate at the local level and while federal education dollars benefit students, they are distributed in a way that is deeply unfair (Boser & Brown, 2015). The end goal for this recommendation is to have a funding formula under ESSA that is not entangled in bureaucratic red tape or unofficially reserved for larger, already well-funded, FSCS systems. Local schools must be provided with opportunities to secure funding and given a certain degree of autonomy for how those funds are spent in relation to what is needed for the FSCS to be implemented or scaled within the context of the particular community. Accountability for funding allocations and subsequent outcomes should be at the community level. The basic funding structure of Title I has remained stagnant and as a nation we have not experienced the desired comprehensive results of these investments. Clearly, the system is broken, not the students, families, or communities in which those systems exist. It is of the upmost importance that we reimagine how federal aid can be dispersed to local schools to enact place-based, community-supported schools.

CONCLUSION AND IMPLICATIONS

School, family, and community engagement scholars agree responsibility for student well-being is shared across a range of actors working authentically within and outside the halls of the school (e.g., Epstein et al., 2018; Ishimaru, 2020; Stefanski, et al., 2016). This is true now more than ever. As the U.S. grapples with a global pandemic of epic proportions, coupled with a national moment of racial reckoning, the time may have finally arrived for education policy changes that attempt to right the wrongs of systems that routinely underserve students marginalized by race and economic status. Any shifts in policy and practice have to be centered in an equity lens and schools alone cannot do this work. Funding allocations under Title I must be readily available if stakeholders are to address multiple determinants of educational disadvantage. Under ESSA, FSCS have potential to thrive, particularly in historically marginalized and underserved communities. Collectively, however government, schools, and communities have to figure out how to work together to implement accountability systems that extend beyond test scores and permit schools to dually focus on academic and non-academic outcomes for students. Only when this fractured system is broken can we achieve the pinnacle goal of educational equity for all students.

REFERENCES

Abrams, L. S., & Gibbs, J. T. (2000). Planning for school change: School-community collaboration in a full-service community school. *Urban Education, 35*(1), 79–103. https://doi.org/10.1177/0042085900351005

Anderson, J. A., Chen, M.-E., Min, M., & Watkins, L. L. (2019). Successes, challenges, and future directions for an urban full service community schools initiative. *Education and Urban Society, 51*(7), 894–921. https://doi.org/10.1177/0013124517747032

Baker, B. D., Farrie, D., & Sciarra, D. (2018, February). *Is school funding fair? A national report card.* Education Law Center. https://edlawcenter.org/assets/files/pdfs/publications/Is_School_Funding_Fair_7th_Editi.pdf

Boser, U., & Brown, C. (2015, July). *5 key principles to guide consideration of any ESEA Title I formula change.* Center for American Progress. https://www.americanprogress.org/issues/education-k-12/reports/2015/07/07/116696/5-key-principles-to-guide-consideration-of-any-esea-title-i-formula-change/

Carey, R. L. (2014). A cultural analysis of the achievement gap Discourse: Challenging the language and labels used in the work of school reform. *Urban Education, 49*(4), 440–468. https://doi.org/10.1177/0042085913507459

Community Schools Playbook. (n.d.). *A project of the partnership for the future of learning.* https://communityschools.futureforlearning.org/

Congressional Research Service. (2019, May). ESEA: The promise neighborhood and full-service community schools program. Author. https://fas.org/sgp/crs/misc/IF11196.pdf

Daniel, J., & Snyder, J. (2015, December). *Community schools as an effective strategy for reform.* Stanford Center for Opportunity in Education. http://nepc.colorado.edu/sites/default/files/community-schools-web11.pdf

Darling-Hammond, L. (2018, April). *Kerner at 50: Educational equity still a dream deferred.* Learning Policy Institute. https://learningpolicyinstitute.org/blog/kerner-50-educational-equity-still-dream-deferred?gclid=CjwKCAjwu5CDBhB9EiwA0w6sLTZgSxw_tifZ4gSrQu7LUXZQDpdlGa4xcsnfhXgJwe7QMf15k41XKRoC0lEQAvD_BwE

Edley, C., & Darling-Hammond, L. (2018, August). *Community schools: A powerful strategy to disrupt inequitable systems.* Learning Policy Institute. https://learningpolicyinstitute.org/blog/community-schools-powerful-strategy-disrupt-inequitable-systems

Epstein, J., Sanders, M. G., Sheldon, S., Simon, B. S., Salinas, K. C., Jansorn, N. R., VanVoorhis, F. L., Martin, C. S., Thomas, B. G., Greenfield, M. D., Hutchins, D. J., & Williams, K. J. (2018). *School, family, and community partnerships: Your handbook for action* (4th ed.). Corwin.

ESSA: A Comprehensive Guide. (n.d.). *SEC. 1001 statement of purpose.* http://www.everystudentsucceedsact.org/title-1-

Frankl, E. (2016). *Community schools: Transforming struggling schools into thriving schools.* Center for Popular Democracy.

Fusarelli, L., & Ayscue, J. (2019). Is ESSA a retreat from equity? *Phi Delta Kappan, 101*(2), 32–36. https://doi.org/10.1177/0031721719879152

Gadsden, V. L. (2017). Gender, race, class, and the politics of schooling in the inner city. *The ANNALS of the American Academy of Political and Social Science, 673*(1), 12–31. https://doi.org/10.1177/0002716217723614

Galindo, C., & Sanders, M. (2019). Achieving equity in education through full-service community schools. In S. B. Sheldon & T. A. Turner-Vorbeck (Eds.), *The Wiley handbook of family, school, and community relationships in education* (pp. 511–530). John Wiley & Sons, Inc. https://doi.org/10.1002/9781119083054.ch24

Galindo, C., Sanders, M., & Abel, Y. (2017). Transforming educational experiences in low-income communities: A qualitative case study of social capital in a full-Service community school. *American Educational Research Journal, 54*(1st suppl.), 140S–163S. https://doi.org/10.3102/0002831216676571

Galindo, C. L., & Sanders, M. G. (2021). Teachers' academic optimism and professional practice in an urban full-service community high school. *Journal of Educational Change.* https://doi.org/10.1007/s10833-021-09430-6

Gopalan, M. (2019). Understanding the linkages between racial/ethnic discipline gaps and racial/ethnic achievement gaps in the United States. *Education Policy Analysis Archives, 27*(154), 1–37. https://doi.org/10.14507/epaa.27.4469

Gordon, N. (2017, February). *What Title I portability would mean for the distribution of federal education aid.* The Brookings Institution. https://www.brookings.edu/research/what-title-i-portability-would-mean-for-the-distribution-of-federal-education-aid/

Green, T. L., & Gooden, M. A. (2014). Transforming out-of-school challenges into opportunities: Community schools reform in the urban Midwest. *Urban Education, 49*(8), 930–954. https://doi.org/10.1177/0042085914557643

Heers, M., Klaveren, C. V., Groot, W., & van den Brink, H. M. (2016). Community schools: What we know and what we need to know. *Review of Educational Research, 86,* 1016–1051. https://doi.org/10.3102.0034654315627365

Hemelt, S., & Jacob, B. (2020). How does an accountability program that targets achievement gaps affect student performance? *Education Finance and Policy, 15*(1), 45–74. https://doi.org/10.1162/edfp_a_00276

Hung, M., Smith, W. A., Voss, M. W., Franklin, J. D., Gu, Y., & Bounsanga, J. (2020). Exploring student achievement gaps in school districts across the United States. *Education and Urban Society, 52*(2), 175–193. https://doi.org/10.1177/0013124519833442

Ishimaru, A. M. (2020). *Just schools: Building equitable collaborations with families and communities.* Teachers College Press.

Jacobson, R. (2016, November). *Community schools: A place-based approach to education and neighborhood change.* The Brookings Institution. https://www.brookings.edu/wp-content/uploads/2016/11/jacobson-final-layout-published-11-16-16.pdf

Jacobson, R. (2019, August). *States lead the way on community school innovation.* The Brookings Institution. https://www.brookings.edu/blog/brown-center-chalkboard/2019/08/01/states-lead-the-way-on-community-school-innovation/

Jimenez, L., & Flores, A. (2019, May). *3 ways DeVos has put students at risk by deregulating education.* Center for American Progress. https://files.eric.ed.gov/fulltext/ED596184.pdf

KIDS COUNT. (2020). *Data book: State trends in child well-being.* The Annie E. Casey Foundation. https://www/aecs/org/m/resourcedoc/aecf-2020kidscountdatabook-2020.pdf

Ladson-Billings, G. (2006). From the achievement gap to the education debt: Understanding achievement in U.S. schools. *Educational Researcher, 35*(7), 3–12.

Lawson, H. A. (2016). Categories, boundaries, and bridges: The social geography of schooling and the need for new institutional designs. *Education Sciences, 6*(3), 1–14.

Lawson, H. A., & van Veen, D. (Eds.). (2016). *Developing community schools, community learning centers, extended-service schools and multi-service schools: International exemplars for practice, policy, and research.* Springer.

Lays, J. (2019, January). *The top 10 issues to watch in 2019*. National Conference of State Legislatures. https://www.ncsl.org/bookstore/state-legislatures-magazine/biggest-issues-to-watch-in-2019.aspx

Learning Policy Institute. (2020, August). *The federal role in advancing education equity and excellence*. https://learningpolicyinstitute.org/product/advancing-education-2020-brief

Maier, A., Daniel, J., Oakes, J., & Lam, L. (2017, December). *Community schools as an effective school improvement strategy: A review of the evidence*. Learning Policy Institute. https://learningpolicyinstitute.org/sites/default/files/product-files/Community_Schools_Effective_REPORT.pdf

Michelman, B. (2016). Title I: The engine of equity and accountability. *ASCD Express, 22*(4), 1–7. http://www.ascd.org/publications/newsletters/policy-priorities/vol22/num04/Title-I@-The-Engine-of-Equity-and-Accountability.aspx

Milner, R. H. (2012). Beyond a test score: Explaining opportunity gaps in educational practice. *Journal of Black Studies, 43*(6), 693–718. https://doi.org/10.1177/0021934712442539

Milner, R. H. (2013). Analyzing poverty, learning, and teaching through a critical race theory lens. *Review of Research in Education, 37*(1), 1–53. https://doi.org/10.3102/0091732X12459720

Mohler, J. (2021, May). *Biden proposes increasing funding for community schools by 15 times the current level*. In the Public Interest. https://www.inthepublicinterest.org/biden-proposes-increasing-funding-for-community-schools-by-15-times-the-current-level/

Morgan, I., & Amerikaner, A. (2018, February). *Funding gaps: An analysis of school funding equity across the U.S. and within each state*. The Education Trust. https://edtrust.org/wp-content/uploads/2014/09/FundingGapReport_2018_FINAL.pdf

Oakes, J., Maier., A., & Daniel, J. (2017, June). *Community schools: An evidence-based strategy for equitable school improvement*. National Education Policy Center. https://nepc.colorado.edu/publication/equitable-community-schools

Oakes, J., Maier, A., & Daniel, J. (2020, July). *In the fallout of the pandemic, community schools show a way forward for education*. Learning Policy Institute. https://learningpolicyinstitute.org/blog/covid-community-schools-show-way-forward-education

Pierce, R. (2021, September). *Community schools: A game changer for public education*? Forbes. https://www.forbes.com/sites/raymondpierce/2021/09/15/community-schools-a-game-changer-for-public-education/?sh=20bced816374

Provinzano, K., Sondergeld, T. A., Ammar, A. A., & Meloche, A. (2020b). A community school reform initiative for middle grades urban and newcomer students: Using mixed methods to examine student academic and non-academic outcomes over time and compared to a matched sample. *Journal of Education for Students Placed at Risk (JESPAR), 25*(4), 293–318. https://doi.org/10.1080/10824669.2020.1744441

Provinzano, K., Sondergeld, T. A., Knaggs, C. M. (2020a). Community schools as a sustainable comprehensive school reform strategy: A transformative mixed methods perspective. *Mid-Western Educational Researcher, 32*(1), 3–30.

Raikes, J., & Darling-Hammond, L. (2019, February). *Why our education funding systems are derailing the American dream*. Learning Policy Institute. https://learningpolicyinstitute.org/blog/why-our-education-funding-systems-are-derailing-american-dream

Sondergeld, T. A., Provinzano, K., & Johnson, C. C. (2020). Investigating the impact of an urban community school effort on middle school STEM-related student outcomes over time through propensity score matched methods. *School Science and Mathematics Journal, 120*(2), 90–103. https://doi.org/10.1111/ssm.12387

Stefanski, A., Valli, L., & Jacobson, R. (2016). Beyond involvement and engagement: The role of the family in school-community partnerships. *School Community Journal, 26*(2), 135–160.

Ushomirsky, N., Smith, A., & Bommelje, S. (2017, December). *Trends in state ESSA plans: Equity Advocates still have some work to do.* Education Trust. https://files.eric.ed.gov/fulltext/ED587197.pdf

CHAPTER 5

MAKE PARENTING EDUCATION UNIVERSAL

Eve Sullivan
Parents Forum

Djamel Bekkai
Tulane and Dillard Universities

OVERVIEW & TERMINOLOGY

The relationship between parenting education and democratic values is the cornerstone of our argument. We believe that children whose parents learn to model and practice responsive communications and positive conflict management at home—and who model civic engagement through their involvement in activities at their children's schools and in their community—are more likely to grow up to be healthy, happy, and productive people and engaged citizens (Kirby-Wilkins et al., 2014)

The January 6, 2021, attack on the U.S. Capitol brought calls from educators for improving civics education (Kawashima-Ginsberg & Dubé, 2021). While the road to a stronger democracy certainly runs *through* the classroom, it does not begin there. In 1994, the United Nations, celebrating the International Year of the

Emerging Trends in Education Policy: Unapologetic Progressive Conversations,
pages 55–73.
Copyright © 2023 by Information Age Publishing
www.infoagepub.com

Family, recognized the family as "the smallest democracy at the heart of society." Children whose ideas and feelings are acknowledged at home and whose parents are active in their communities are more likely to become thoughtful, engaged citizens. While effective family governance is more benevolent dictatorship than democracy, parents who listen to their children and allow them age-appropriate choices are, in important ways, teaching civics.

We will provide a capsule history that describes some current parenting education programs and discuss, briefly, the context within which parenting education takes place. We see the primary barrier to establishing universal parenting education to be the often subtle, sometimes blatant, stigma associated with parenting programs that stems from its link to child protective services. These must often identify parents or others in parenting roles as perpetrators of child neglect and abuse.

First let us clarify the terms used to describe programs for parents: parent education, parenting education, family development, family life education, family science and family support. The phrase 'parent education' implies that the parent is the target, while 'parenting education' focuses on the process rather than the person and seeks to involve anyone caring for a child. 'Family development' and 'family life education' (Kirby-Wilkins et al., 2014) further broaden the scope of programming and 'family science' is often preferred by professional parenting educators who have certification or professional licensure, for example, in social work or psychology. The term 'family support' covers a range of activities and services that meet a variety of parents' and children's needs.

The term 'family engagement', now commonly used to include parenting education, is not, in our view, focused enough for our purposes. We seek to support parents, of course, including fathers, and we recognize the unfortunate reality that parents are often sidelined in many well-intentioned efforts to foster children's and family wellbeing and promote children's learning.

Further, we want to highlight the format in which parenting programs are delivered: lectures, discussions, a combination of the two, or individual consultation, as well as where programs are offered: in the home, by visitors trained to work with parents, or in school or community settings, and now, more often than not, online. We see group discussion, with minimal lecture-style presentations, as the most effective. Guided by a trained facilitator, parents in groups can develop shared leadership practices and problem-solving skills. Requesting parents' evaluation of programs is key, as the process further hones parents' sense of efficacy in their roles at home and in the community.

The term 'family support' became common in the late 1970s to describe local programs for parents with young children. Like the settlement houses of over a century ago often serving immigrants, community-based family support programs are publicly funded and provided at locations called family centers or family resource centers. These are voluntary and open to all parents and caregivers in a neighborhood, town, or city.

We use the term 'parenting education' which we see as both narrower and deeper than the others. We see 'parent engagement' as a term best used to describe various activities for parents related to their children's learning and recreation and to school governance.

To the above terms, we add 'parent peer support', an informal part of many professionally led parenting programs. Parent peer support is, in fact, the focus of the program led by the co-authors of this article. Growing recognition of the value of lived experience has led to paraprofessionals, sometimes called family advocates, family liaisons or parent liaisons, being hired by schools, social service agencies, public health clinics and medical practices. The 'granddaddy' of peer support programs, Alcoholics Anonymous, founded in 1935 in Akron, Ohio, now has offshoots supporting recovery from addictions. The value of peer support is recognized by Mental Health America and some commercial ventures, like Weight Watchers, make peer support a central plank in their organizational structure.

Let us define parenting education as we see it. It has three elements: emotional, cognitive, and behavioral. It...

- offers emotional support and social connections to parents and other caregivers, essentially social-emotional learning or SEL,
- provides information about child development and appropriate expectations for each developmental stage,
- models and encourages behaviors and speech that effectively support and guide children at each stage of their development and that develop parents' problem-solving and leadership skills.

The second element, providing information, is the easiest and, therefore, may be over-emphasized, leading to emotional and behavioral support being sidelined. The format most conducive to accomplishing all three goals is a group setting. Lectures and informational handouts often miss the mark which is positive change in parents' behaviors in their day-to-day interactions with their children.

There is no one-size-fits-all parenting education model, however. Parents in various circumstances may need or want programs tailored to their interests, life situation or cultural background. These include programs for fathers/mothers/couples, teen parents (teen mothers and fathers may be together or in separate groups), parents of children of a particular age (e.g., parents of teens), adoptive parents, foster parents, immigrant or refugee parents, grandparents raising grandchildren, incarcerated or formerly incarcerated parents, parents serving in the military and/or their spouses, parents of children with special needs, parents who themselves or whose children are experiencing (or have experienced) addictions or mental health challenges and parents who are divorcing or have divorced.

It is worth mentioning that, as of 2014, about half the 50 US states require co-parenting classes for divorcing parents with minor children. More than one participant, according to Dr. William Sharp, a colleague who teaches these mandatory classes in Massachusetts, has said that if they had had parenting classes earlier, they might not have divorced.

Concern for fathers' participation in parenting education programs deserves special mention, as only since the 1990s have men's issues been considered as distinct. Traditionally, many fathers have not been directly involved in the day-to-day tasks of childrearing or in parenting programs, but we believe that parenting education must be universal and must explicitly include fathers.

There are many parenting education curricula on the market, at varying costs, some requiring professional or trained lay facilitators (Bartlett et al., 2016). Note that the presenter's training and experience is often more important than the curriculum. Mary Crowley, OBE, former head of Parenting UK, a national umbrella body for people working with parents, and former chair of the International Federation for Parent Education, has said that she found a good facilitator using a mediocre curriculum more effective than a mediocre facilitator using a good curriculum.

The challenges for all parenting education programs, whatever the curriculum and whoever the presenter, are to offer support, provide information and encourage positive behaviors and problem-solving—in about equal measure—and do these three things in ways that lift parents up rather than put them down. It can be done.

BACKGROUND

Family, church, and school have long served as the three institutions that guide young people's learning and development (Bartlett et al., 2016). Literacy and formal schooling became more widespread during the 1800s and schools took on a larger role, especially as the industrial revolution required parents to work outside the home (Vinovskis, 1987). The moral aspect of children's upbringing, however, remained primarily parents' responsibility. Children were to be taught right from wrong and, if children got into trouble, the church, and the community, then schools, blamed their parents. Children could be removed from their families, as they still are today, when parents failed to provide adequate care and supervision.

Punitive removal of children from parents' care has included forced separation of children from their enslaved parents, relocation of indigenous children to white settlers' families and their enforced assimilation in mission schools, as well as suppression of native languages, including sign language among the Deaf. This backdrop makes clear why services for parents were, and still are, more often viewed with suspicion than welcomed and accepted.

The kindergarten movement originated in Germany in the early 1800s and came to the US in the 1860s. Despite the significant growth in appreciation for children's learning that the movement brought and the variety of creative and effective initiatives in early education by educators and psychologists over the last 150 years, parenting programs have until relatively recently remained remedial, if not punitive.

Positive and preventive services for parents, mostly mothers and most often those in immigrant families and poor communities, were provided in settlement houses in the late 1800s and early 1900s. These focused on children's early years and practical aspects of promoting children's health, emphasizing sanitation and nutrition. In 1899, at the Lake Placid Conference, the term 'home economics' was selected as the name for the nascent field. Activists then began to call for home economics to be taught, mostly to girls, in schools across the country. In 1909 Ellen Swallow Richards founded the American Home Economics Association. Nearly a century later, in 1994, the organization was renamed the American Association of Family and Consumer Sciences to make the field's offerings appealing to both boys and girls. Consumer sciences curricula include child development along with life skills and practical tasks necessary for managing a household.

Over the years, programs for parents recognized, and some were created specifically to focus on, parents' role in helping their children learn basic academic skills, that is, 'school-readiness.'

The end of World War II and the subsequent, if uneven, prosperity that followed, first in the US then more widely, was accompanied by significant growth in the field of psychology and greater understanding of children's stages of development. Still, programs for parents were the exception, with extended family taking the primary role in supporting and guiding parents. To provide context for our thesis that parenting education can play a key role in responding to the current crises in public health, social justice, and democratic engagement, we present the following chronology of previous efforts in the field.

HISTORY

This selective review describes parenting education initiatives and nonprofit and academic programs on parenting and family life issues, some international but mostly US-based. We recognize that many other countries have a tradition of robust government-supported childcare, parental leave, and other parent support policies (Daly et al., 2015; Williams & D'Addato, 2012;). By focusing on the United States, we want to highlight the assets and contributions of American entities but at the same time acknowledge that society-wide deficits in the US clearly contribute to the difficulties many families in this country experienced in 2020 and will continue to experience without improved and coordinated support for parents. One such effort is the American Rescue Plan Act of 2021, which included revision of the Child Tax Credit, making it more like the family allocation programs provided to parents in many European countries.

LITERATURE REVIEW

1938. The National Council on Family Relations, NCFR was founded as a professional association focused on family research, practice, and education. Its members, from more than 35 countries and all 50 US states, now include scholars, professionals and students in family science, family life education, human development, marriage and family therapy, sociology, psychology, anthropology, social work, theology, child development, health and more. NCFR certifies professionals in Family Life Education. We will discuss later our concern for recognition of the value of the 'lived experience' that paraprofessionals bring as presenters of parenting education programs.

1946. The International Federation for Parent Education, IFPE, was created as an outgrowth of Belgian 'parent schools.' The organization, based in Paris, is still in existence in a small way, but the organization's name, with the word 'parent' rather than 'parenting', reveals the persistent bias that parents' programs are directed at a person, rather than being about a process.

1948. The Society for Human Resource Management / SHRM, first called the American Society for Personnel Administration, was founded to represent the personnel profession, and provide professional development opportunities. SHRM's 2021 national campaign, "When I grow up" uses an early childhood lens—pictures of adorable babies—to call for an end to discrimination, exclusion, and harassment in the workplace. We hear that as an argument for parenting education that would help people become better managers, as well as better parents.

Mid-1960s. The International Federation for Family Development, IFFD began with support programs for parents based on the 'case method' and the organization now works in 70 countries with an extensive network of volunteers.

1970s. The term 'family support' emerged during this decade to describe programs for parents with young children offering a variety of resources and services, including nutritional support and parenting education. Three notable early childhood education programs launched during this time are the Nurse-Family Partnership / NFP, founded by David Olds in Elmira, NY, now united with Child First; the Carolina Abecedarian Project, a controlled experiment conducted in 1972 at the University of North Carolina Chapel Hill; and Zero To Three, launched in 1977 as the National Center for Clinical Infant Programs.

1970. Harlem Children's Zone, HCZ was founded in New York City to provide free parenting workshops, preschool and other educational and health programs to poor children and their families. Programs start with pre-natal support and now continue through college years and beyond with the Center for Higher Education and Career Support. HCZ is one of the longest-lasting programs created as a result of the social unrest of the 1960s which led to grass-roots educational and parent support initiatives in both African American and Latino communities.

Among those initiatives were the Black Panther Party's free breakfast program for school children in Oakland, California, that grew, from 1969 to 1980, to serve 23 cities across the US, feeding over 10,000 children daily. In 1975, the party helped pressure Congress to expand the free breakfast program to all public schools.

1973. Avance Mother-Infant Program, now Avance, meaning "advance" or "progress," was created in Dallas to meet the needs of low-income families and now serves parents in a half dozen cities, mainly in Texas. Its programs "take a two-generation approach to family success."

1978. Fran Litman at Wheelock College (now Wheelock College of Education & Human Development at Boston University) founded the Center for Parenting Studies to address the impact on parents and children of the profound structural and demographic changes then occurring in American culture. Litman was convinced that mothers working outside the home were being unjustly blamed for increased divorce rates and believed that American society needed to develop new attitudes about family structure and, in particular, new supports for families.

1980s. This decade brought concern for work/life balance, as both men and women experienced increasing job-related stress. Employers began to recognize the benefits—to their employees and their bottom line—of offering positive, preventive support on family life issues.

1983. The Global Family Research Project is the successor to the Harvard Family Research Project (1983–2016) and separated from the Harvard Graduate School of Education at the start of 2017. The project focuses on defining and advancing the fields of family, school and community engagement and offers advice and technical assistance to national educational organizations, school districts and community-based nonprofits.

1983. Minnesota legislator Jerome Hughes initiated the Early Childhood and Family Education, ECFE program for parents of children birth to age five which continues to the present day. The state program is unique in offering financial support and requiring local school districts to opt-in, share costs and pay trained parenting educators salaries on a par with classroom teachers. Parents who participate in ECFE remain involved in their children's pre-school and primary schools. Parenting education clearly serves as a steppingstone to parent engagement Mueller, Armson, & Rader, 2003).

1988. Fran Litman, the Wheelock College professor mentioned above, co-founded Families First to provide seminars for parents in the Boston area. With the Children's Trust Fund the organization hosts an annual conference on parent education, "A View from All Sides." In 2020 Families First "continues to provide early childhood parenting education, family engagement and parent leadership."

1994. The United Nations declared 1994 the International Year of the Family, celebrating the family as "the smallest democracy at the heart of society," and organizes annual conferences on family themes each year on or near May 15, named International Day of Families. Also, in 1994 Marilyn Dalrymple of Lancaster, California, called for August 1 to be observed as Respect for Parents Day.

1994. The National Fatherhood Initiative was organized to improve the well-being of children by increasing the proportion of children with involved, responsible and committed fathers. Also, in 1994 the Collaborative for Academic, Social and Emotional Learning / CASEL was formed with the goal of establishing high-quality, evidence-based social and emotional learning as an essential part of preschool through high school education.

1996. The Fathers & Families Coalition of America was formed to provide leadership and professional development as well as advocacy for children, families and those who work to improve the lives of children.

1996. A group of parenting practitioners in the US came together to support and strengthen the field of parenting education, creating the National Parent Education Network, NPEN. In the early 2000s the organization was renamed the National Parenting Education Network to recognize that parents are not alone in doing the work of childrearing. NPEN provides a state-by-state listing of parenting programs, articles on choosing and evaluating such programs as well as reports on both professional and paraprofessional parenting educator competencies.

2000. Susan Linn founded Campaign for a Commercial Free Childhood, CCFC to work with policymakers, health, and child development experts in order to help children thrive in an increasingly commercialized, screen-obsessed culture. The organization works to end marketing to children and help parents reduce children's screen time.

2006. The Doha International Family Institute, DIFI, a global policy and advocacy institute, was established by the Qatar Foundation for Education, Science and Community Development. It seeks to advance knowledge of Arab families and promote evidence-based polices to support families in the Arab world. DIFI also convenes high-level conferences on family issues in the Gulf Region and beyond.

2011. The National Family Support Network, NFSN. founded as a membership-based organization, comprises "statewide networks of two or more-family support and strengthening programs working together to ensure coordinated quality support for families."

2011. Minnesota Teacher of the Year Katy Smith was the first parenting educator in the US to be honored with such an award, an important advance for the field of parenting education.

2012. At the urging of the Mission of Qatar, the UN General Assembly declared June 1 Global Day of Parents, providing an opportunity to "appreciate all parents for their selfless commitment to children and their lifelong sacrifice to nurturing parent-child relationships."

2016. The Boston Basics, later renamed The Basics, was launched as an outgrowth of the Achievement Gap Initiative founded by Harvard University professor Ron Ferguson. The Basics helps parents learn and apply five science-based parenting and caregiving principles that support their children's social, emotional, and cognitive development. The work builds on that of James Heckman, University of Chicago Nobel Prize-winning economist (García et al., 2017).

2016. The Collaborative on Healthy Parenting in Primary Care / HPPC was formed within the National Academies of Sciences, Engineering and Medicine. It seeks to recognize the evidence of the effectiveness of family-focused prevention programs in promoting the physical and behavioral health and the emotional well-being of children from birth through adolescence. HPPC's 2020 policy options paper calls for universal parenting education and for funding, including insurance reimbursement, to support program provision.

2016. The Confess Project, founded to build a culture of mental health for boys, men of color, and their families through capacity-building and advocacy, uses a unique model: training barbers to become mental health advocates with their customers and in the community.

2017. The Early Childhood Development Action Network (ECDAN) is an alliance of over a hundred organizations and networks and thousands of members committed to improving the lives of young children from conception to five years around the world. They are collaborating to launch a global movement, spur investment, and help countries achieve the Sustainable Development Goals (SDGs) by meeting young children's developmental needs.

2018. DIFI and IFFD, along with seven other nonprofit organizations, published a Civil Society Statement on Parenting (Doha International Family Institute, 2018), disseminated at the October 2018 International Conference on Parenting, Child Wellbeing and Development in Doha.

2019. Educating for American Democracy / EAD was organized in recognition of the broad failure in recent decades "to prepare young Americans for self-government." It seeks parents' support for its Roadmap, a framework that "weaves history and civics together and inspires students to learn by asking difficult questions."

2020. In August the UN Focal Point on the Family, within the Division of Economic and Social Affairs / DESA, polled member states and UN entities on various family issues. The 'Note Verbale' inquiry specifically mentioned investments in parenting education as a tool to enhance children's well-being (Department of Economic and Social Affairs, 2020).

In closing this historical review, we want to mention that the 2021 theme for the UN International Day of Families / IDF, May 15th, was Families and New Technologies. This was the first mega-trend to be explored in preparation for the 30th anniversary of the International Year of the Family in 2024 and the discussion included the role of digital technologies in parenting education.

We hope that the programs described above give readers a sense of the diversity of offerings to parents as well as the increasing attention paid by researchers to work in the field of parenting education. A number of agencies list such programming: Blueprints for Healthy Youth Development (a national registry), the Child Welfare Information Gateway of the US Administration for Children and Families, the National Parenting Education Network / NPEN and the National Family Support Network / NFSN.

CONTEXT

The background and history above touch high points in a solid tradition of informal and formal support for parents but do not recognize many long-established parenting education programs in the US or other countries. In this section we mention several of these.

Two organizations in the US that address parenting education concerns in their work are the Society for Prevention Research, founded in 1991, and the Center for Humane Technology, launched in 2018. The latter grew out of concerns of founder Tristan Harris, a design ethicist at Google, about the "threats that the attention economy poses to our well-being, relationships, democracy and shared information environment."

Commercial parenting education endeavors include coaching and there are at least three parent coaching organizations: The Parent Coaching Institute, established in 2000, Academy for Coaching Parents, formed in 2004, and the Family Life Coaching Association, founded in 2015. The significant challenges of making parenting education pay are evident in the brief rise of Isis Parenting, founded in 2003 as Isis Maternity in Boston, and its bankruptcy in 2014.

Programs that engage parents, but that lie outside our immediate concern, include those that help parents, especially disadvantaged parents, prepare their children for success in school. These include Barbershop Books, Libraries Without Borders, Raising a Reader, Reach Out and Read, Room to Grow, and the Thirty Million Words Initiative. Programs addressing the challenges parents face due to economic hardship include Cradles to Crayons.

A host of program have been organized by and for parents themselves, some long-established, like the National Parent Teacher Association, PTA, founded in 1897, some new like the National Parents Union, NPU, organized in 2020. The latter runs a Facebook Live channel, with parent activists across the country leading panels on topics related to children's access to educational opportunities, social justice, and school improvement.

Programming directed to medical care providers includes the Collaborative for Healthy Parenting in Primary Care, HPPC, mentioned above, and the Brazelton Touchpoints Center. The latter builds on the work of T. Berry Brazelton, MD, internationally renowned pediatrician, and supports families, providers, and communities in applying knowledge of early childhood development to practice and policy.

Hollywood, Health & Society, HHS, founded in 2001, studies the role of media in shaping public opinion on matters of health and provides information to program creators on health and medical issues. NPEN has advocated with HHS for recognition of parenting education themes in television show story lines.

Places where parenting education can take place include, really, anywhere parents happen to be, starting with schools and health care settings. We see the workplace as an under-utilized venue that could serve parents by providing parenting education programs. Unexplored as a venue for parenting education are youth-serving agencies like Boys & Girls Clubs and the Family Y. A search of these organizations' websites reveals that both seek to engage parents, primarily as volunteers with children's programs. Perhaps mini sessions for parents could be offered while children and youth are involved in their activities.

We hope that the above chronology adequately shows the progress that society has made over the last 150+ years toward improving parenting resources. Two key themes that have emerged in recent decades are the importance of cultural competence in programs and their presenters the need for targeted efforts to reach fathers, grandparents and others involved in children's lives.

But we have a difficult topic to address next. As noted in the abstract, there is a legitimate, but stigmatizing, association of parenting education with child abuse prevention. Unless we face this important issue head-on, we cannot expect to achieve success for the bold policy initiative we propose: to make parenting education universal.

CHILD ABUSE PREVENTION

The sad reality is that many parents and others in parenting roles were themselves neglected or abused as children. The groundbreaking Adverse Childhood Experiences Study, ACES, conducted by Kaiser Permanente from 1995 to 1997, documented the link between childhood abuse, neglect and household challenges and poor outcomes in later-life health and well-being (The Child & Adolescent Health Measurement Initiative, 2017; National Center for Injury Prevention and Control, Division of Violence Prevention, 2020). While we believe that all parents want to create safe, stable, and nurturing homes for their children—these are the three criteria recognized by the CDC as necessary for a healthy family environment—we also believe that, without intervention, specifically without parenting education, parents who suffered neglect or abuse as children may all too easily pass their own childhood deficits and harms on to their children.

Child abuse in the U.S. is staggering. In 2018 there were 677,529 reported cases of child abuse, about four deaths every day and the most common form of maltreatment was neglect (Duffin, 2021). The problem is not confined to the US, as a 2010 UNICEF report (UNICEF, 2010) describes:

> Although widespread and pervasive, violence against children remains hidden and socially condoned. Widely perceived as a social taboo or a needed form of discipline, it is seldom reported… and, openly or implicitly, children feel pressured to conceal incidents of violence and abuse, particularly when perpetrated by people they know and trust.

We believe, and studies have shown, that parenting education can play a vital role in breaking the intergenerational transmission of violence (Wessels et al., 2013). To break this cycle and build, or re-build, the foundations of a democratic society, we must work broadly, deeply, and consistently with parents. We must approach parents with as much care as we approach children. Only by doing this can we help parents reflect on the pain and sadness that they may carry within and which, despite their best intentions, they may perpetuate in their families.

A mantra in addictions recovery is that "hurt people hurt people." Too many parents have themselves experienced parental neglect or abuse. Sociology professor Murray Strauss did ground-breaking research on family violence, devoting much of his career to the study of spanking and corporal punishment, accumulating evidence that these practices were associated with increased subsequent aggression among children and reduced warmth between them and their parents. Because boys are more often subject to corporal punishment than girls, according to Human Rights Watch the ill effects of corporal punishment fall more directly on men but, of course, ripple out to others in the family (Farmer et al., 2008).

Traditional societies put the father at the head of the household but at the same time leave him at a distance from the day-to-day responsibilities of parenting (Department of Economic and Social Affairs, 2020). While this is changing (DESA, 2011), many programs in contemporary societies still direct parenting services primarily to mothers, perpetuating if not actively creating a disconnect and imbalance in the family structure that does not serve the child, the mother, or the father.

RECOMMENDATION

We support policy and practice initiatives that make parenting education available, accessible, affordable, and attractive to all parents and caregivers to support children's wellbeing and healthy development from birth through young adulthood. The words 'available, accessible, affordable and attractive' are chosen to make clear that parenting education should be available—offered to all parents and caregivers of children birth to age three, during children's pre-school, grammar school, middle and high school years and into college, especially at important transition points like those from middle school to high school and high school to college, accessible—offered with appropriate accommodations for people with physical disabilities, including hearing impairment, for those who speak a language other than the dominant one, and in locations that normalize participation, like workplaces, as well as through faith communities and organizations especially likely to engage fathers, like sports associations, affordable—provided with insurance coverage for fees charged by parenting educators and with local sponsorship for costs of peer support activities, attractive—promoted by public health campaigns and social marketing from various community partners in a variety of broadcast and interactive media.

CONCLUSION AND IMPLICATIONS

We see and want to accelerate a shift towards the perception of parenting education as a positive and normal activity. The default for schools, social service agencies, workplaces and other venues should be to offer parenting education and, similarly, the default for parents should be to participate. Ultimately, we can move both personal and public perception away from parenting education as remedial, while still offering such programs as needed.

We want to involve in coordinated advocacy not only educators and pediatricians, already on board, but also human resource professionals, along with parent leaders like those in the National Parents Union and the PTA. We want to add the voices of leaders and staff in youth-serving agencies of America, sports association, faith communities, the media and, as The Confess Project does, barbers and hairdressers.

The depth and breadth of the current physical and mental health crises, compounded by political divisions and economic distress, may call for something like a national truth and reconciliation commission. While that may seem an extreme measure, we recognize that many citizens—white, black, and brown—have deep-seated feelings of being unheard, discounted, and disrespected. These feelings profoundly affect their ability to take a positive role in their communities. Parents cannot give what they do not have. If we want all our children to be raised in an atmosphere of curiosity, courtesy, and compassion we must approach parents in that same manner.

We acknowledge that this chapter does not address the challenges of program funding and note that financial support for program monitoring and evaluation are important along with that for the programming itself. We sincerely hope that readers will take up our call for advocacy with local, state, and federal entities in all sectors of society—government, business, and community organizations—in order to advance the cause. Programming, monitoring and evaluation all need financial and policy support.

The recommendation above, "We support policy and practice initiatives that make parenting education available, accessible, affordable and attractive to all parents and caregivers in order to support children's wellbeing and healthy development from birth through young adulthood" is endorsed by the American Academy of Pediatrics, Mental Health America, Trust for America's Health, Zero to Three, National Prevention Science Coalition, the Center for the Study of Social Policy and the Collaborative on Healthy Parenting in Primary Care of the National Academies of Sciences, Engineering and Medicine.

This manifesto is available for free download on the website of Parents Forum, the parent peer support program we co-lead, for interested individuals and institutions to share in physical and virtual spaces wherever parents gather.

Two entities in the US already support making parenting education universal: the Collaborative for Healthy Parenting in Primary Care (HPPC) and the National Parenting Education Network (NPEN). We will continue, as individuals and through our organization, Parents Forum, to advocate for this cause. We invite you, our readers, to use your personal, professional, and organizational connections to help make parenting education universal to improve the lives of children, to support parents and others who love and guide them and to promote democratic values in families and communities.

ACKNOWLEDGEMENTS

The authors sincerely appreciate former NPEN council member Mary Kay Stranik's careful reading of several drafts of this chapter, especially her help with the overview, terminology, and history. We are also very grateful to the editors and reviewers of this book, *Emerging Trends*, and to you, the reader.

SOME PROGRAMS MENTIONED

Abecedarian Project, Avance, CASEL: Collaborative for Academic, Social and Emotional Learning, CCFC: Campaign for a Commercial-Free Childhood, Center for Humane Technology, DESA: Department of Economic and Social Affairs at the UN, DIFI: Doha International Family Institute, EAD: Educating for American Democracy, ECDAN: Early Childhood Development Action Network, ECFE: Early Childhood and Family Education (MN), Families First (MA), FFCA: Fathers & Families Coalition of America, GFRP: Global Family Research Project, HCZ: Harlem Children's Zone (NY), HHS: Hollywood, Health and Society, HPPC: Collaborative for Healthy Parenting in Primary Care, IFFD: International Federation for Family Development, IFPE: International Federation for Parent Education (also known as FIEP, the French acronym), NFI: National Fatherhood Initiative, NCFR: National Council on Family Relations, NFP: Nurse-Family Partnership, NPEN: National Parenting Education Network, NPU: National Parents Union, NSFN: National Family Support Network, PTA: Parent Teacher Association, Society for Prevention Research, Zero to Three.

REFERENCES

Bartlett, J. D., Sparrow, J., Ayoub, C., Alleyne, K., & Muniz, J. (2016). *Compendium of parenting interventions.* Unpublished. https://doi.org/10.13140/RG.2.1.1397.0962.

The Child & Adolescent Health Measurement Initiative. (2017). *ACEs resource packet: Adverse childhood experiences (ACEs) basics.* National Data Resource Center for Child and Adolescent Health.

Daly, M., Bray, R., Bruckauf, Z., Byrne, J., Margaria, A., Pecnik, N., & Samms-Vaughan, M. (2015). Family and parenting support: Policy and provision in a global context. *Innocent Insight.* UNICEF Office of Research, Florence.

Department of Economic and Social Affairs (DESA). (2011). *Men in families and family policy in a changing world* (issue brief). United Nations. www.un.org

Department of Economic and Social Affairs. (2020, August 6). *Good practices in family policy making.* United Nations. https://www.un.org/development/desa/family/2020/08/06/family-policy-making/

Doha International Family Institute. (2018, October 22). *Civil society statement on parenting.* DIFI. https://www.difi.org.qa/civil-society-statement-on-parenting/

Duffin, E. (2021, March 2). *Child abuse in the United States—Statistics & facts.* Statista. https://www.statista.com/topics/5910/child-abuse-in-the-united-states/

Farmer, A., Neier, A., & Parker, A. (2008). *A violent education: Corporal punishment of children in US public schools.* Human Rights Watch.

García, J. L., Heckman, J., Leaf, D. E., & Prados, M. J. (2017, June). Quantifying the life-cycle benefits of a prototypical early childhood program. *National Bureau of Economic Research.* doi:10.3386/w23479

Kawashima-Ginsberg, K., & Dubé, L. (2021). *The road to a stronger democracy begins in the classroom.* Boston GLOBE. https://www.bostonglobe.com/2021/03/08/opinion/road-stronger-democracy-begins-classroom/

Kirby-Wilkins, J., Taner, E., Cassidy, D., & Cenizal, R. (2014). *Family life education: A profession with a proven return on investment* [White Paper]. National Council on Family Relations. https://www.ncfr.org/sites/default/files/ncfr

Mueller, M. R., Armson, R., & Rader, S. (2003). *Parent involvement in kindergarten and third grade education: What former participants in early childhood family education and other parents report.* Minnesota Center for Survey Research. http://ecadmin.wdfiles.com/local--files/literature-research/Parent%20Inv%20and%20former%20ECFE%20part.pdf.

National Center for Injury Prevention and Control, Division of Violence Prevention. (2020, April 3). *adverse childhood experiences (ACEs).* Centers for Disease Control and Prevention. https://www.cdc.gov/violenceprevention/aces/index.html.

UNICEF. (2010). *Child disciplinary practices at home: Evidence from a range of low and middle-income countries.* Author.

Vinovskis, M. A. (1987). Family and schooling in colonial and nineteenth-century America. *Journal of Family History*, *12*(1–3), 19–37. https://doi.org/10.1177/036319908701200102.

Wessels, I., Mikton, B., Ward C. L., Kilbane, T., Alves, R., Campello, G., Dubowitz, H., Hutchings, J., Jones, L., Lynch, M., & Madrid, B. (2013). *Preventing violence: Evaluating outcomes of parenting programmes.* World Health Organization. www.who.int

Williams, A., & D'Addato, A. (2012). *Early intervention and prevention in family and parenting support: Compendium of inspiring practices.* Eurochild. www.eurochild.org

APPENDIX

PARENT PARTICIPATION LADDER AUGUST 2014

Eve Sullivan

INTRODUCTION

The following definitions of roles are intended to be descriptive rather than confining. An individual may act in one or another role, or in multiple roles, at different times. Similarly, the definitions of strategies are not exclusive. An activity may be part of one or more strategy or part of several strategies at different times. *The writer's hope is that the terms and definitions offered below will be distributed widely and adopted by parents themselves as well as by policy makers, parenting services practitioners, providers, and staff.*

ROLES

Parent / Caregiver: Any individual who has or had primary responsibility for the care of a child of any age.

Practitioner / Provider / Staff: An individual, in a paid or volunteer position, affiliated with a program or organization offering parenting education, training and support.

It is important to note that the above two main roles often overlap: Practitioners, providers and program staff are very often parents themselves. Further, an individual parent or caregiver has various sorts of interaction—and often follows a natural progression in his or her interaction—with a parenting services program or organization, as follows:

1. **A parent or caregiver starts out as a participant.** At this stage his or her primary activity involves receiving the benefits of the program: education, training, support.

2. **A parent may become involved** more regularly with a program and take an active role for shorter or longer periods, bringing materials home,

offering feedback, for example, and these activities may inspire other participants to follow his or her example.

3. **A parent may then choose to become engaged** in a wider variety of activities and make a longer-term commitment. This involves taking on more responsibilities, including communicating about program events and organization with other parents and with practitioners, providers and / or staff and helping plan and organize program activities.

   Note: The term "parent engagement" also describes efforts by school departments and other community agencies to include parents in activities and programs, often under the heading "family and community engagement."

4. **Ideally, the interactions described above lead to parents becoming empowered** and both more confident and more competent in their family roles as well as in their roles in the community, including in parenting services program.

5. **Finally, an individual may become a parent leader: someone who has taken part in one or more of above activities, first participating, then becoming involved, engaged, and finally empowered to take on major responsibilities.** These include independent advocacy and/or meaningful advisory roles within or for a parenting program on issues of program planning, policy and evaluation. These can include advocacy and advisory roles, as well, for other community programs that benefit children and parents, for example, recreation, sports and arts programs.

Clearly, individuals should be able to move from one sort of interaction to another as their children grow and develop and they should be able to move back to simple participation if their needs dictate. A common thread in all these interactions is parent peer support, a vital complement to the education, training and support offered by practitioners, providers and staff who work in parenting programs.

Usually, parents fill the roles described above as volunteers, but parents also may move into practitioner, provider or staff roles. It should be noted that financial support (stipends, expense reimbursements and other practical support including meals, child care and transportation) offered to for fulfilling any of the roles from participant through leader may blur the nonprofessional/professional distinction. However, the value of parents' time and the wide, deep and long-lasting social benefit of parents and caregivers becoming good at raising children, should be recognized and can legitimately be remunerated.

STRATEGIES

Public, private and community-based organizations committed to community-building should incorporate the above sorts of interactions and should support parents in taking on whatever roles they need, want, and can take on, depending on their and their families' situation. These strategies include:

- Parent participation
- Parent involvement
- Parent engagement
- Parent empowerment
- Parent leadership

Further, the collaboration between parents and practitioners that takes place in the course of parenting services being offered and that results in parents' increasing competence and confidence can develop into parent-practitioner partnerships that take a variety of forms. Parents and practitioners may partner with each other along a continuum from individual family support to program planning, policy and evaluation.

Ideally, parents' needs are met, their voices are heard and their confidences are respected in all the strategies. Similarly, good management practices in parenting services respect the needs and foster the career development of practitioners, providers and staff alike.

CONCLUSION

The above schema is offered as a contribution to the national dialogue on parenting resources in a variety of fields: education, human services, medicine, public health, public safety and workforce development. I hope it will serve to raise awareness of the importance of a strengths-based approach to parenting services that recognizes parents as most knowledgeable about their families and communities and will, ultimately, serve to improve the health and wellbeing, educational attainment, and life success of all our children.

—Eve Sullivan, Cambridge, Massachusetts USA
eve@parentsforum.org / *617-233-7890*

NOTES

In distributing this Parent Participation Ladder, kindly provide credit to Eve Sullivan, Founder, Parents Forum, Cambridge, Massachusetts USA / eve@parentsforum.org (and on twitter: @evesullivan) / Founder, Parents Forum / http://www.parentsforum.org / Author: *Where the Heart Listens: a handbook for parents and their allies in a global society*

The 'ladder' schema was created as a follow-up to the FRIENDS Network for Action Meeting held June 21+22, 2011, Alexandria VA, and is based on the Parent Leadership / Partnership Working Document presented at the June 21, 2011, 11am session at that meeting.

In spring 2013 I completed a project for Teachers21 (www.teacher21.org), co-writing standards for 'family and community engagement' submitted to Massachusetts DESE Dept. of Elementary and Secondary Education. In those standards we used Family and Community Engagement as the overarching term, and wrote "family engagement," "parent engagement" and (in Boston) 'family and student engagement' as shorthand.

I understand the term 'engagement' to mean the school's responsibility for outreach to parents and others in parenting roles, that is, family members responsible for children's and youth's care and guidance. Parents as individuals then have a responsibility to participate, become involved and empowered and, as they are able and willing, assume leadership roles in school/home partnerships.

I urge these activities to be considered steps on a ladder: participation, involvement, engagement, empowerment and leadership, with parents responsible for the first two and the last two, and school and agency staff—who, of course, are often parents themselves—responsible for engagement. An individual parent or caregiver can step up or down on the ladder, depending on his or her time, interest and expertise.

SECTION III

ROLE OF COLLEGES

In the corner of a coffee shop where they had gathered, outside of the traditional EPFP meeting calendar, one of Danielle's peers commented that "the industrial revolution influenced not just the world but also education in the United States." Danielle listened carefully as Ed, a high school teacher, progressed through his notes for their group's Learning Teams presentation and facilitation of the next EPFP session. Ed went on to say, "By the 1900s, America had adopted the factory model of education. It was highly influenced by standardized testing. This process is strikingly like factory quality control. The factory model of education is based on three main ideas: 1) the school as a factory, 2) the child as a product, and 3) standardized testing as a form of quality control. Education was so closely related to the factory model that the Smith-Hughes Act was passed in 1917, an act that provided funding for vocational training." Danielle and her group appreciated Ed's careful research and eloquent reporting. They were shocked at how little had changed since the 1900s in their experiences of education. They wondered how alternative models that valued innovative programming options, worked to meet each student's needs, and genuinely included diverse, equity-oriented faculty could change the game. On the other hand, the group considered how frustrations over high stakes testing and the rising cost of tuition could make people question the point of college altogether. While their attention was primarily centered on delivering an excellent session for their peers, Danielle's group appreciated it when someone at a table near them turned to say that their conversations reminded him of debates that he read about between W.E.B. Du Bois and Booker T. Washington. Hearing that comment, her small group felt confident that they had enough current and historical information to get the full EPFP cohort to consider the flaws of modern instructional practices, how they influence post-secondary decisions, and what colleges and universities can learn from different voices. At their session, they would frame the current conversation around the contemporary role of colleges and highlight the need for authentic leadership to realize education's promises. As the group began packing up their laptops, notes, and presentation materials, Danielle smiled, knowing that her team would have the most relevant, well-evidenced, and engaging presentation of her cohort.

CHAPTER 6

INVOLVED FATHERS

The Missing Link in Education Policy Reform

Theodore S. Ransaw

Michigan State University

Here are the questions that my father clients could easily answer: If your son could be a super hero, what would his power be?, What kind of monsters do your kids fear?, How high does your daughter feel comfortable flying in a swing?, What makes your son feel defeated?

> —*Marylin York*
> *Man's Rights Attorney (York, 2020)*

INTRODUCTION

In 2019 the United States spent $129.8 billion on education (U.S. Department of Education, 2019). However, in 2019, the annual cost of father absence in the U.S. was $100 billion (Nock & Einolf, 2008). There are more than monetary implications for children who grow up in father-absent homes. But the fact that fathers are not even considered as potential allies in school improvement plans is a form of deficit thinking that leaves an entire group of allies without a voice.

Emerging Trends in Education Policy: Unapologetic Progressive Conversations,
pages 77–93.

For example, even though children who grow up in fatherless homes have adverse educational outcomes, a high mortality rate of four times a greater risk of living in poverty, more likely to have behavioral problems, more than seven times more likely to become pregnant as a teen, more likely to suffer from child abuse and neglect, more likely to abuse alcohol, twice as likely to suffer from obesity, twice as likely to drop out of high school, more likely to commit a crime, and more likely to go to jail (Fatherhood.org, 2016; Pascoe et al., 2016; Radi et al., 2017), surprisingly, 86 % of Americans say a single parent and child constitute a family (Pew Research Center, 2010). What is more alarming is that according to the U.S. Census Bureau, 80 percent of single-parent families are headed by single mothers (U.S. Census Bureau, 2022). And since fatherless homes are more likely to be affected by poverty (U.S. Census Bureau, 2017), children raised in impoverished families are more likely to have toxic stressors that lead to dropping out of school (Shonkoff & Garner, 2012).

To be clear, educators are taking academic achievement in schools seriously (Berger, 2018; Garcia, & Weiss, 2017; Kyriakides et al., 2019). Most school improvement plans have some form of social-emotional support as well as social-cultural support. For example, culturally relevant pedagogy, culturally sustaining pedagogies, and culturally proficient pedagogies are popular topics for increasing cultural competency (Ladson-Billings, 1995). Popular topics that advocate for school improvement include helping teachers to use empathy for better classroom interactions, facilitating opportunities for teachers to develop empathy, and trying to better understand how bullying is tied to a student's low sense of empathy (Warren, 2014; Black & Phillips, 1982; Jolliffe, & Farrington, 2006). Many researchers suggest cultural competency as a critical component in effective school reform (Boykin 1994; Derman-Sparks & Edwards 2009; Laird 2015; Paris & Alim, 2017; Warren 2014).

OVERVIEW

The following section will include essential terms related to fathering involvement, followed by the frameworks used to ground policy recommendations to increase fathering involvement in schools.[1] Next, you will see the literature review highlighting ways fathers contribute to closing achievement gaps, cultural competency, empathy, behavior, cognition, and literacy. Lastly, you will find the policy recommendations that support the idea that involved fathers are the key to improving educational outcomes.

---

[1] The author acknowledged that there are studies on -sex parenting. However, same-sex parenting and child outcomes are mixed, and many gaps in the research remain. And since research on same-sex parenting is beyond the chapter's scope and premise, this chapter unapologetically advocates, advances, and articulates for more fathers to be involved in schools regardless of sexual orientation.

TERMS

Positive forms of father involvement include participating in child-related activities, engaging multiple forms of involvement, and developing a positive father-child relationship (Adamson & Johnson, 2013). Father involvement comprises three components: (1) direct interaction (or engagement) with the child in the context of caretaking, play, or leisure; (2) accessibility (or availability), being physically or psychologically available to the child; and (3) responsibility, assuming responsibility for the child's welfare and care, including organizing and planning his/her life (Tamis-LeMonda & Cabrera, 1999). This model is presently the most widely accepted definition of father involvement, as it focuses on his feelings and society's perceptions of masculinity (Pleck & Pleck, 1997).

Please note that fathering involvement is an academic term that includes engagement, availability and responsibility and is different than parenting involvement. Parenting involvement and parenting engagement are two related terms. Parent involvement is not consistently defined in the literature but often described as two-way communication between parents and teachers and parent engagement is often referred to as parent being engaged in their child's learning in home and school (National Improvement Hub, 2022). However, there is a continuum between parental involvement and parental engagement, and it is not "always easy to say whether something is 'parental involvement' or 'parental engagement'" (National Improvement Hub, 2022). However, the focus for this chapter is to support fathers being engaged in all school and schooling activities. Additionally, play will be defined as "a mix of physical, social, emotional, and intellectual rewards at all stages of life" (Eberle, 2017, p. 217), that fathers typically engage in to bond, connect and teach their children.

THEORETICAL FRAMEWORK

This chapter makes use of two interrelated theories. The first is Bandura's Social Learning Theory (1977). Social Learning Theory, S.L.T. asserts that learning is a social function comprised of attention, retention, reproduction, and motivation (Bandura, 1977), all key factors in effective mentoring. Fathers are the first mentors (Boone, 2016). The second is Social Cognitive Theory, S.C.T. (Bandura, 1986; Miller & Dollard, 1941) that views learning as a process learned from observing the behavior of others. Successful cognitive learning occurs when there is close identification with the observed such as a relatable mentor.

Cultural Competency

The importance of cultural competency cannot be overstated. In addition to being a popular topic in archeology, anthropology, history, psychology, policy, criminal justice, occupational therapy, medicine, and nursing (Smith, 1997), cultural competency is one of the most cited topics in education (Muniz, 2019). In fact, despite its popularity, there is still no consensus about the definition of cultural competence nor its components (Fantini, 2018; Muniz, 2019). However, there is research that asserts that cultural competence is a form of emotional intelligence or *E.I.* (Guntersdorfer & Golubeva, 2018; Riess, 2017). Fortunately, Emotional Intelligence, E.I. does have a definition. *E.I.* was defined by Mayer and Salovey as a "subset of social intelligence that involves the ability to monitor one's own and others' feelings and emotions, to discriminate among them and to use this information to guide one's thinking and actions" (1990, p. 189) and later refined to include "thinking about feelings" (1997, p. 10). Commonly used in intercultural competence (I.C.), E.I. encourages social and emotional development through a combination of self-awareness, self-regulation, motivation, social skills, and empathy (Guntersdorfer & Golubeva, 2018). Weilenmann et al. (2018) assert that regulating emotions, empathy, and mindful listening are the most cited components of emotional intelligence. Tucker et al. (2012) attest that emotional intelligence can predict student intercultural growth and decreased ethnocentric communication apprehension. Having said that, empathy cannot be forced in a classroom. "When empathy occurs, we find ourselves experiencing it, rather than directly causing it to happen" (Davis, 1990, p. 707). Simply put, there is a direct connection between E.I., I.C., and empathy.

Empathy

While similar to cultural competency in that there is not a consensus on defining it, empathy seems to be comprised of at least two components (Weilenmann et al., 2018). The first is sharing of another's emotions—an affective component and the second is understanding how a person feels—the cognitive component (Weilenmann et al., 2018). In addition to material needs, fathers provide a positive emotional model for their children and foster empathy in them (Rapini, 2016). In fact, children who grow up with a father in the home are much better at self-regulation than children who are raised fatherless (Rapini, 2016). Additionally, fathers can positively influence their children's sense of self-control and can help instill a feeling of empathy toward others (Popenoe, 2017). Understanding is more than a feeling but a process that can be useful in predicting and understanding social behavior (Lahvis 2016).

Sharing, being in the moment of another's emotion, and understanding how a person feels the way they do are essential elements that are related to healthy socialization (Eisenberg & Fabes, 1998). Although people think of roughhousing when they hear the word 'Dad,' fathers make a significant contribution to their children's emotional wellbeing and resilience through modeling their unique form of sensitivity and empathy for someone hurting (Rapini, 2016).

Empathy is a vital element to fathering involvement as there are distinct ways that fathers nurture empathy and the moral emotions of their children independent of mothers, as well as the different ways children respond to their father form of empathy (Antonopoulou et al., 2012; Papaleontiou & Omari, 2020; Strayer & Roberts, 1989). In fact, according to Thurston (2014), father-infant—not mother-infant—attachment stimulates the desire to connect with others and to understand them because fathers are the first 'other,' i.e., the first person other than the mother a child comes in contact with. Empathy is such a powerful component to father parenting that children who have involved fathers are better at identifying other children's feelings and taking steps to make them feel better (Cummings, & O'Reilly, 1997; Palkovitz, 2002). The ability to empathize with others and to see their point of view is a type of "decentering," the ability to be in touch with one's own feelings and the willingness to self-regulate (Byram, 1997).

Similar to decentering, having theory of mind, the capacity to understand the mental state of others, and in turn, predict and explain their behavior is also a social part of being empathic (DeBernardis et al., 2014; Premack & Woodruf, 1978). Social cognitive skills such as empathy (matching the emotional state of another) and theory of mind (understanding others' mental states) are crucial for everyday interactions, cooperation, and cultural learning (Goldstein &Winner, 2012). Empathy and theory of mind *ToM*, are distinctive psychological constructs in predicting children›s social functioning (Wang & Wang, 2015).

One method that fathers use to help their children better understand themselves and others is through rough and tumble play. Social play, especially rough-and-tumble play R.T., is intimately associated with communication. Play communication may be among the most sophisticated communication systems seen in humans and non-humans (Palagi et al., 2016). Rough and tumble play mimics physically vigorous, playful fighting that "mimics" aggressive behaviors between at least two consenting partners (DiPietro, 1981). Since fathers are more likely to engage in rough and tumble play than mothers (Paquette & Dumont, 2013), and rough and tumble play "promotes the development of empathy" (Carlisle, p. 308, 2009), fathering involvement is a gendered specific way that fathers facilitate empathy in their children.

Rough and tumble play is important to regulating emotion and managing aggression and positive emotional expressiveness (LaFreniere, 2013; Lindsey & Colwell, 2013). Rough and tumble play stimulates the cerebral cortex and the hippocampus, important factors in learning, memory, mental flexibility, improving social problem skills, and increasing the capacity to manage emotions (Bekoff & Pierce, 2009; DeBenedet & Cohen, 2011; Pellegrini, 1987; Sunderland, 2007). Rough and tumble play is essential to regulating emotion and managing aggression and the positive emotional expressiveness of children (LaFreniere, 2013; Lindsey & Colwell, 2013).

Limits set by fathers that often occur during rough and tumble play can contribute to the development of empathy, and father affection positively influences empathy in girls during middle childhood and early adolescence (Antonopoulou et al., 2012). Children with involved fathers have more satisfying lives, are more likely to have long-term marriages and fewer divorce rates, have less depression, have less emotional distress, and experience fewer negative feelings like fear and guilt (Paquette, 2004). It seems that a father's love is just as important as a mother's love in psychological wellbeing and behavioral health (Rohner, & Veneziano, 2001).

Behavior

Fathering involvement reduces behavioral problems in boys, psychological issues in young women, and a child's social and emotional wellbeing (Adamson & Johnson, 2013; Sarkadi et al., 2008). Boys with an engaged father have fewer behavioral problems during their early school years and are slightly more socially advantaged than children with less involved fathers in their preschool years (Aldous & Mulligan, 2002; Howard et al., 2006). Daughters who have an involved father are more likely to have higher academic achievement than those who do not because an involved father encourages his daughter to take secure risks like enrolling in more challenging courses (Leman & Sorensen, 2000).

Furthermore, father involvement has a protective effect against criminality for both sexes (Coley, 2001), and school-aged children of involved fathers are more likely to achieve higher academically than those of non-involved fathers (Nord & West, 2001). *There also seems to be a link between consistent fathering involvement and child regulation* roles (Bocknek et al., 2014).

Children born in single-mother homes show higher levels of aggressive behavior than children born to married mothers (Osborne, & McLanahan, 2007). In fact, McLanahan, Tach, & Schneider, 2013) assert that, statistically, father absences are responsible for many social and behavioral problems. Put simply, it is clear that fathers make positive contributions to their children's behavioral development, particularly in cognitive and social domains (Black et al., 1999; Bocknek et al., 2014; Cabrera et al., 2006).

Cognition

In addition to supporting behavioral health, fathering involvement enhances cognitive development and academic achievement (Sarkadi et al., 2008; Adamson & Johnson, 2013). A father's involvement in his children's schooling is associated with the likelihood of a student getting mostly A's (Adamsons & Johnson, 2013). The association between fathering involvement and likelihood for mostly A's holds true for biological fathers, stepfathers, and single-parent families (Adamsons & Johnson, 2013). In fact, a father's positive influence on his child's cognitive and educational outcomes starts as early as five months old. By the first year, involved fathers have higher cognitive functioning children, their toddlers have better problem-solving skills, and by age three have better problem-solving skills and a higher I.Q. (Rosenberg & Wilcox, 2006).

A father's academic support is positively related to a son's motivation to try harder in school and to place a higher value on education (Alfaro et al., 2006). Additionally, "fathers tend to have a unique style of disciplining their children . . . [and] are more likely to use strict and demanding parenting behaviors when dealing with boys" (Malone-Colon & Roberts, 2006, p. 2). As Paquette (2004), as well as Naber et al. (2010), asserted, the parent's and the child's gender play important and intertwined roles in parenting. These positive aspects of fathers' involvement are not limited to just boys; however, daughters are also often more mentally competent as a result of positive fathering involvement (Pruett, 2000).

Findings yielded by Newland et al.'s (2013) international study indicated that a father's involvement is related to his children's beliefs about teachers and perceptions about invitations for involvement. Additionally, a father's involvement is relevant to his children feeling secure, exploring the world, and their willingness to embrace academic challenges (Newland et al., 2013). Finally, Williams and Kelly (2005) contended that the level of a father's involvement and the quality of his relationship with his children could predict whether they will internalize or externalize problems in school.

Literacy

Regarding language, fathers positively contribute to early language development in ways that are separate and independent of a mother (Pancsofar & Vermon-Feagans, 2010). In general, fathers ask more challenging who, where, when, and what questions than mothers (Rowe et al., 2004). These types of challenging questions help to improve language development and self-confidence (Palkovitz, 2002). Consequently, a father's homework assistance strategies and reading engagement during storytime with his children complement mothers who tend to ask more emotive questions in soothing tones (Palkovitz, 2002). Additionally, involved fathers promote reading opportunities, recognize their children's achievements, interact positively with their children; s literacy practices, and model being a reader (Morgan et al., 2009). A father's early involvement in his child's literacy activities helps to develop their reading and writing skills (Stile, & Ortiz, 1999). The time a father spent reading with his child was the strategy that predicted emergent literacy outcomes most consistently (Brooks, 2015).

The research is clear. Fathering involvement positively influences current trends in school reform practices, including increasing cultural competency, facilitating empathy, sustained behavioral support, improving cognition, and encouraging early literacy development (Ransaw, 2015). Having said that, the key to fathers supporting their children's educational outcomes is to have an involved father. Involved fathers make a difference. To that end, there are many programs, resources, best practices, and funding opportunities to support fathers to be involved in the lives of their children.

Programs

The Family Literacy in Prisons, *FLIP* program was designed to encourage fathers and to highlight the importance of early literacy development through literacy-orientated family visits. Success in the FLIP program was demonstrated by the fact that theories of early literacy development were successfully shared with incarcerated fathers and incorporated into the literacy-oriented family visits. (Nutbrown et al., 2019).

24/7 Dad is a community-based curriculum that helps men develop the attitudes, knowledge, and skills they need to get and stay involved with their children. Preliminary analyses reveal statistically significant increases in parenting knowledge and conflict resolution skills (Perry, 2019).

The Doctor Dad Program created by healthcare professionals, helps new dads learn the basics of child health and safety, increasing their knowledge and confidence while strengthening their parenting skills. Fathers completing the pre/post surveys on average scored 45% mastery on the pre-test and 87% mastery on the post test (Casey et al., 2004)

Boot Camp for New Dads is an English and Spanish father-to-father, community-based workshop that inspires and equips men of different economic levels, ages, and cultures to become confidently engaged with their infants, support their mates, and personally navigate their transformation into dads. Ninety percent of participants reported a boost of confidence in taking care of a new baby, taking care of a new mom, and working with her to build a family (Bootcampfornewdads.org, 2020).

The Nurturing Father's Program is a 13-week group-based program for developing attitudes and skills for male nurturance. Participants improved in their understanding of developmental capabilities of children, improved their ability to demonstrate empathy toward children, improved in the use of alternate strategies to corporal punishment, increased understanding, and acceptance of the needs of self and children, and showed an increase of value placed on children feeling empowered (Daire, no year).

WATCH D.O.G.S. (Dads of Great Students) is the father involvement initiative of the National Center for Fathering that organizes fathers and father figures to provide positive male role models for students and to enhance school security. WATCH D.O.G.S has been recognized on the floor of Congress as a program that "can be a great tool in our efforts to prevent school violence and improve student performance because it can increase parental initiative and involvement in their children's education" (Congressional Record, 2023, Senate Bill S393, 2022).

InsideOut Dad™ Fathers Reentry Program is designed to address the specific needs of incarcerated fathers. Statistically significant improvements in parenting self-efficacy, knowledge, attitudes, and contact with children (Block et al., 2014).

Resources

There are school-based resources for dads from the National Fatherhood Initiative, including a P.T.A. recruitment kit and activities for dads to engage their children at various stages of development (preschool, elementary school, and adolescence). Engaging Absent Fathers is an online curriculum developed by the Pennsylvania Child Welfare Training Program. RISE, a magazine written by and for parents with children in the child welfare system, focuses on the rights and roles of fathers. Involving Fathers has practice tips for child welfare caseworkers to involve fathers, written by the Iowa Department of Human Services (Just Partners, 2011). The Annie Casey Foundation has a 40+ Top Fatherhood Resource guide available online at: https://www.aecf.org/resources/40-top-fatherhood-resources/.

BEST PRACTICES

While no single approach is applicable to all situations, according to the National Academies of Sciences, Engineering, and Medicine (Breiner et al., 2016), there are a few strategies for increasing participation and retention of parenting program participants.

They include viewing parents as equal partners in determining the types of services that would most benefit them and their children; tailoring interventions to meet the specific needs of families; integrating services for families with multiple service needs; creating opportunities for parents to receive support from peers to increase engagement, reduce stigma, and increase their sense of connection to other parents with similar circumstances; addressing trauma, which affects a high percentage of individuals in some communities and can interfere with parenting and healthy child development; making programs culturally relevant to improve their effectiveness and participation across diverse families; and enhancing efforts to involve fathers, who are underrepresented in parenting research (Breiner et al., 2016).

POSSIBLE FUNDING

On July 9, 2008, President Obama attempted have a "national conversation on responsible fatherhood and healthy families" (Obama, 2009). The resulting Responsible Fatherhood and Healthy Families Act of 2009 bill announced June 19, 2009, was intended to provide grants to promote economic opportunity for low-income parents, reverse federal funding cut from child support programs, repeal a $25 child support fee charged to parents, require all collected child support to be paid to families, address the issue of unpaid child support debt, expands the Earned Income Tax Credit (EITC), and create career pathways that require a good education. "We need [men] to realize that what makes you a man is not the ability to have a child—it's the courage to raise one" (Obama, 2009). However, the Responsible Fatherhood and Healthy Families Act was met with pollical opposition and was replaced with the My Brother's Keeper mentorship program. The inclusion of this information in not a criticism of a political party but a fitting example of a lack of attention and minimal awareness of the need to support fathers. Consequently, other than the Fatherhood Research and Practice Network FRPN. org, funding sources to support fathering involvement in schools are typically found in grant funding organizations that support parenting involvement/engagement in general. For example, the U.S. Department of Health and Human Services (H.H.S.) and the U.S. Department of Education fund education programs that support parenting practices associated with healthy child development (Breiner, Ford, Gadsden, 2016) at an ongoing rate of $150 million a year.

Macro funding databases to search for parenting involvement/engagement funding include Grants.gov, a federal site that aggregates all federal grant opportunities, and Healthy Marriage and Responsible Fatherhood Grants acf.hhs.gov that offers $150 million per year for programs provided by the US Department of Health and Human Services. Additional possible funding sources that may support fathering involvement/engagement include the Kellogg Foundation Family Engagement Current Grantees, wkkf.org, Lastly, the Centerforpolicyresearch.org, offers resources for fathers aggregated by federal, state and local sources.

POLICY RECOMMENDATIONS

Based on the literature review and supplemental information above, the following three-pronged approach is suggested to advocate and sustain positive father involvement in our school. *Policies* to inform, encourage and support fathering involvement, facilitating *networking* to change the narrative of a father as the silly parent into the view of dad as a child›s first hero, and employer *Leadership* that enables fathers to be full participants in their children›s lives by facilitating equitable, flexible parental leave time.

These policy recommendations are based on the idea that learning is a social function (Bandura, 1977) and the realization that learning is a learned process through observations of those who are close to us (Bandura 1986; Miller & Dollard, 1941). Consequently, *S.L.T.* (Bandura, 1977), *S.C.T.* (Bandura 1986; Miller & Dollard, 1941) were suitable frameworks in which to examine fathering involvement and its impact on educational outcomes. Taking steps to make sure fathers are involved in their children›s lives puts students on the right path toward better school experiences and higher grades.

Policies. Political strategies that inform fathers, mothers, schools, and organizations about the importance of fathers in parenting a whole child that helps to make schools more father friendly are needed. This entails making a conscious effort to invite, welcome, and include fathers in parent-teacher conferences, Parent Teacher Associations *P.T.A.'s,* and Parent Teacher Organizations, *P.T.O. emails, notes that are sent home, and homework support. We need to change* the hearts and minds to make schools more father-friendly.

Networking. Establishing and creating communities that educate, share information and resources to support a father's capacity to be an involved parent is the next step. Networking may include parenting, child behavior, and homework assistance training classes designed to enhance a father's instinctive nurturing style. It is also critical to utilize social media, to send encouraging words to dads, to make sure that fathers know their rights, and to inform mothers that father's parent differently but effectively.

Leadership. Administrator and supervisor support in the form of endorsing fathers who take a half-day off to visit a school to read to children or allow him to leave a few minutes early to attend a parent conference, attend P.T.A. meetings, participate in take your kid to work day or to read to kids at school is the final component. Providing equal maternity leave time and supporting fathers on bringing your child to work day are also suggested. Leadership entails employers proactively encouraging and helping fathers to support their children whenever possible. The more time fathers spend with their children, the better it is for both the fathers, their families, and their children.

The research is overwhelmingly clear. When it comes to improving educational outcomes, such as increasing cultural competency, facilitating empathy, sustained behavioral support, improving cognition, and early literacy development, fathers can make significant contributions but are rarely encouraged to participate in school reform policies. Let's help fathers to be more involved in their children's lives through *Policies t*o inform, encourage and support fathering involvement, facilitating *Networking* to change the narrative of a father as the silly parent into the view of dad as a child›s first hero, and employer *Leadership* that enables fathers to be full participants in their children›s lives by facilitating equitable parental leave time.

REFERENCES

Adamson, K., & Johnson, S. K. (2013). An updated and expanded meta-analysis of nonresident fathering and child well-being. *Journal of Family Psychology, 27,* 589–599.

Aldous, J., & Mulligan, G. M. (2002). Father's childcare and children's behavioral problems. *Journal of Family Issues, 23*(5), 624–647.

Antonopoulou, K., Dimitrios, A., Alexopoulos, K., & Maridaki-Kassotaki, K. (2012) Perceptions of father parenting style, empathy, and self-esteem among greek Preadolescents. *Marriage & Family Review 48*(3), 293–309, DOI: 10.1080/01494929.2012.665016.

Bandura, A. (1977). *Social learning theory.* General Learning Press.

Bandura, A. (1986). *Social foundations of thought and Action: A Social cognitive theory.* Prentice Hall.

Bekoff, M., & Pierce, J. (2009). Wild justice: The moral lives of animals. University of Chicago Press.

Berger, T. (2018, February). *Closing the achievement Gap with SEL. Edutopia.* https://www.edutopia.org/article/closing-achievement-gap-sel

Black, H., & Phillips, S. (1982). An intervention program for the development of empathy in student teachers. *The Journal of Psychology, 112*(2), 159–168. DOI:10.1080/00 223980.1982.991537

Block, S., Brown, C. A., Barretti, L., Walker, E., Yudt, M., & Fretz, R. (2014). A mixed-method assessment of a parenting program for incarcerated fathers. *Journal of Correctional Education, 65,* 50–67.

Bocknek, E. L., Brophy-Herb, H. E., Fitzgerald, H. E., Schiffman, R. F., & Vogel, C. (2014). Stability of biological presence as a proxy for family stability: Cross-racial associations with the longitudinal development of emotion regulation in toddlerhood. *Infant Mental Health Journal, 35,* 309–321.

Boone, T. (2016, April). *Black students and Black teachers: Separating the myths from the facts*. Keynote presented at the Black Male Summit, Akron, Ohio.

Bootcampfornewdads.org. (2020). *Validating research*. https://www.bootcampfornewdads.org/validating-research#research

Boykin, A. W. (1994). Afrocultural expression and its implications for schooling. In E.R. Hollins, J. E. King, & W.C. Hayman (Eds.), *Teaching diverse populations: Formulating a knowledge base* (pp. 243–56). State University of New York Press.

Breiner, H., Ford, M., & Gadsden, V. L. (2016, November). *Parenting matters: Supporting parents of children ages 0–8*. National Academies of Sciences, Engineering, and Medicine.

Brooks, C. (2015). Father book reading behaviors and pre-kindergarten emergent literacy. *AllGraduate Theses and Dissertations* (p. 2522). https://digitalcommons.usu.edu/etd/2522.

Byram, M. (1997). *Teaching and assessing intercultural communicative competence*. Multilingual Matters.

Cabrera, N., Shannon, J. D., West, J., & Brooks-Gunn, J. (2006). Parental interactions with Latino infants: Variation by country of origin and English proficiency. Special Issue on Race. *Ethnicity, and Culture in Child Development,74*, 1190–1207.

Carlisle, R. P. (2009). *Encyclopedia of play in today's society*. Sage.

Casey, K. A., Holleran L., & Stone, S. A. (2004). *Summary of formative evaluation findings: Doctor dad pilot test*. Center for Social Work Research. University of Texas at Austin. https://cdn2.hubspot.net/hub/135704/file-563789141 pdf/Research_Eval_Files/18_Evaluation_DoctorDad_UT_102406.pdf.

Coley, R. L., & Medeiros, B. L. (2007). Reciprocal longitudinal relations between nonresident father involvement and adolescent delinquency. *Journal of Child Development, 78*(1) 132–147.

Congressional Record. (2023).The Watchdogs Program. *Congressional Record, 146*(9). https://www.congress.gov/congressional-record/volume-146/issue-9/senate-section/article/S392-2

Cummings, E. M., & O'Reilly, A. W. (1997). Fathers in family context: Effects of marital quality on child adjustment. In M. E. Lamb (Ed.), *The role of the father in child development* (3rd ed.). Wiley.

Daire, A. P., Greenidge, W. L., & Johnson, N. M . (2020, Manuscript under review). *Parental attitudes and behaviors of participants in the Nurturing Father's Program. Fathering*. dadsofgreatstudents.com

Davis, C. M. (1990). What is empathy, and can empathy be taught? *Physical Therapy, 70*(11), 701–711.

DeBenedet, A. T., & Cohen, L. J. (2011). *The art of roughhousing*. Quirk Books.

DeBernardis, G. M., Hayes, L. J., & Fryling, M. J. (2014). Perspective taking as a continuum. *Psychological Record, 64*(1), 123–31.

Derman-Sparks, L., & Edwards, J. O. (2009). *Anti-bias education for young children and ourselves*. National Association for the Education of Young Children.

DiPietro, J. A. (1981). Rough and tumble play: A function of gender. *Developmental Psychology, 17*(1), 50–58.

Eberle, S. G. (2017, March). The elements of play: Toward a philosophy and a definition of play. *American Journal of Play, 6*(2), 214–233.

Eisenberg, N., & Fabes, R. A. (1998). Prosocial development. In W. Damon (Ed.), *Handbook of child psychology. social, emotional, and personality development* (pp. 701–78). Wiley & Sons.

Fantini, A. (2018, May). *Exploring intercultural communicative competence: Concepts, components and assessment (A Multinational Perspective).* Paper presented at the ICC 2018—Intercultural Competence and Mobility: Virtual and Physical. Tucson, AZ.

Fatherhood.org. (2016). *The father absence crisis in America.* National FatherhoodInitiative. https://cdn2.hubspot.net/hubfs/135704/NFIFatherAbsenceInfoGraphic071118.pdf

Garcia, E., & Weiss, E. (2017). *Reducing and averting achievement gaps. Key findings from the 'Education inequalities at the school starting gate' and comprehensive strategies to mitigate early skills gaps.* Economic Policy Institute. https://www.epi.org/publication/reducing-and-averting-achievement-gaps/.

Goldstein, T. R., & Winner, E. (2012) Enhancing empathy and theory of mind. *Journal of Cognition and Development, 13*(1), 19–37, DOI: 10.1080/15248372.2011.573514

Guntersdorfer, I., & Golubeva, I. (2018). Emotional intelligence and intercultural competence: Theoretical questions and pedagogical possibilities. *Intercultural Communication Education, 1*(2), 54–63.

Howard, K. S., Lefever, J. E., Borkowski, J. G., & Whitman, T. L. (2006). Fathers' influence in the lives of children with adolescent mothers. *Journal of Family Psychology, 20*(3), 468–476.

Jolliffe, D., & Farrington, D. P. (2006). Examining the relationship between low empathy and bullying. *Aggressive Behavior, 32,* 540–550.

Just Partners. (2011). *40+ Top fatherhood resources.* Annie E. Casey Foundation. https://www.fatherhood.gov/sites/default/files/Resource%20Files/e000002271_0.pdf

Kyriakides, L., Charalambous, E., Creemers, H. P. M., & Dimosthenous, A. (2019). Improving quality and equity in schools in socially disadvantaged areas. *Educational Research, 61*(3), 274–301, DOI: 10.1080/00131881.2019.1642121

Ladson-Billings, G. (1995). But That's just good teaching! The case for culturally relevant pedagogy. *Theory Into Practice, 34*(3), 159–165.

LaFreniere, P. (2013). Children's play as a context for managing physiological arousal and learning emotion regulation. *Psychological Topics, 22,* 183–204.

Lahvis, G. P. (2016). Social reward and empathy as proximal contributions to altruism: The camaraderie effect. In M. Wöhr & S. Krach (Eds.), *Social behavior from rodents to humans* (pp. 127–157). Springer International Publishing.

Laird, L. (2015). Empathy in the classroom: Can music bring us more in tune with one another? *Music Educators Journal, 101*(4), 56–61.

Leman, R., & Sorensen, E. (2000). Father involvement with their nonmarital children: Patterns, determinants, and effects on their earnings. *Marriage and Family Review, 29*(2/3), 137–158.

Lindsey, E. W., & Colwell, M. J. (2013). Pretend and physical play: Links to preschoolers' affective social competence. *Merrill-Palmer Quarterly, 59*(3), 330–360.

Malone-Colon, L., & Roberts, A. (2006). *Marriage and the well-being of African American boys. A comprehensive literature review.* Institute for American Values.

Mayer, J. D., & Salovey, P. (1997). What is emotional intelligence? In P. Salovey & D. Sluyter (Eds.), *Emotional development and emotional intelligence: Implications for educators* (pp. 3–31). Basic Books

McLanahan, S., Tach, L., & Schneider, D. (2013). The causal effects of father absence. *Annual Review of Sociology, 39,* 399–427.

Miller, N. E., & Dollard, J. (1941). *Social learning and imitation.* Yale University Press.

Morgan, A., Nutbrown, C., & Hannon, P. (2009). Fathers' involvement in young children's literacy development: Implications for family literacy programmes. *British Educational Research Journal 35*(2), 167–185.

Muñiz, J. (2019, March). *Culturally responsive teaching: A 50-state survey of teaching standards.* New America.

Naber, F., Van Ijzendoorn, M. H., Deschamps, P., Van Engeland, H., & Bakermans- Kranenburg, M. J. (2010). Intranasal oxytocin increases fathers' observed responsiveness during play with their children: A double-blind within-subject experiment. *Psychoneuroendrcrinology, 35*(10), 1583–1586.

National Improvement Hub. (2022). *What is 'parental involvement' and parental engagement'?* Education Scotland Denholm House Livingston Scotland. https://education.gov.scot/improvement/research/what-is-parental-involvement-and-parental-engagement/

Newland, L. A., Chen, H.-H., & Coyl-Shepherd, D. D. (2013). Associations among fathers beliefs, perceptions, life context, involvement, child attachment and school outcomes in the U.S. and Taiwan. *Fathering, 11*(1), 3–30.

Nock, S. L., & Einolf, C. J. (2008). *The one hundred-billion-dollar man: The annual public costs of father absence.* National Fatherhood Initiative.

Nord, C. W., & Jerry West, J. (2001). *Fathers' and mothers' involvement in their children's schools by family type and resident status.* U.S. Department of Education, National Center for Education Statistics.

Nutbrown, C. P., Stammers, L., Emblin, N., & Summer Alston-Smith, S. (2019). Family literacy in prisons: fathers' engagement with their young children, *Research Papers in Education, 34*(2), 169–191, doi: 10.1080/02671522.2017.1402085.

Obama, B. (June 19, 2009). *Healthy families, active fatherhood.* Active Fatherhood Washington, D.C. Office of Family Assistance. https://www.acf.hhs.gov/ofa/programs/healthy-marriage-responsible-fatherhood

Osborne, C., & McLanahan, S. (2007). Partnership instability and child well-being. *Journal of Marriage and Family, 69,* 1065–1083.

Palagi, E., Burghardt, G. M., Smuts, B., Cordoni, G., Dall'Olio, S., Fouts, H. N., Řeháková-Petrů, M., Siviy, S. M., & Pellis, S. M. (2016). Rough-and-tumble play as a window on animal communication. *Biological Review, 91,* 311–327. doi:10.1111/brv.12172.

Palkovitz, R. (2002). Involved fathering and child development: Advancing our understanding of good fathering. In C. S. Tamis-LeMonda, & N. Cabrera (Eds.), *Handbook of father involvement* (pp. 33–64). Lawrence Erlbaum.

Pancsofar, N., & Vermon-Feagans, L. (2010). Fathers' early contributions to children's language development in families from low-income rural communities. *Early Child Research Quarterly, 25*(4), 450–463.

Papaleontiou, E., & Omari, O. A. (2020). The (neglected) role of the father in children's mental health. *New Ideas in Psychology, 59,* 1–3.

Paris, D., & Alim, H. S. (2017). *Culturally sustaining pedagogies: Teaching and learning for justice in a changing world.* Teacher's College Press.

Paquette, D. (2004). Theorizing the father–child relationship: Mechanisms and developmental outcomes. *Human Development, 47*, 193–219.

Paquette, D., & Durmont, C. (2012). Is father–child rough-and-tumble play associated with attachment or activation relationships? *Early Child Development and Care, 183*(6), 760–773, doi: 10.1080/03004430.2012.723440.

Pascoe, J. M., Wood, D. L., Duffee, J. H., & Kuo, A. (2016). Mediators and adverse effects of child poverty in the United States. *Journal of the American Academy of Pediatrics, 137*(4), 20160340.

Pellegrini, A. D. (1987). Rough-and-tumble play: Developmental and educational significance. *Educational Psychologist, 22*(1), 23–43, doi: 10.1207/s15326985ep2201_2

Perry, A. P. (2019). *24/7 dad ® in a multi-site parent education intervention for nonresident fathers: Preliminary project evaluation.* https://cdn2.hubspot.net/hubfs/135704/Research%20Evaluation%20Files/247Dad_Louisville_Univ_preliminary_eval_final.pdf?__hstc=162717731.55858456951591101ea5c1763c1cd6 8c.1616768627382.1616768627382.1616768627382.1&__hssc=162717731.6.16 16768627383&__hsfp=1927323894&hsCtaTracking=e8f622db-218f-49c1-ac36-244e30b3016b%7Cd4dd8d88-7f21-402e-8b16-ef46b57649de

Pew Research Center. (2010, November). *The decline of marriage and rise of new families.* https://www.pewsocialtrends.org/2010/11/18/the-decline-of-marriage-and-rise-of-new-families/

Pleck, E. H., & Pleck, J. H. (1997). Fatherhood ideals in the United States: Historical dimensions. In M. E. Lamb (Ed.), *The role of the father in child development* (3rd ed., pp. 33–48). Wiley.

Popenoe, D. (2017). *War over family.* Routledge.

Premack, D., & Woodruff, G. (December 1978). Does the chimpanzee have a theory of mind? *Behavioral and Brain Sciences, 1*(4), 515–526.

Pruett, K. D. (2000). *Fatherneed: Why father care is as essential as mother care for your child.* The Free Press.

Radi, J., Salazar, L., & Cebolla-Boado, H. (2017). Does living in a fatherless household compromise educational success? A comparative study of cognitive and non-cognitive skills. *European Journal of Population. European Journal of Population / Revue Européenne de Démographie, 33*(2), 217–242.

Ransaw, T. (2012). A *father's hands: African American fathering involvement and the educational outcomes of their children.* UNLV Theses, Dissertations, Professional Papers, and Capstones. 1612.https://digitalscholarship.unlv.edu/thesesdissertations/1612

Rapini, M. (2016, June). *A dad's influence in raising empathetic and considerate children.* Chron. https://blog.chron.com/loveandrelationships/2016/06/a-dads-influence-in-raising-empathetic-and-considerate-children/.

Rosenberg, J., & Wilcox, W. B. (2006). *The importance of fathers in the healthy development of children.* U.S. Department of Health and Human Services, Administration for Children and Families Administration on Children, Youth and Families, Children's Bureau, Office on Child Abuse and Neglect.

Rohner, R. P., & Veneziano, R. A. (2001). The importance of father love: History and contemporary evidence. *Review of General Psychology, 5*(4), 382–405.

Rowe, M. L., Cocker, D., & Pan, B. A. (2004). A comparison of fathers' and mothers talk to toddlers in low-income families. *Social Development, 13*(2), 278–291.

Riess, H. (2017). The science of empathy. *Journal of Patient Experience, 4*(2), 74–77.

Salovey, P., & Mayer, J. D. (1990). Emotional intelligence. *Imagination, Cognition, and Personality, 9*, 185–211.

Sarkadi, A., Kristiansson, R., Oberklaid, F., & Bremberg, S. (2008). Fathers' involvement and children's developmental outcomes: a systematic review of longitudinal studies. *Acta Paediatrica, 97*, 153–158.

Shonkoff, J. P., & Garner, A. S. (2012). The lifelong effects of early childhood adversity and toxic stress. *Pediatrics, 129*, 232–246.

Smith, L. S. (1997). Concept analysis: Cultural competence. *Journal of Cultural Diversity, 5*(1) 4–10.

Spinrad, T. L., Losoya, S. H., Eisenberg, N., Fabes, R. A., Shepard , S. A., Cumberland, A., Guthrie, I. K., & Murphy, B. C. (1999). The relations of parental affect and encouragement to children's moral emotions and behavior. *Journal of Moral Education, 28*(3), 323–337.

Stile, S., & Ortiz, R. (1999). A model for involvement of fathers in literacy development with young at-risk and exceptional children. *Early Childhood Journal, 26*, 221–224.

Strayer, J., & Roberts, W. (1989). Children's empathy and role taking: Child and parental factors, and relations to prosocial behavior. *Journal of Applied Developmental Psychology, 10*(2), 227–239. doi:10.1016/0193-3973(89)90006-3

Sunderland, M. (2007). What every parent needs to know: *The incredible effects of love, nurture and play on your child's development.* Dorling Press.

Tamis-LeMonda, C. S., & Cabrera, N. (1999). Perspectives on father involvement: Research and social policy (with commentary by Ross Thompson). *Society for Research in Child Development, Social Policy Report, 13*(2), 1–26.

Thurston, C. (2014). *The* Dad Difference: *Five ways you impact your child and your world.* Still Point Press Design Studio.

Tucker, M. L., Gullekson, N. L., & Esmond-Kiger, C. (2012, June). Accounting for EI: Does emotional intelligence predict greater intercultural growth? *Journal of International Business and Cultural Studies, 8.* http://www.aabri.com/manuscripts/141787.pdf.

U.S. Census Bureau. (2022). *America's families living arrangements: 2022.* https://www.census.gov/data/tables/2022/demo/families/cps-2022.html

U.S. Department of Education. (2019). *President's FY 2021 budget request for the U.S. Department of Education.* https://www2.ed.gov/about/overview/budget/budget21/index.html

Wang, Z., & Wang, L. (2015). The mind and heart of the social child: Developing the empathy and theory of mind scale. *Child Development Research*, 1–8. https://doi.org/10.1155/2015/171304

Warren, C. A. (2014). Towards a pedagogy for the application of empathy in culturally diverse classrooms. *Urban Review, 46*(3) 395–419.

Weilenmann, S., Schnyder, U., Parkinson, B., Corda, C., von Känel, R., & Pfaltz., M. C. (2018). Emotion transfer, emotion regulation, and empathy-related processes in physician-patient interactions and their association with physician well-being: A theoretical model. *Front Psychiatry.* 9(389), 1–19. doi: 10.3389/ fpsyt.2018.00389

Williams, S. K., & Kelly, F. D. (2005). Relationships between involvement, attachment and behavioral problems in adolescence: Examining father's influence. *Journal of Early Adolescence, 25*(2), 168–196.

York, M. [TEDx University of Nevada] (2020, March 20). [Video]. *What representing men in divorce taught me about fatherhood.* YouTube. https://youtu.be/RlSwsE22nX0

CHAPTER 7

ADVANCING THE PROMISE OF CAREER PROGRAMMING IN HIGH SCHOOL

Critical Components Driving Key Student Outcomes

Avery D. D. Newton

Strategic Data Project

INTRODUCTION

In recent years, CTE programming during high school has been found to positively predict student engagement, satisfaction with school, attendance, and graduation rates (Advance CTE, 2017; Walsh et al., 2019). Beyond high school, CTE participation is associated with higher rates of 2-year and 4-year college enrollment (Walker & Farmer, 2018) and labor market outcomes (Dougherty et al., 2020; Rosen et al., 2018). Much of the available evidence on these outcomes, however, is observational. As such, it is often difficult to pinpoint whether and how CTE programming is truly driving these outcomes or merely correlated with them.

Emerging Trends in Education Policy: Unapologetic Progressive Conversations,
pages 95–109.
Copyright © 2023 by Information Age Publishing
www.infoagepub.com

To clarify some of these causal relationships, this chapter profiles several career exploration models around the country that have been evaluated in experimental or quasi-experimental settings. The use of these research methodologies enables causal linkage between program and outcomes in a way that other observational methodologies cannot guarantee. In focusing on these methodologies, this chapter contributes to the growing CTE research literature through clarifying the specific components of Career and Technical Education that influence critical outcomes in high school, college, and beyond.

By drawing upon the best practices as outlined in causal research on CTE, it is possible to consider consistent features across programs as potentially key drivers of target outcomes for students. Throughout this chapter, four exemplar/pilot programs are featured: New York City's P-TECH 9-14 program (Rosen et al., 2020); Wake County, North Carolina's Career Academies (Hemelt et al., 2019); Arkansas' SmartCore Curriculum (Dougherty et al., 2019); and Massachusetts' Innovation Pathways & Early College Pathway Program (ICF, 2020). These programs were selected because they reflect diverse settings and programming approaches, though they all leverage specific research and evaluation methodologies that enable direct causal inference. For each of these programs, features, scope, and causal outcomes from evaluations are outlined. The degree to which elements of these programs drive key student outcomes then informs a discussion of successful elements and limitations. Following this discussion, the chapter concludes with an overview of how these learnings inform policy alongside a series of specific state-level recommendations. These recommendations include incorporating both academic and career-related learning as high school graduation requirements; cultivating systems for early access to postsecondary education and coursework; and creating (or continuing) a coalition of government, school, college, and employer leaders to help unify the mission, priorities, and target outcomes for CTE statewide.

Background

Causal research in CTE is limited relative to other areas of educational research. As is the case in other fields, causal research using experimental or quasi-experimental methods clarifies the direct impact of an initiative on measured outcomes. Hemelt et al. (2019, p. 176) articulate the promise of causal research in the CTE space, writing,

> as districts and states assemble portfolios of reform initiatives and interventions, they must be armed with causal evidence on how those initiatives and programs affect different types of students in different settings. Only with such evidence can policymakers knit a tapestry of reform activities capable of improving outcomes for all students.

Accordingly, a causal evidence base enables a more intimate understanding of the features and limitations of CTE programming, which in turn carries the promise of serving a wider spectrum of students most effectively.

One of the limiting factors preventing more widespread CTE research is the length of time separating early high school from later education and entry into the workforce. Due to this barrier, the true *impact* of Career and Technical Education on students' future outcomes remains somewhat unknown. Until recently, the literature around the causal impact of CTE was largely furnished by James Kemple based on career programming throughout the 1990s (e.g., Kemple, 2001, 2004; Kemple & Willner, 2008, 2011). In the last few years, however, as CTE programming has increased in popularity around the country, several researchers have made notable inroads to understanding how CTE impacts important outcomes in high school, postsecondary education, and early career. To this end, four high school career programs are introduced below, alongside key research and evaluation findings related to the relationship between career programming and important student outcomes. The recency of the available evidence limits the collective understanding of the full longitudinal impact of these and similar CTE interventions, but the methodological strength of the programs profiled in this chapter offers strong early indications of "what works" in varied settings.

After presenting an overview of each program, reviewing the methodology and findings, and sharing concluding thoughts and limitations, the best practices and key lessons learned from this body of research informs three policy recommendations in the next section.

NEW YORK CITY'S P-TECH 9-14
PROGRAM (ROSEN ET AL., 2020)

Program Overview. New York City's Pathways in Technology Early College High School (P-TECH) program serves students in grades 9–14 as they persist through high school (grades 9–12) and eventually community college (grades 13–14). Originally established by IBM, the P-TECH program involves a partnership between a public high school, a community college, and one or more employers. Together, these partners aim to accomplish two central goals: to address and close skills gaps in regional economies and to provide underserved youth with a clear pathway toward higher education and the world of work. Students in P-TECH high schools leave the program with a high school diploma, a cost-free industry-recognized associate's degree, and work-based learning experience (e.g., internships, mentorship, job shadowing).

Evaluation Methods and Data. The program's use of a lottery admissions system allowed for effective estimation of causal program impact through the random assignment inherent to lottery-based selection. As a result, students selected for the P-TECH program and those who were not selected were effectively identical on observed characteristics and assumed to be identical on unobserved characteristics, meaning that any differences measured between the groups over time could be attributed directly to participation in the P-TECH program. While not every student was assigned via a lottery, the authors contend that the use of these admissions processes meet the criteria for a random assignment study in the form of a natural experiment. In total, the study included 3,161 students in cohort 1, 2,164 in cohort 2, and 1,203 in cohort 3.

Evidence collected at the end of each year in high school revealed the following:

- P-TECH students earned more credits than students in other schools, including more *nonacademic* credits in topics including work-based learning, technology, engineering, and human services
- P-TECH students were more likely to take and pass Regents exams, which in turn qualify them for CUNY enrollment
- P-TECH students were eligible to dual enroll in CUNY at a younger age and at a higher rate than their peers

Considered together, the available evidence suggests that P-TECH students are not only on target for high school graduation at a higher rate than their peers, but that they are also gaining career-related skills (including earning relevant credits) and are better equipped for higher education through higher rates of dual enrollment eligibility. Furthermore, because these findings hold for academically low-performing students, the P-TECH model may be well-suited to keeping those who might otherwise be "at risk" on a pathway to graduation and postsecondary access.

Program Conclusions and Limitations. Thus far, the available evidence supports a causal link between P-TECH participation and improved outcomes in academic credits earned, non-academic credits earned, and improved college access through the Regents exams and dual enrollment offerings. However, because the program and the research reflect interim findings, the available evaluation results can neither speak to the "overall efficacy" of the P-TECH 9-14 model nor the long-term impacts on postsecondary completion or career (as well as what may mediate these eventual impacts; Rosen et al., 2020, p. 36).

WAKE COUNTY, NC'S CAREER ACADEMIES
(HEMELT ET AL., 2019)

Program overview. The Wake County Public School System in North Carolina offers a career academy model to students housed within district high schools. Broadly, features of career academies include a multi-year model, CTE coursework, project-based learning opportunities, and career-adjacent activities such as internships, shadowing, events, and related activities (Levesque et al., 2008). Beyond these logistical features, stated goals of many career academies include boosting student engagement through career relevance and engaging local employer partners.

In Wake County, Apex High School is home to the Academy of Information Technology. Students are selected for the program via random lottery prior to their 9th grade year and commit to four years of participation. The program includes a paid internship, four years of information technology coursework, cohort-based programming, and soft skills training in addition to students' non-CTE requirements as a part of the general high school experience.

Evaluation Methods and Data. This evaluation estimated causal effects of career academy participation on high school and college outcomes using random assignment approximating a true experiment. In this program, treatment and comparison groups were determined through a lottery-based selection process. Over 90 percent of those who entered but were not selected in the lottery enrolled in the traditional track within Apex High School, leading to a high-quality comparison group ripe for estimation of treatment effects.

The authors included four 9th grade cohorts in their analyses, spanning from those entering high school in 2009 through those entering in 2012. Treatment effects were estimated using a two-stage least squares model across an analytic sample of 469 total students. Results from the models revealed the following:

- Career academy students' 9th grade absences were 38 percent lower than non-academy students' absences, which translates to a difference of 1.4 extra days of school. This effect is notably driven by students who previously has high rates of absenteeism and serves as a compelling proxy for student engagement.
- Career academy students and non-academy students did not differ in academic achievement, nor in patterns of advanced course taking
- Career academy students were twice as likely as non-academy students to earn an industry-relevant certification during high school (a difference of 23 percentage points)
- Career academy students were more likely to graduate from high school than non-academy students by 8 percentage points. Academy enrollment was found to boost graduation likelihood both for on-time graduation and graduation at any time, and most of the graduation impacts were driven by differences between male students in the academy versus those outside the academy.
  - The impact of career academy participation on high school graduation is "at least partially" mediated by absenteeism and industry certification (Hemelt et al., 2019, p. 172)
- Male career academy students were more likely than their non-academy counterparts to enroll in college within a year of on-time high school graduation

Program Conclusions and Limitations. This study revealed several positive impacts of the Apex career academy on attendance, industry certification, graduation, and college enrollment. The graduation and college enrollment effects were driven largely by differences among male students in the academy versus those not in the academy, suggesting that boys may be more responsive to this type of CTE programming. Despite this gender gap, the positive impact of career academies on high school graduation and college enrollment held for students at varying levels of academic achievement.

One of the benefits of the career academy model is the juxtaposition of career programming and traditional high school programming. At Apex High School, the career academy provides an integrated curriculum to its students, which includes time for teachers from the CTE courses as well as teachers from the "traditional" academic courses to "weave common content and relevant applications" from both domains as a part of the CTE program experience (Hemelt et al., 2019, p. 174). As another way of integrating career and academic learning, the program provides students the opportunity to take college-level coursework during their senior year, which provides students with exposure to college-level material as well as access to a smooth transition into college with already-earned credits.

The power and promise of these results are hindered by external validity in that the program is housed within a single school in a relatively high-performing and well-resourced district. Additionally, the program includes a paid internship, which can be cost-prohibitive in other districts depending on employer involvement. Finally, this study did not include longer-term outcomes such as college completion data or early career data.

ARKANSAS' SMARTCORE CURRICULUM (DOUGHERTY, ET AL., 2019)

Program Overview. Beginning with the high school class of 2014, Arkansas implemented a statewide policy around the "Smart Core" curriculum, which required students to complete six or more career-related courses to graduate. The goal of this program was to improve academic and labor market outcomes through greater exposure to CTE.

While specialized career academies and technical schools are available throughout the state, at the time of publication approximately 90 percent of students taking CTE coursework in the state did so at a traditional high school. CTE offerings differ from district to district and from school to school, but all students (unless opted out of Smart Core via a waiver) must complete Career Focus courses in order to graduate from high school.

Evaluation Methods and Data. In this statewide study, the authors drew on Arkansas administrative data to explore the relationship between CTE course taking and academic and employment outcomes. Data came from three cohorts of entering 9th graders in 2008, 2009, and 2010, from high school entry through one year after on-time high school graduation. Unlike many states, Arkansas tracks students longitudinally not just in K–12 but through postsecondary education and the workforce as well; this enabled a unique analytic opportunity to track students' post-high school regardless of their chosen pathway.

The study employs quasi-experimental research methods, which enhance the power of the research by enabling causal inference. The authors employ instrumental variables estimation to measure the impact of CTE coursework on academic and labor market outcomes. Ordinary least squares [OLS] coefficients likely bias effective interpretation of statewide CTE effects as they do not control for the unobserved student and contextual (county- and district-level) characteristics driving selection bias in CTE participation. An instrumental variables approach reduces this bias and isolates causal effects by accounting for endogenous characteristics impacting CTE exposure, including district-level variability in course offerings over time.

Results revealed that CTE course taking positively predicted:

- Students graduating from high school (on-time and overall)
- Students' likelihood of enrolling in a 2- or 4-year college
- Students being employed
- Students netting higher initial earnings in their jobs

Program Conclusions and Limitations. Broadly, this study found that higher rates of CTE coursework during high school drove an array of positive educational and labor market outcomes. Participating in one additional CTE course led to a higher likelihood of on-time high school graduation, a higher likelihood of enrolling in college, and both employment rates and earnings. Results revealed positive impacts for students who were college-bound as well as for those who were not. Like the Wake County model, this suggests that CTE carries promise for a wide array of students irrespective of postsecondary pathway. On a related note, the authors concluded that the results speak to both an alignment between career and academic learning and the utility of career learning in postsecondary access: "That we find relationships between course taking and high school completion suggests that CTE may provide an applied pathway that helps improve student engagement in high school. Likewise, the link between CTE course taking and enrollment in college suggests to some degree that these courses may help to strengthen the school-to-college pipeline for many students" (Dougherty et al., 2019, p. 440).

A central limitation of this study is the statewide setting; while important for the evaluation of policy decisions and widespread trends, the diversity of curricular offerings across the state inhibits a clear understanding of the extent to which specific courses drive specific outcomes or how teaching, grade level, and other classroom-level characteristics may factor in. As the authors note, future qualitative research may help in elucidating these and other impacts. Additional limitations include access to just one year of post-high school data as well as the timing of the data collection in the immediate aftermath of the 2008–2009 economic recession.

MASSACHUSETTS' INNOVATION PATHWAYS & EARLY COLLEGE PATHWAY PROGRAM (ICF, 2020).

Program Overview. In 2017, Massachusetts received a $1.95 million New Skills for Youth Grant to strengthen and scale high-quality career education for students in the Commonwealth. Part of this grant was used to establish the Innovation Pathways program, designed to connect students in public high schools with industry-relevant coursework and work experience in partnership with local employers from in-demand sectors. One of the primary goals of this initiative is to help provide high-quality career learning to students who are not attending a dedicated vocational high school, where the number of waitlisted students statewide is nearly 5,000. Importantly, students are not trained for a specific occupation, but rather given opportunities for academic and hands-on learning in a broad industry or employment sector. To this end, several grantees have developed course content covering employability skills, which includes study skills, interviewing, communication, and writing resumes.

Each participating high school offers one or more Innovation Pathways in areas such as information technology, environmental & life sciences, healthcare & social assistance, maritime STEM, and other topics relevant to the local economy. The program provides students with the ability to graduate high school armed with college credit and at least 100 hours of internship or work-based learning experience.

Evaluation Methods and Data. The 2020 evaluation report employed a quasi-experimental methodology to estimate causal effects of the Innovation Pathways program. Propensity score matching was used to match participating v. non-participating students within the same school on a series of demographic and academic characteristics. Once matched (i.e., once these observed characteristics were statistically controlled for), differences in key outcomes between the student groups could be estimated and attributed more directly to participation in the program.

The potential of the findings is limited by a relatively small sample size: 124 students each in the Innovation Pathways and the comparison groups. Nonetheless, a series of significant effects was detected:

- Innovation Pathways students were more than twice as likely to graduate having completed the Massachusetts Core Curriculum (a college readiness indicator)
- Innovation Pathways students had significantly higher attendance rates
- Innovation Pathways students had 40 percent fewer reported disciplinary incidents

Program Conclusions and Limitations. Despite being a young program with limited cohorts available to be studied, the Innovation Pathways program has already shown promise in its impact on student outcomes during high school. In particular, student engagement (attendance), behavior, and rates of completing of a statewide curriculum geared toward college readiness were all improved following Innovation Pathways participation.

One of the central limitations is that this initial program evaluation was conducted only on a limited number of original designee schools and only included students for whom a comparison group match could be found (126 out of 147 eligible students). As such, certain subgroups such as grade level were sometimes too small to be evaluated, and indicators such as high school graduation could only be tested for 12 students in each group—far too few to speak to program efficacy on late high school, college, or employment indicators at this point in time.

RECOMMENDATIONS AND EVIDENCE

While the four programs profiled in this chapter are far from representative of the full gamut of CTE programming across the country, the associated research and evaluation studies are especially valuable in the CTE literature for their inclusion of methodologies enabling causal, rather than just observational inference. Although correlational research may reveal similar results and inspire comparable policy recommendations, it risks a relative lack of precision in connecting programming mechanisms to relevant outcomes. With respect to advancing policy recommendations, the methodological strength of the included studies is more directly impactful than observational or correlational studies in terms of identifying where and to what extent CTE programming affects high school, postsecondary, and labor market outcomes.

Based upon the body of research surrounding existing career programming during the high school years, selected program elements appear to be the primary drivers of improved student outcomes in high school, postsecondary education, and early career: work-based learning, curricular CTE exposure, and access to early college and dual enrollment. While expanding these offerings is the overall conclusion and recommendation of this chapter, specific policy recommendations are directed at the state level and are three-fold:

1. **Reconsider high school graduation requirements at the state level** to include all of the following: academics, lifelong learning skills development, and technical skills development (Jimenez, 2020).

Key elements of successful CTE programs include uniting career and academic learning. The Arkansas Smart Core program demonstrated that policy change involving adding career learning requirements in high school boosted high school graduation, college matriculation, employment, and earnings. At a statewide scale, integrated career education requirements—whether technical or related to other types of skills—are able to drive positive outcomes for college-bound and non-college-bound students alike. Similarly, in Wake County, central to program efficacy is the weaving of "common content and relevant applications through both sets of courses [academic and career]" (Hemelt et al., 2019, p. 174).

The four profiled programs demonstrate that impactful high school offerings unite the academic and career learning spheres to accomplish the following:

- Harness the practicality and labor market responsiveness of workforce-centered training;
- Incorporate the high expectations and academic rigor of postsecondary preparation programs;
- Promote authenticity through a combination of classroom and hands-on learning; and
- Drive student outcomes across the student engagement, high school, postsecondary, and labor market domains

By incorporating career learning explicitly alongside the existing academic requirements for high school completion, "integrated curriculum" offerings such as in Wake County might become the rule rather than the exception. At its best, CTE operates as a supplement, rather than as a replacement, for academic learning in the high school setting. As Massachusetts has seen, the demand for vocational high schools has skyrocketed in recent years. Rather than building additional dedicated vocational schools, embedding career learning more deeply into the traditional public high school setting can help to alleviate this demand while simultaneously reducing the perceived divide between the academic and career learning spheres.

A 2021 report by American Student Assistance and Bellwether Education Partners profiles work-based learning policies in all 50 states and the District of Columbia (Robson et al., 2021). The comprehensive policy evaluation rubric included a criterion for work-based learning as a high school graduation requirement. At the time of publication, students could earn credit for work-based learning in all states and the District of Columbia, but it was not a state-level graduation requirement in any location. The evidence base for improved student outcomes is strong in those districts and schools where this policy is already in place; centering the unity between academic and career learning at the state level is recommended to maintain and expand these encouraging findings.

2. **Cultivate systems for college access, matriculation, (and, ideally, persistence)**, including dual enrollment and similar opportunities for students to earn college credit while still in high school.

While CTE coursework alone has been found to boost the likelihood of college enrollment, "Dual enrollment—earning college credit while still in high school—magnifies the impact of an additional CTE course by doubling the probability that a student will enroll in a two-year college the year after graduation" (Dougherty, 2016, p. 5).

The P-TECH program includes a partnership with CUNY, enabling eligible students to earn an associate's degree free of charge as a part of their extended high school experience. P-TECH students gain access to this college pathway through a qualifying score on the state's Regents exams, which the program offers to students on an "accelerated" timeline. By offering opportunities to qualify for college and enroll in courses earlier in high school, students have earlier, more frequent, and more numerous points of entry into postsecondary education. Similarly, Wake County's program includes the opportunity for students to take at least one college-level course for credit and completing Arkansas' Smart Core curriculum provides access to scholarships and opens the opportunity for admission to certain state colleges. In Massachusetts, Innovation Pathways participation improved MassCore completion rates. MassCore includes dual enrollment, access to online college courses for credit, and was specifically designed to help reduce the need for remedial coursework in college (https://www.doe.mass.edu).

As of 2019, New York was the only state *without* a codified dual or concurrent enrollment policy in place (Education Commission of the States, 2019). However, the specific program features and guidelines differ substantially from state to state. Funding is often the responsibility of the student or their family (with locally varying types of support available), though in states such as Maine, the state education agency will fund 50% of up to 12 credit hours per academic year at an eligible institution. Beyond financial access, guidelines regarding logistics, program quality, and transferability continue to vary. Ensuring equitable access in addition to offering dual enrollment is a critical second step in relevant state-level public policy.

3. **Create a coalition from the Governor's office, the state department of education, the state department of labor or workforce board, public and community colleges, school district leadership, and industry** to strategize locally appropriate methods for embedding the critical components identified above at the school (and particularly high school) level;

This policy recommendation carries at least two potential benefits: clarifying the shared goals and target outcomes of career learning; and involving employers more directly as partners.

As results from the four exemplar programs suggest, career learning does not exist in a vacuum and implementing effective CTE programming is not as straightforward as introducing a new curriculum. P-TECH engages schools, community colleges, and employers in a three-way partnership; Innovation Pathways incorporates a focus on regionally specific in-demand industries as well as work-based learning in partnership with local employers; and Wake County offers students paid internships and other work-based learning experiences outside the classroom. Accordingly, program implementation and success are dependent in part upon alignment across schools, employers, institutions of higher education, and others. Aligning learning experiences from K–12 to post-secondary requires strong authentic leadership that cuts across grade level boundaries.

Engaging state and local governments and workforce boards in these collaborative initiatives is essential for encouraging alignment, expanding CTE offerings, and prioritizing (and progressing toward) target outcomes in high school, postsecondary education of all kinds, and the labor market. To ensure these outcomes can be effectively captured and leveraged, policymakers should direct funds and personnel toward measuring student outcomes, including associated evaluation and advocacy efforts. This includes tracking program implementation supports and barriers and embedding career learning efforts within existing state longitudinal data systems. Arkansas provides a compelling model for expanding longitudinal data systems with its inclusion of postsecondary and labor market data beyond K–12.

Finally, building a cross-sector coalition offers a more direct role for employer partners. Recent research out of the University of Missouri noted that more than 85 percent of surveyed business leaders believed that CTE provided students with transferable skills and 90 percent agreed that there should be partnerships between schools and local employers to help students gain real-world education and training (Russell & White, 2020). However, just half of surveyed businesses reported any sort of partnership with a CTE program, and less than half offer internships or other work-based learning opportunities to students.

A survey of employers in Massachusetts in 2016 produced similar results. Of the four issues identified to be at the top of an ideal policy agenda, three were directly related to CTE: developing students' applied skills, increasing hands-on experiential learning opportunities, and creating greater access to vocational and technical education (MassINC, 2016). Additionally, 94 percent of employers cited partnering with local companies as an effective idea to improve career education in the Commonwealth. The demand among employers is clear, as they face direct incentives in ensuring a prepared next-generation workforce. The opportunities, however, are relatively scarce. Broad coalitions of leaders, educators, and employers can collaborate in expanding access to these partnerships, and where necessary, policymakers can consider offering tax and other incentives for employers in various sectors to leverage these collaborations to build capacity for on-the-job training, mentorship, and work-based learning experiences.

Career Connect Washington [CCW] represents a response to this widespread demand and serves as the only existing instance of a multi-sector career education coalition created by a governor and funded by the state legislature (JFF, n.d.). CCW is a coalition of "business, labor, education, and community leaders who are creating work-based and academic programs for young people to explore, learn, and earn money or college level credit" (Career Connect Washington, n.d.). The goal is to establish a comprehensive state-wide system for career learning, leveraging various partners and committing to annual progress reports for added accountability and outcomes tracking. Washington state offers a detailed policy model and sets a notable precedent for building and sustaining an inclusive coalition in support of career learning.

DISCUSSION AND IMPLICATIONS

The four programs profiled in this chapter represent the growing but limited literature on CTE programs at the high school level for which causal impacts can be estimated. While the programs here are far from representative of CTE in the United States at large, the exemplar programs intentionally reflect four very different contexts: statewide (Arkansas Smart Core), select districts (Massachusetts Innovation Pathways), large city (New York P-TECH), and single school (Apex Career Academy). The lessons learned from each program help clarify the diverse conditions and settings under which CTE drives important student outcomes.

Due to the relatively limited causal research base, many of the extant CTE policy platforms are necessarily drawn from observational evidence rather than rigorous examination of how CTE programming truly *drives* specific outcomes. The programs profiled in this chapter help in clarifying and specifying the mechanisms through which it is possible to impact student outcomes directly and with the highest likelihood for success. While the policy recommendations advanced in this chapter are neither wholly new nor uniquely reflective of the lessons conferred by the profiled programs, the discussions throughout this chapter illustrate and ensure that these policies are directly linked to causal impact evidence.

The urgency is clear; the Carl D. Perkins Vocational and Technical Act was reauthorized in 2018 [Perkins V] and American Institutes for Research has established a CTE Research Network with the express mission of "expanding the evidence base for career and technical education" (American Institutes for Research, n.d.). State-level policies in the career education space are already active, with studies like those profiled in this chapter and others in the CTE Research Network poised to strengthen and expand the causal evidence base driving policy and practice.

By uniting the career and academic spheres in a high school setting through a reconstruction of high school graduation requirements, states can prioritize career learning opportunities (and their associated benefits) for students from all backgrounds. By prioritizing and expanding access to higher education, states can help remove some of the major barriers to college access, enrollment, and completion—namely, credits and the necessity of remedial education. Finally, by creating a broad coalition of government leaders, schools, colleges, and employers, states will promote a unified vision for career education and target outcomes while also more effectively and more comprehensively engaging the business community statewide and regionally.

Taken together, these policy recommendations reflect best practices found in various CTE programs throughout the United States. The causal evidence base offers further support and sustainable foundation upon which to develop public policy. Future research featuring rigorous methodologies and longitudinal data systems are positioned to clarify the efficacy and the implementation considerations of the proposals advanced in this chapter.

REFERENCES

Advance CTE. (2017). *The value and promise of career technical education: Results from a national survey of parents and students.* Advance CTE.

American Institutes for Research. (n.d.). *Expanding the evidence base for career and technical education.* Career and Technical Education Research Network. Retrieved September 29, 2021, from https://cteresearchnetwork.org/.

Anderson, N. S., & Nieves, L. (2020). *Working to Learn.* Palgrave Macmillan.

Career Connect Washington. (n.d.). *About us.* Retrieved September 29, 2021, from https://careerconnectwa.org/about-us/

Dougherty, S. M. (2016). *Career and technical education in high school: Does it improve student outcomes?* Thomas B. Fordham Institute.

Dougherty, S. M., Gottfried, M. A., & Sublett, C. (2019). Does increasing career and technical education coursework in high school boost educational attainment and labor market outcomes? *Journal of Education Finance, 44*(4), 423–447.

Dougherty, S., Macdonald, I. H., Ecton, W. G., & Kreisman, D. (2020). *Increasing individuals' economic stability through Massachusetts' Career and Technical Education.* Georgia Policy Labs Reports, 38. https://scholarworks.gsu.edu/cgi/viewcontent.cgi?article=1037&context=gpl_reports doi: https://doi.org/10.57709/30728988

Education Commission of the States. (2019). *50-state comparison: Dual/concurrent enrollment policies.* Education Commission of the States. Retrieved September 29, 2021, from https://www.ecs.org/dual-concurrent-enrollment-policies/.

Hemelt, S. W., Lenard, M. A., & Paeplow, C. G. (2019). Building bridges to life after high school: Contemporary career academies and student outcomes. *Economics of Education Review, 68,* 161–178.

ICF. (2020). *Massachusetts Innovation Pathway & Early College Pathway program evaluation impact report.* ICF.

JFF. (n.d.). *Spotlight: Career connect Washington.* Policy Agenda and Supporting Strategies. Retrieved September 29, 2021, from https://www.jff.org/resources/equitable-pathways-hypotheses-spotlights/policy/.

Jimenez, L. (2020). *Building a strong middle class through career pathways programs: Case studies of Germany, Singapore, and Switzerland.* Center for American Progress.

Kemple, J. J. (2001). *Career academies: Impacts on students' initial transitions to postsecondary education and employment.* Manpower Demonstration Research Corporation.

Kemple, J. J. (2004). *Career academies: Impacts on labor market outcomes and educational attainment* (pp. 1–106). MDRC.

Kemple, J. J., & Willner, C. J. (2008). *Career academies: Long-term impacts on labor market outcomes, educational attainment, and transitions to adulthood* (pp. 1–47). MDRC.

Kemple, J. J., & Willner, C. J. (2011). *Technical resources for "Career Academies: Long-term impacts on labor market outcomes, educational attainment, and transition to adulthood."* (pp. 1–130). MDRC.

Levesque, K., Laird, J., Hensley, E., Choy, S. P., Cataldi, E. F., & Hudson, L. (2008). *Career and technical education in the United States: 1990 to 2005. Statistical analysis report. NCES 2008-035.* National Center for Education Statistics.

MassINC. (2016). *2016 MA employer survey on education and workforce readiness*. Retrieved from: https://www.mbae.org/wp-content/uploads/2016/11/FINAL-Report-2016-MBAE-Employer-Poll-for-web.pdf

Robson, K., Scheiss, J. O., & Lammers, J. (2021). *Working to learn and learning to work: A state-by-state analysis of high school work-based learning policies*. American Student Assistance.

Rosen, R., Byndloss, D.C., Parise, L., Alterman, E., & Dixon, M. (2020). *Bridging the school-to-work divide: Interim implementation and impact findings from New York City's P-TECH 9-14 schools*. MDRC.

Rosen, R., Visher, M., & Beal, K. (2018). *Career and technical education: Current policy, prominent programs, and evidence*. MDRC.

Russell, R., & White, M. C. (2020). *Perceptions of career and technical education in Missouri*. Institute of Public Policy. https://truman.missouri.edu/institute-public-policy/publication/perceptions-career-and-technical-education-missouri

Walker, R., & Farmer, A. (2018). The impact of a career and technical education on the graduation rates and college enrollment of high school students. *The Journal of Academic Development and Education, 10*. http://dx.doi.org/10.21252/KEELE-0000030

Walsh, M., O'Kane, L., & Noronha, G. (2019). *Where credentials meet the market: state case studies on the effect of high school industry credentials on educational and labor market outcomes*. ExcelinEd & Burning Glass Technologies. https://files.eric.ed.gov/fulltext/ED612442.pdf

CHAPTER 8

TRANSFORMATIONAL CHANGE

Lessons From Workforce Diversification Efforts in California's Community Colleges

Daisy Gonzales and Nadia Leal-Carrillo
California's Community Colleges

OVERVIEW

The California Community Colleges (CCC) serves 2.2 million students among its 116 colleges and is a key driver in ensuring educational opportunity and success for Californians. As an open-access institution, the system serves a diverse student population in terms of race and ethnicity, age, and levels of educational attainment. While the system excels at ensuring access, student success remains a challenge and opportunity gaps persist as only 48 percent of students who enter a community college complete a degree, certificate, or transfer to a four-year university within six years. These opportunity gaps disproportionately impact African American, Latino, and Native American students.

In response to this problem, the Chancellor's Office (CO) examined the impact of faculty and staff diversity on student success and convened a Diversity, Equity, and Inclusion Task force (Task force), to develop a cultural change framework to

Emerging Trends in Education Policy: Unapologetic Progressive Conversations,
pages 111–122.
Copyright © 2023 by Information Age Publishing
www.infoagepub.com
111

increase faculty and staff diversity as an integral component of the system's *Vision for Success* (California Community Colleges Chancellor's Office, 2017). The work of the Task force served as a call to action for colleges to reach their full potential as vehicles for social mobility. Specifically, the Task force theory of action asserted that faculty and staff diversity is a driver for the educational achievement and the social mobility of students, and that students who benefit from a diverse faculty are "better educated and better prepared for leadership, citizenship, and professional competitiveness" (Taylor et al., 2010). Furthermore, this effort was centered on the need for an organizational shift from a practice of compliance to partnerships across systems to design, implement and reinforce policies, procedures, and behaviors that cultivate an inclusive ecosystem.

In September 2019, the Board of Governors (Board) of the California Community College system, adopted a set of recommendations from the Task force that included the adoption of 1) a statement on diversity, equity and inclusion (DEI) that acknowledges that institutional discrimination and systemic racism exist, and 2) a systemwide DEI Integration Plan (Integration Plan) consisting of 68 hiring, recruitment and retention strategies to increase racial and ethnic diversity among faculty and staff (California Community Colleges Board of Governors, 2019). By adopting both, the Board endorsed the need for regulatory changes to reform existing hiring practices, the allocation of resources, the faculty tenure review processes, and existing retention strategies. To fully implement the Integration Plan, the CO called on the various associations within the system to create internal infrastructures to implement the cultural reforms guided by the systems transformational change framework.

INTRODUCTION

Nationwide, 44% of undergraduates attend a community college and one out of every four community college students in the nation attends a California community college (Jenkins & Fink, 2020). Roughly 2.2 million students attend one of California's 116 community colleges. Of these students, 69% identify as members of one or more underrepresented student populations. Low persistence and completion rates for Latinx (Latinos/Hispanic), African American, Native American, and Asian students represent a long-standing challenge that education leaders strive to address. In California, the race and ethnic diversity of California community college faculty and staff populations continues to be significantly less diverse than the student population. As open-access institutions of education, closing educational opportunity gaps by race and ethnicity is an equity imperative and a moral obligation.

A critical element for education leaders striving to address student success for historically underserved and minoritized students is the ability to create a safe, inclusive, and anti-racist campus culture. As such, a diverse workforce and inclusive curriculum are at the core of this work. This chapter will assist the next generation of leaders to expand their knowledge, skills and practice of higher education diversity, equity, and inclusion policy implementation. Education leaders will be presented with a roadmap to empower a cultural transformation that begins with a review of existing policies, practices, and behaviors to diversify faculty and staff. For full disclosure, the authors of this chapter are intimately involved in the implementation of diversity, equity, and inclusion efforts in California's Community College. This work is grounded in the transformational change framework we developed, and we wish to share our observations and reflections of progress to date in hopes that this information may support leaders at other institutions engage stakeholders to advance diversity, equity, and inclusion work.

Understanding the Importance of Faculty Diversity and Transformational Change

Before convening the Task force for a six-month process of deliberations on faculty and staff diversity, a review of the literature was conducted to help frame and guide discussions. Our review of the literature revealed the need for system level commitment to faculty, staff, and student diversity to ensure we are supporting our students towards completion of their academic goals and closing opportunity gaps among historically underserved and minoritized student populations. That is, student success is dependent on faculty and staff diversity. A broad section of the literature on student retention focuses on the importance of a clear institutional commitment to diversity to maintain and serve a diverse student population. Tinto (2006, 2017) looks at efforts to enhance student retention and places the responsibility back on the institution to take a student-centered approach in developing and implementing student success policies and practices. Gregerman et al. (1998) highlights that it is essential to the academic success and retention of African American students to have interactions with faculty of color. Within this context, retaining a diverse student population is connected to faculty teaching and institutional accountability. Quaye and Harper (2007) discuss how accountability in terms of the assessment of student learning outcomes goes hand in hand with institutions choosing to make diversity a priority at the system level.

In addition, the literature also points to the need to hold faculty accountable for including diversity in their teaching but cautioned against the weight of this work being carried by a subset of staff such as faculty of color. Harper and Hurtado (2007) state faculty should be "challenged to consider their roles as accomplices in the cyclical reproduction of racism and institutional negligence." The same expectation should be placed on all college administrators and staff. Departments within an institution need to be committed and prioritize matters such as implicit bias both in the classroom and as part of campus wide professional development training. An institutional commitment with support from key administrators is vital in bringing about transformational change.

The role of leadership in transformational change is emphasized in the literature because to change cultures, the authors note, leaders cannot simply make a statement in support of diversity, it requires a critical examination of programs (Harper & Hurtado, 2007). Harper and Hurtado (2007) speak about transformational change, a holistic institutional cultural upheaval that requires key administrative leadership to guide it. This type of cultural change requires equity-minded practices that consist of actions aimed at addressing "racialized structures, policies, and practices that produce and sustain racial inequities" (Bensimon & Malcolm, 2012, pp. 17–44). Other equity minded education policy reformers recommend hiring diverse faculty and staff is necessary to dismantle systematic bias and racism. Combined, transformational change advances educational change and policy towards equity by centering the role of an institution and its impact of existing operations that have perpetuated racial disparities, promoting equity, adopting sustainable racial equity and inclusion efforts. In short, transformational change that advances diversity, equity and inclusion must systematically examine organizational practices, policies, structures, and transform culture.

Advancing DEI Through A Transformational Change Framework

Responding to external pressures to address the lack of diversity among faculty and staff, the Chancellor's Office convened system leaders, led by the Deputy Chancellor and the President of the statewide academic senate, to develop a transformational change framework to increase faculty and staff diversity as an integral component of the system's *Vision for Success* (California Community Colleges Chancellor's Office, 2017). The Task force included faculty, campus presidents, trustees, human resources experts, students, and researchers. Over the course of six months, the DEI Task force met monthly to review and discuss key topics related to the lack of faculty and staff diversity and its impact on student outcomes in the context of the system's equity goals and commitments. A process and culture of inquiry was nurtured by the co-chairs who provided space for open dialogue, communal learning, reflection, and collaboration. Through deep dive study session and the examination of institutional policies, this process allowed the Task force to recognize the historical nature of discriminatory and oppressive policies such as redlining that have had lasting effects on communities of color and their ability to achieve social mobility (Lawrence et al., 2004). In particular, the communities of color many of our colleges serve.

Therefore, to engage meaningfully in transformational change and address systemic racism the Task force had to authentically engage in diversity, equity, and inclusion. The work began by defining diversity at a system level and utilizing the transformation change agenda as a foundation.

In broad terms, diversity is commonly used to refer to social differences or differences among people (Blaine & McClure Brenchley, 2018). Those differences are defined by social characteristics that speak to the type of discrimination or disadvantages people have or may experience. In the case of a workplace definition of diversity there is not a universal definition of diversity that is used across organizations and employers. With this understanding, the Task force felt it was important to adopt a definition of diversity that promoted a collective understanding and appreciation for the system's rich diversity. Specifically, the Task force focused on the perspective that concern for social justice implies both inclusion and equity are at the forefront of system efforts to increase faculty and staff racial and ethnic diversity. This perspective recognizes stereotypes that can cause or justify discrimination towards specific groups (Blaine & McClure Brenchley, 2018). Combining this with an organizational context, the result was the adoption of a diversity, equity, and inclusion statement that in part, states:

> With the goal of ensuring the equal educational opportunity of all students, the California Community Colleges embrace diversity among students, faculty, staff, and the communities we serve as an integral part of our history, a recognition of the complexity of our present state, and a call to action for a better future. Embracing diversity means that we must intentionally practice acceptance and respect towards one another and understand that discrimination and prejudices create and sustain privileges for some while creating and sustaining disadvantages for others... (California Community Colleges Chancellor's Office, 2020)

However, to carry this work forward, members of the Task force had to accept the personal responsibility to lead transformational change. To bridge diversity to transformational change, we must be authentic leaders who, by definition, promote a positive ethical climate to foster greater self-awareness, an internalized moral perspective, and positive self-development among followers (Walumbwa et al., 2008). In this case, members of the Task force needed to come to terms with the personal responsibility of engaging at a system level by modeling equity-minded behavior and actions which meant they would need to stand on important social justice issues by proactively communicating their morals and beliefs. As an example of this, when faculty of color were invited to speak to the Task force and share raw personal experiences with microaggressions and racism in the workplace and the impact this has had on their health, the members became cognizant of the urgency of transforming the system's culture. This became a pivotal moment for this work. This panel was the first opportunity for authentic leadership and providing a space to listen to others' experiences, which brought the members together with renewed commitment and urgency. Combined with exercises where the group examined diversity hiring practices and approaches from other state and national higher education college systems, the Task force was able to imagine what progress could look like and what practices the CCC system could model and borrow from others. Ultimately, they unanimously identified 68 DEI strategies for immediate implementation with the goal of having these recommendations serve as a strategic plan for structural transformation.

To fully implement all 68 recommendations in the Integration Plan, the Chancellor's Office created the DEI Implementation Workgroup. The workgroup was structured to function as an oversight entity for three years. Members of the workgroup were tasked with serving as the primary liaisons responsible for reporting and tracking progress, providing assistance, and identifying resources needed to the Board and the Chancellor's Office. Unlike the Task force, the workgroup included labor union associations and external social justice partners along with faculty, presidents, trustees, human resources experts, students, researchers, chief instructional officers, classified staff, and chief budget officers to mobilize a cultural transformation at the district and campus-level. To achieve this, representatives were asked to develop internal structures to implement recommendations and, where specific associations were identified as key stakeholders, advance this work via association level subcommittees, steering committees, or a task force. This work required each association to: 1) adopt DEI as a priority in their annual goals; 2) integrate DEI into organizational structures; 3) urgently develop professional development and online modules for their members; and 4) collaborate with system partners to implement the Integration Plan recommendations.

As a three-year term workgroup, members focused their first year on the implementation of tier 1 recommendations, which are strategies that can be achieved within a one to two-year timeline and with existing resources. These recommendations include professional development on bias and anti-racism; integrating the student voice into hiring processes; amending EEO plans to be publicly discussed and approved annually and standardizing minimum qualifications for faculty hiring. For example, California Education Code states that there are two faculty minimum qualifications: 1) a master's degree in the discipline of the assignment, and 2) being able to demonstrate sensitivity to teaching a diverse student population in terms of academic, socioeconomic, and ethnic backgrounds. How each of these minimum qualifications is measured, assessed, and weighted as part of the hiring process becomes consequential to faculty diversity, equity, and inclusion. In this case, to advance DEI hiring practices, California community college districts must move away from checking off a simple yes or no answer, and instead must embed the minimum qualification into every question and evaluate responses based on the positive impact to a diverse student population. Simply put, a candidate's preparation and knowledge to serve a diverse student population can only adequately assessed when we fully understand who they have previously served, what actions or best practices they have acted on and what the related student outcomes are. Conversations about dismantling and reimagining structures and practices that present barriers to diverse hiring and EEO are critical and difficult to lead, particularly in a unionized work environment. In the next section, a set of recommendations will be presented to help leaders interested in engaging in this work navigate institutional structures and political dynamics to systematically transform culture.

RECOMMENDATIONS TO LEAD
SYSTEMIC DIVERSIFICATION EFFORTS

Launching an isolated goal of increasing diversity will not yield long-term transformational change, particularly in a resource scarce environment. Reflecting on the efforts by the CO to advance diversity, equity, and inclusion work at the system level we offer to leaders at any institution, a transformational change framework based on four recommendations. For authentic leadership to make lasting transformation change, we recommend that DEI leaders: 1) create the conditions for honest and intentional dialogue on diversity, equity and inclusion by communicating a clear commitment to diversity and elevating the voices of marginalized employees; ; 2) ensure that diversity, equity and inclusion efforts are integrated to student success reforms by conducting a review hiring policies and practices to make clear the connection that employee behaviors and pedagogy impact student outcomes; 3) develop a strategic plan and allocate resources accordingly by identifying a set of strategies for sustainable change that will give equal weight to equity issues and racial groups; and 4) give agency to transformational leaders to do away with organizational silos and lead cultural change by normalizing honest conversations about race and partnering with affinity groups. While the suggested approaches presented here are informed by the California community college system context, the recommendations can be applied within any context and by leaders in any higher education segment. To complete this work, authentic leaders need to be unapologetic and honest about the problem they are solving and why, while simultaneously being vulnerable when they do not have the answers. As we will discuss in the next sections, a level of humility and vulnerability from leaders at all levels of an organizational structure is required to shift attention from a set of goals or a plan to action and accountability.

FACILITATING HONEST AND INTENTIONAL DIALOGUE

The first component a leader must put into place is the establishment of honest and intentional dialogue about diversity, equity, and inclusion. This can be done in several ways, but we will highlight three examples that helped us in facilitating open dialogue around these topics at a system-wide level. DEI starts with intentional and vulnerable leadership that must model the type of transformation that you are advocating for. You cannot establish honest and intentional dialogue about the issue if, as an employer, you have not made the transformation you are advocating for or are unwilling to take an honest look at your own organizational deficiencies. In the case of the CO, this required an assessment of the hiring practices, acknowledging the lack of diversity among staff, and an evaluation of workplace climate. By taking an internal look at our organizational practices and processes, we signaled to stakeholders that we are part of the cultural transformation, and this is a change we would be undertaking together. We then developed a common understanding of the community college history and the broader historical context for diversity, equity, and inclusion. We affirmed common facts about our institutions, including that as an institution of higher education in the United States we were originally created to only serve the educational needs of White males and any previous attempt to dismantle racism in our country have been met with institutionalized pushback and in some cases the explicit affirmation to support segregated schools. Understanding our historical context allowed leaders in the room to vet, critique, and examine the purpose and history of our system's recruitment, hiring and retention policies. This was not facilitated out of distrust or blame of existing system leaders, but rather because existing structures were designed to institutionalize and perpetuate discrimination. As institutions of learning, this process was a unique and particularly appropriate tool as we committed to learning together.

The last example we wish to highlight is the development of a theory of change. It is important to note that leading DEI work is a long-term commitment. Our Board provided a clear message that this effort was about moving from compliance to empowerment. They pronounced that system diversity efforts must transform institutions, departments, and individuals to fundamentally alter our system's workforce and culture. In doing so, they grounded this approach in a theory of change. The theory of change is based on empowering local district leaders and the communities that elect and fund them. The accountability of this approach is built into the recommendations to make data public, standardize processes, and change funding structures to embed incentives for diversity, equity, and inclusion. We will elaborate on this point in our third recommendation specific to the development of an Integration Plan. The focus of our second recommendation is on the integration of DEI efforts into student success reforms to avoid the perception that these efforts are lesser than or separate from an institution's package of reforms.

INTEGRATING DEI WITH STUDENT SUCCESS

The second component leaders at any institution must do to lead DEI work is to ensure those efforts are integrated with student success reforms. For example, aligned with the system's ambitious reform agenda and goals identified in its *Vision for Success*, efforts to advance DEI for the community colleges represent an effort to accelerate equity-minded hiring, retention, and support practices and policies to meet the needs of a diverse student population. Consequently, equity and inclusion are the driver for student success. To this end, having a strategic plan is fundamental to establish clarity around the goals and mission of an institution. In this case, the *Vision for Success* served as the framework for equity, but the Integration Plan is the vehicle by which student success reforms and local efforts are aligned to further student completion among historically underserved and minoritized students. As leaders, it is important to expose the notion of a "silver bullet" when implementing changes to existing policies and practices. Instead, there needs to be intentionality around the outcomes the institution wants to achieve to make sure reforms in place are complementary to one another and advance equity work. The idea that each reform is a lever to unveil inequalities in organizational policies, procedures and practices is key to any institution wishing to lead equity work at the system level-this is where emphasis on intentionality is important. Intentionality needs to be supported by active leadership seeking to maintain DEI at the core of any student-centered reform.

To achieve this, first, it is fundamental to align diversity, equity and inclusion strategies to an institution's mission, goals and or commitments. For the California community colleges, this meant the DEI strategies were clearly aligned to one of the seven core commitments of the *Vision for Success*. These commitments include student-centered approaches such as designing and deciding with students in mind, focusing relentlessly on students' end goals, and enabling action and thoughtful innovation, among others (California Community Colleges Chancellor's Office, 2017). Aligning DEI strategies with the system core commitments enabled the activities that ensued to support meaningful and action-oriented deliverables such as changes to existing Title 5 regulations to revise EEO plans to make hiring practices more equitable. Another important factor is the integration of roles and responsibilities within organizational departments. As part of the Chancellor's Office internal efforts to drive equity, the executive team was provided with a work plan to operationalize DEI work in every division. This meant that any reform moving forward needed to align to the same core principles established in the *Vision for Success* with an equity lens to specifically target historically underserved and minoritized student populations. Other mechanisms included developing a communication plan so that each statewide association and department can disseminate the same message to its constituency and model actions and behaviors expected of the campuses. Moreover, integrating and aligning reforms and departments within the organization was complemented by the alignment and integration of financial resources to support the advancement of DEI efforts.

INCENTIVIZING DEI OUTCOMES

The third component we offer to leaders is the alignment of financial resources to incentivize equitable outcomes. For background, California's community college system is funded by three state sources that require alignment to support DEI work: state funds, local district resources and community college foundation dollars. For the CO, the alignment of resources was done through regulatory changes and increased oversight. The regulatory changes included changes to district EEO Plan regulations and EEO fund allocation formula. Simple changes like requiring a standardized submission deadlines for all districts and requiring the adoption of the plan in a public meeting under action (not consent) provide an opportunity to conduct a longitudinal system analysis and enlist communities to hold districts accountable. In addition to this, the EEO fund allocation has been amended to incentivize colleges to follow best practices such as the use of funds to support adding students to the hiring process, faculty mentorship programs, and interview travel expenses. By tying funding to best practices and the adoption of local EEO plans in a public meeting, we ensure early adoption of recruitment, hiring, and retention strategies found in the Integration Plan.

Increasing accountability for implementation and systemwide cultural transformation also includes the transformation of the associations and entities responsible for statewide oversight and accountability. Leaders wishing to replicate this process must provide centralized professional development and funding to support internal transformations. Each statewide association in the DEI Implementation Workgroup was provided with a work plan outlining key strategies and activities for them to lead at a state level. To integrate resources and align outcomes associated with the implementation of the Integration Plan, the associations were provided financial support to assist them with the development of professional development tools for their members. The CO was able to discourage this work being performed in silos by requiring each association to track and report back on progress at each convening and take ownership and participate in accountability efforts. Further, to ensure the integration of efforts and the alignment of financial resources, the CO incentivized best practices by providing a statewide best practice manual modeling equity-minded hiring practices for the system.

AGENCY TO LEAD CULTURAL CHANGE

The fourth component to leading diversity, equity and inclusion work is to give agency to organizational leaders to focus on culture change as they lead transformational change. To do so, is to allow for honest dialogue and give cover to minoritized employees in the system so they can speak out unapologetically. There is a level of humility and vulnerability that needs to be recognized when individuals are empowered to share their perspective. This takes courage and willingness from leaders at all levels to step into uncomfortable and emotional situations knowing their perspective may not be supported by their administrators and peers. The CO maintained a level of resilience in providing consistent and frequent communication to allow space for dialogue, community, and action. The CO engaged in a two-year process to engage members of the college community to 1) normalize a shared understanding of how faculty and staff diversity is critical to student success; and 2) engage the field and affinity groups in dialogue to continue momentum. The CO took a cultural change approach to community engagement that encompassed leading change with intentional alignment of structures, ensuring staff and stakeholder participation, clear and frequent communication regarding the cultural change, and managing any emotional response to the change (Wuthnow, 1992).

One of the initial mechanisms by which the CO gave agency to organizational leaders to lead transformational change was by hosting Town Hall meetings with stakeholder groups at every campus to allow for honest discussions regarding the lack of staff and faculty racial and ethnic diversity. As Chancellor of the system, Chancellor Oakley modeled this behavior with a statewide Town Hall where he publicly supported structural changes and normalized dialogue to about race, racism, and equity as a part of the institution's culture. Following the tragic death of George Floyd, the tenor and tone of Chancellor's Office communication shifted to give others a place to speak truth and voice the pain being felt among faculty and staff of color. Providing an open space for dialogue within the system was elevated by recruiting diverse perspectives to share personal stories during system-level webinars. In some instances, this meant inviting faculty and staff of color to speak and omitting the perspective of White faculty from the discussion. Additional system communication went beyond explaining why diversity, equity, and inclusion is important but rather acknowledging the deeply rooted structures of racism that exist among higher education institutions across the country. In other words, dedicating airtime to address structural racism by amplifying the role of students and staff dedicated to equity work and giving agency to those voices and perspectives was intentional. This strategy was both a strategy to ensure DEI remained a priority, but also a tool to provide agency to system stakeholders. As a system, our commitment to engaging in dialogue and learning was furthered affirmed by launching a systemwide book club challenge and deploying tools such as a glossary of common terms that could be used by our college community in their pursuit of honest and intentional dialogue on DEI across 116 colleges.

CONCLUSIONS AND IMPLICATIONS

Moving forward, the California community college system will continue to embark on system-wide implementation of diversity, equity, and inclusion policies and practices. The next phase of this work will consist of advocating for additional state funds to support the hiring of ethnic and racial diverse faculty and staff. As such, phase two of this work will require another layer of strategic planning and communication. In the meantime, DEI work is not being postponed or being further delayed. As presented in this chapter, cultural change is possible with the understanding that leaders must be willing to engage in a process where perspectives and institutional norms are challenged, emotions will run high, and advancing related activities and tasks will be taxing but impactful work.

Our recommendations for effective leadership of diversification efforts consists of four components: first, we presented facilitating honest and intentional dialogue. You cannot establish honest and intentional dialogue about the issue if as an employer, you have not made the transformation you are advocating for. Second, we discussed the need to integrate DEI efforts with system-wide student success reforms. There needs to be intentionality around the outcomes the institution wants to achieve to make sure reforms in place are complementary to one another and advance equity work. Third, we highlighted a few examples of how the Chancellor's Office incentivized DEI outcomes. This requires the alignment of financial resources to incentivize and fund activities that will result in equitable outcomes. Lastly, we emphasize the importance of providing agency to lead cultural change. Specifically, allow for honest dialogue and give cover to voices of minoritized employees to speak out unapologetically. In each of the four components presented, the underlying thread is authentic leadership and vulnerability and empathy in approaching DEI work as leaders. Further, it is the realization that generations of historically underserved and minoritized students cannot wait for our system to adapt and change. As educational leaders, we must accept and lead change that evolves our behaviors and practices in service of our diverse student population and prepare for sustainable implementation. Many of our colleges have already responded to the call to action and our work continues.

REFERENCES

Bensimon, E. M., & Malcolm, L. (2012). *Confronting equity issues on campus: Implementing the equity scorecard in theory and practice.* Stylus.

Blaine, B. E., & McClure Brenchley, K. J. (2018). *Understanding the psychology of diversity* (4th ed.). Sage.

California Community Colleges Board of Governors. (2019, September 16). *Board of governors meeting agenda.* Retrieved December 17, 2019, from https://www.cccco.edu/-/media/CCCCO-Website/Files/BOG/2019/bog-agenda-09-16-17-2019.

California Community Colleges Chancellor's Office. (2017). Vision for success: Strengthening the California community colleges to meet California's needs. *Foundation for California Community Colleges.* Retrieved October 8, 2020, from https://foundationccc.org/Portals/0/Documents/Vision/VisionForSuccess_web_2019.pdf

California Community Colleges Chancellor's Office. (2020). *Vision for success diversity, equity and inclusion task force.* Retrieved February 17, 2020, from https://www.cccco.edu/-/media/CCCCO-Website/Files/Communications/vision-for-success/cccco-dei-report.pdf?la=en&hash=FAB1854B05779EA47FBA10D1E5DED7A290D5C9E1

Gregerman, S. R., Lerner, J. S., Von Hippel, W., Jonides, J., & Nagda, B. A. (1998). Undergraduate student-faculty research partnerships affect student retention. *The Review of Higher Education, 22*(1), 55–72.

Harper, S. R., & Hurtado, S. (2007). *Nine themes in campus racial climates and implications for institutional transformation.* New Directions for Student Services. http://inclusion.uci.edu/wp-content/uploads/sites/13/2017/09/2007-HARPER-HURTADO-nine-themes-in-campus-racial-climates-and-implications-for-institutional-transformation.pdf

Jenkins, D., & Fink, J. (2020). *How will COVID-19 affect community college enrollment? Looking to the great recession for clues.* Community College Research Center.

Lawrence, K., Sutton, S., Kubisch, A., Susi, G., & Fulbright-Anderson, K. (2004). *Structural racism and community building.* The Aspen Institute.

Quaye, S. J., & Harper, S. R. (2007). *Faculty accountability for culturally inclusive pedagogy.* Liberal Education, Association of American Colleges and Universities. https://files.eric.ed.gov/fulltext/EJ775570.pdf

Taylor, O., Apprey, C. B., Hill, G., McGrann, L., & Wang, J. (2010). Diversifying the faculty. *Association of American Colleges and Universities, 12*(3). https://www.aacu.org/publications-research/periodicals/diversifying-faculty

Tinto, V. (2006). Research and practice of student retention: What next? *Journal of College Student Retention: Research, Theory & Practice, 8*(1), 1–19.

Tinto, V. (2017). Reflections of Student Persistence. *Student Success, 8*(2), 1–8.

Walumbwa, F., Avolio, B., Gardner, W., Wernsing, T., & Peterson, S. (2008). Authentic leadership: Development and validation of a theory-based measure. *Journal of Management, 34*(1), 89–126. https://doi.org/ 10.1177/0149206307308913

Wuthnow, R. (1992). Cultural change and sociological theory. In H. Haferkamp, H. & N. J. Smelser (Eds.), *Social change and modernity* (pp. 256–277). University of California Press.

SECTION IV

ROLE OF PHILANTHROPY

At each EPFP session that she attended, Danielle heard about imaginative policy ideas to revolutionize schools and challenge oppressive education practices that dominated the status quo. Being the realist that she was, though, Danielle constantly asked herself how the speakers she listened to planned to finance their efforts. Inequitable funding was why the students she knew bundled up in patched coats during winter math classes while youth five miles away frolicked during recess in designer ones that they shed before gleefully returning to their toasty classrooms. Similarly, inadequate funding explained her sister's reliance on substitute teachers and paraprofessionals at her school to keep classes functioning while pupils at rival institutions heard from educators with master's degrees, backed by a seemingly endless supply of instructional assistants, specialists, and support staff. Over time, some of Danielle's concerns were assuaged by peers that flagged the possibility of identifying new pools of support, petitioning policymakers for broad legislative changes around school funding, and connecting with local foundations in the hopes of them democratically including educators in their ambitious efforts to redesign neglected communities. Additionally, Danielle questioned how education leaders could build the support they needed to spur the adoption of their solutions. She had seen other reformers rejected and deterred from making waves when they attempted grandiose shifts, and she knew that others' aspirations would be mediated by the imperfect policy and political ecosystems surrounding them. Danielle also knew that her peers faced local, state, and federal policies governing a range of topics, from the assessments they had to administer to the accountability systems grading their performance. Here, she drew optimism from other Fellows that highlighted their ability to find ways to inject their values and ideals into the uncertain spaces, discretion, and delegation built into these pre-existing policies and parlay this engagement into more radical changes. Engaging in these reforms focused on proximate problems without losing sight of her desired structural change designed to ameliorate root causes was challenging but feasible with Danielle's eyes set on her end goal. She was determined to find a way around the barriers to reform.

CHAPTER 9

A NEW NORTH STAR

The Role of Progressive Policy Reform In Re-Envisioning More Equitable Educational Goals, Assessments, and Accountability

Christopher A. Shearer
Third Sector Strategy LLC

INTRODUCTION

Progressive critics of the present U.S. education system's limitations often cite the aspirations, policies, and practices of other, more educationally successful and equitable nations. It has become a cliché to compare the U.S. to Finland to throw into high relief the differences in vision, pace, and outcomes of school reform—pathways, ironically, that have been successfully informed by U.S.-based progressive researchers and reformers abroad but not at home. However, well into the 21st century, the United States is wildly unlikely to pattern itself on a northern European nation with a modest economy, a congenial civil society, and a small, relatively homogenous population. What is needed is the emergence of an American Finland—a domestic model for coherent systemic realignment, whether holistically within a single influential state or parsed across several. That will require

Emerging Trends in Education Policy: Unapologetic Progressive Conversations,
pages 125–141.

getting to an order of magnitude greater scale for progressive education reform. And *that* will require focused and sustained attention by educators, advocates, and funders not just to classroom and district innovations, but to the very policies that undergird what the country defines as the purpose of equitable public education, desirable outcomes, and allowable practices.

THEORETICAL FRAMEWORK

One framework that is helpful to guide engagement in policy research and design, piloting, advocacy, and reform has been developed by Viennet and Pont at the Organisation for Economic Co-operation and Development (OECD). Its central tenets are that effective policy implementation reflects a "purposeful and multidirectional change process aiming to put a specific policy into practice and which may affect an education system on several levels."[1] The OECD frame requires that actors at every level of the system can engage in designing and implementing reforms that respond to seminal changes in demographics and culture, are pertinent to a clear policy problem, inclusive of stakeholder engagement, acknowledge the current policy context, and promise policy coherence when implemented at the local level. This proposed approach—while not exhaustive or formally aligned with the present situation in the U.S., offers progressive educators a strong framework for deliberate engagement in the policy reforms necessary for greater coherence and impact at scale.

A Legacy Mindset. Despite the recent belated reauthorization of the major laws governing K–12 education in the U.S., relatively little has changed in the dominant "standards and assessment" mindset, which has long held sway. Introduced by the Goals 2000: Educate America Act and the Improving America's Schools Act (IASA) of 1994 and driven by the No Child Left Behind Act of 2001 (NCLB), this approach gives primacy to the importance of "ensuring high standards" and "improving accountability, as well as teaching and learning, by using State assessment systems."[2] As a practical matter, the process of establishing high standards under IASA codified a set of ten separate academic subjects; subsequent school accountability formulas under NCLB further narrowed academic content prioritization to the three that were measured regularly. State agencies were required to "measure the proficiency of students in, at a minimum, mathematics and reading or language arts" annually and "the proficiency of students in science"[3] in grade bands. Requirements to develop and implement "a single statewide State accountability system"[4] generated severe penalties for schools that did not make

---

[1]   Viennet, R. & Pont, B. (2017, December). *Education policy implementation: A literature review and proposed framework; OECD Education Working Paper No. 162*. Organisation for Economic Co-operation and Development. https://www.oecd.org/officialdocuments/publicdisplaydocument-pdf/?cote=EDU/WKP(2017)11&docLanguage=En

[2]   PL 103-382 oct 20 1994 Section 1001 d 1 and 8

[3]   PL 103-382 oct 20 1994 Section 1111 b 3 v

[4]   PL 103-382 oct 20 1994 Section 1111 b 2 A

Annual Yearly Progress on student scores in these academic subjects. Educators at the local level predictably responded by refocusing their attention on this limited instructional palate guided by proscriptive testing.

Accordingly, since the '90s many schools and districts have in practice attended disproportionately to the Three Rs, overemphasizing a discouragingly low-level target of basic student competency defined largely by assessment cut scores—selected points on the score scale of a test that indicate, for example, a judgement that a learner has met "proficiency" in a subject[5]. As noted by the Educational Policy Improvement Center, "For better or for worse, cut score proficiency defined by standardized testing has operated as the North Star of education policy since the turn of the millennium."[6] Current accountability systems and reports demonstrate that this remains largely true despite new state-level flexibility over accountability systems afforded by the Every Student Succeeds Act of 2015 (ESSA), which succeeded NCLB[7]. Under their ESSA plans, most states are beginning the transition to an accountability system featuring multiple measures of school quality. However, state policies have yet to significantly change in order to align with their ESSA plans[8]. This is because nearly every element of a state's education system is framed by, driven by, or enmeshed in standardized end-of-year assessments—a relationship referred to by former education commissioner Gene Wilhoit as a "web of interdependence."[9] This lock-step policy approach has weakened the country's ability to focus on achieving its aspirational policy rhetoric regarding the purposes of an education. Testing results themselves have done more to highlight persistent achievement gaps than to address them. Instead, the education system has been drawn to a more anemic outcome of recall, recognition, and basic application rather than robust analysis and critical thinking. This has kept the U.S. education system in a long-standing period of stasis.

Looking Through the Lens of Equity. Of note, neither enough sophistication nor depth has accompanied the national discussion of equity following the shift from the seminal Elementary and Secondary Education Act in 1965 to its more directive successors described above—regardless of the important position that equity has played as an aspiration behind any individual piece of legislation in the iteration of federal policies. There is now, however, a wealth of frameworks

---

[5] Zieky M., & Perie, M. (2006). *A primer on setting cut scores on tests of educational achievement. (P.2)*. Educational Testing Service. https://www.ets.org/research/policy_research_reports/publications/publication/2006/dbkw

[6] Beach, P., Their, M., Lench, S. C., & Coleman, M. (2015). *Defining a new north star: Aligning local control accountability plans to college and career readiness. (P.1)*. Educational Policy Improvement Center. https://eric.ed.gov/?id=ED571643

[7] PL 114–95 dec 2015 Section 1005 c 4 B

[8] Education Commission of the States. (2018, May). *50-state comparison: States' school accountability systems*. https://www.ecs.org/50-state-comparison-states-school-accountability-systems/

[9] Wilhoit, G. (2020, September). *A letter from Gene Wilhoit: How might we respond to secretary DeVos?* Center for Innovation in Education. https://www.leadingwithlearning.org/post/as-you-respond-to-secretary-devos-letter-you-may-want-to-consider

and strategic approaches with powerful implications for more equitable policy and practice design. A recent one is the Building Equitable Learning Environments (BELE) Framework created by the BELE Network, a group of education researchers, foundations, intermediaries, and district networks.[10] The framework places students at the center of the educational enterprise and proffers specific recommendations in four categories of learning contexts and conditions: teaching and learning; schoolwide systems and structures; family, caregiver, and community partnerships; and district and state policies. Where most applicable, the BELE Framework recommendations are referenced below as a way to illustrate how progressive education policy reform can intentionally reflect emerging theory and attend to racial justice and equity both in practice and in places and vice versa. The aim here is not to endorse any one frame, but rather to demonstrate how it is quite possible to anchor any discussion of policy evolution in much greater depth regarding equity than has been common in large-scale reform in the U.S.

A New Age of Reform. As scholar, educator, and advocate Linda Darling-Hammond and her colleagues have argued, "No system should be frozen for extended periods of time to the point where we find ourselves now: in a place where the system inhibits our ability to do what we learn is best for the students we serve."[11] Darling-Hammond's critique of policy stagnation gives voice to the complaints of innumerable education activists. Indeed, interest in education reform has rarely been greater. Reformers in the United States are motivated by a range of poor outcomes such as stagnated growth in student achievement, seemingly intractable racial achievement gaps, and the dilatory pace of technological innovation. Their work has taken on urgency in the face of poor international education comparisons, the progressively obvious disconnect between the aspirations and behaviors of the present education system and both community desires and the demands of the 21st century, increased attention to racial justice, and the immense challenges posed by the coronavirus pandemic.

As the reform environment has heated up, however, the earlier bipartisan policy consensus for the role and goals of government in education has begun to fray. Education has become ever more of a stalking horse for political ideologies entangling issues ranging from taxation to what constitutes appropriate academic subject matter. Excited by diverse theories of change, foundations and other funders have fueled the emergence of a wide spectrum of reform—from charter schools to community schools, from high stakes student testing to performance-based assessment, from value-added teacher evaluation to teacher capacity development, and more. The result has been what philanthropic leader Kent McGuire has called "a competition of ideas"—a panoply of sometimes opposed top-down education

---

[10] Building Equitable Learning Environments Network. https://belenetwork.org/library_resources/the-bele-framework/

[11] Darling-Hammond, L., Wilhoit, G., & Pittenger, L. (2014). Accountability for college and career readiness: Developing a new paradigm. *Education Policy Analysis Archives, 22*(86), 5. https://doi.org/10.14507/epaa.v22n86.2014

reform initiatives, models, and tactics that has been underinformed by communities and learners and has bred reform fatigue at the local level.

It is possible to classify the varying aims and approaches of today's reformers into differing ideologies. Two broad strands of innovation—politically separated—push against one another. Conservative education reformers, although not a homogenous group, are generally vexed by a government monopoly on K–12 schooling; ossified education regulations and structures; and the snail's pace of innovation. They tend to promote policy and practice approaches gleaned from the business world, such as consumer choice among schooling venues, tax refunds or vouchers to support individual purchasing of educational services, and more flexible delivery models, such as charter or online schooling. Progressive education reformers—also a varied group—are, in turn, animated by concerns over the idea of schooling as a marketplace and that education has come to be seen as a commodity to be consumed primarily for individual advancement. They argue for the value of public education as a public good, as a means of actively embracing the new diversity in the U.S., and for fostering community engagement.

The Progressive Agenda. The OECD framework posits that effective policy implementation is, "purposeful to the extent that the process is supposed to change education according to some policy objectives."[12] Attendant to philosophical underpinnings like those noted above, progressives advocate for related school reform approaches. One collaborative group of nonprofits and foundations—the Partnership for the Future of Learning—offers an illustrative set of progressive premises: Expand the purposes of education; Practice student-centered instruction; Foreground diversity, equity, and inclusion; Reanimate the civic mission of schooling; and Emphasize educator professional capacity.[13] The Partnership's statement of values aligns well with the BELE Framework, which suggests such elements as equity-focused teaching and learning practices and policies (e.g., provide opportunities for critical thinking and metacognition, student choice, project-based learning, and civic education and engagement) and schoolwide systems and structures (e.g., structure time in the school day for frequent teacher collaboration and professional learning).[14] Such approaches have been put into practice in a host of classroom-, school-, and district-wide reforms. Schools working in this vein use a variety of monikers: deeper learning, 4 Cs, competency-based, project-based, and more. Together, they represent the latest wave of effort to elevate U.S. public schooling from its earlier Industrial Era conceptualization—one in a series

[12] Viennet, R., & Pont, B. (2017, December). *Education policy implementation: A literature review and proposed framework; OECD Education Working Paper No. 162.* (P.27). Organisation for Economic Co-operation and Development. https://www.oecd.org/officialdocuments/publicdisplaydocumentpdf/?cote=EDU/WKP(2017)11&docLanguage=En

[13] National Public Education Support Fund. (2016). *Updating American public education: Keeping the foundation while preparing for the future.* (P. 2). https://www.npesf.org/networks/partnership-for-the-future-of-learning/

[14] Building Equitable Learning Environments Network. https://belenetwork.org/library_resources/the-bele-framework/

of ebbs and flows stretching from work done at the at the turn of the 20th century, such as constructivism, Montessori Education, and John Dewey's Chicago Laboratory Schools[15], to Bloom's taxonomy in the middle of the century, and the Partnership for 21st Century Skills "4 Cs" movement in the early aughts[16], which at its height promoted learning centered on collaboration, communication, critical thinking, and creativity among 16 state partners.

The most recent wave of progressive reform has seen impressive growth. For example, the Deeper Learning Network of Schools convened in 2010 by the William and Flora Hewlett Foundation comprise more than 500 sites operated or coached by ten charter and school support organizations.[17] Seeking to learn more about deeper learning reforms *in situ*, researchers Jal Mehta and Sara Fine identified 30 high schools to study, ranging from "no excuses" schools to International Baccalaureate and Advanced Placement schools to small schools, project-based schools, and comprehensive high schools emphasizing greater rigor and higher-order thinking.[18] These models advance such instructional practices as high-quality project-based learning, community-connected "expeditions," interdisciplinary study, learning progressions, proceed-when-ready learning, performance-based assessment, and others. Such progressive education is not limited to purpose-built schools. Even though most public school systems still conform largely to the model of core academic subjects, teacher-centered instruction, and high-stakes end-of-year testing there is now significant evidence of progressive approaches at district and school levels nationwide. As Mehta and Fine noted, "The good news is that such learning is happening *somewhere* in virtually every school that we visited."[19]

The Wet Blanket of Policy. Yet, for all today's energy and excitement around new models of progressive schooling, traditional policies put a "wet blanket" on the scope and scale of such reforms, which are still ultimately beholding to a framework of individual academic subject standards; low-level, high stakes assessments; and rigid accountability formulae. These strictures reify a gap between what a progressive vision intends and what the present system delivers. They mean that many reforms are categorized by districts or states as experimental rather than as systemic in intent, offered to those with the resources to be successful already under the dominant system—perhaps even further widening inequities. As a result, local practitioners end up spending considerable time and effort backmapping their innovations onto the dominant system—for example, keeping two sets of books, one for internal purposes tracking student achievement in an

[15] Wikipedia (n.d.) *University of Chicago Laboratory Schools.* https://en.wikipedia.org/wiki/University_of_Chicago_Laboratory_Schools

[16] California Department of Education. (2019, May). *Partnership for 21st century skills.* https://www.cde.ca.gov/eo/in/cr/p21cskls.asp.

[17] Alliance for Excellent Education. (n.d.). *Deeper learning network schools.* https://deeperlearning4all.org/enabling-deeper-learning-in-schools/

[18] Mehta, J., & Fine, S. (2019). *Deeper learning: The quest to remake the American high school.* (pp. 19–21). Harvard University Press.

[19] Ibid. (p. 31).

interdisciplinary, project-based course, and one for externally reporting grades that are parsed back into traditional stand-alone subjects. As a result, Superintendents may limit their embrace of progressive reforms, seeing them as a pressure relief valve for local reform impulses or as one-off learning exercises. Many may simply view it as too great a risk to the rewards their status confers in a rank-order hierarchy under traditional practice and assessment measures. Access to this more rigorous learning agenda is, therefore, often reserved for higher income communities, or charter or private schools, and much of it is offered in out of school venues requiring additional private payment, computer technology, and Internet access. Together, these circumstances leave major elements of systemic racism and inequity in the education systems largely in place.

Progressives appear to be insufficiently aware of the critical role of the intertwined frames of Standards, Assessments, and Accountability policy or of how to impact them. What is clear is that their vision is commonly overcast by financial and legal structures that rest on meeting seat time requirements and basic student test proficiency in at least a limited number of academic subjects. It is likely that ignorance of how to change the drivers of the system in which progressives work hampers their effectiveness as change agents and has hindered efforts to take promising educational innovations to scale. In effect, the disconnect between the progressive agenda and the establishment vision for schooling is a wide one. Their practices are also radically different from traditional education. Further, standards-based multiple choice testing is a poor measure of applied academic rigor, higher-order thinking skills, and learning dispositions: it poses a significant potential risk to reformers who are likely to endanger their school's testing scores, which undergird both traditional practices, such as summative ratings, and newer accountability considerations, such as student growth. This threatens their license to operate reforms by potentially exposing sponsoring district and state leaders to criticism under single state accountability models. Together, these policies serve as systemic structural barriers to greater expectations and improved outcomes for at-risk students, especially children who are Black, Indigenous, and People of Color (BIPOC). (By contrast, the BELE Framework suggests altering systems and structures to move, for example, to a school-wide system of competency-based grading and establishing competency-based graduation pathways.)[20] The net result has been to limit progressive educational reform to relatively small scale, often site-specific innovation that challenges the core frameworks of U.S. education content, assessment, and accountability policy only on a per classroom or per school basis. The OECD framework highlights the need for education policy to address the effects of shifts in culture, demography, politics, and economy.[21]

---

[20] Building Equitable Learning Environments Network. https://belenetwork.org/library_resources/the-bele-framework/

[21] Viennet, R., & Pont, B. (2017, December). *Education policy implementation: A literature review and proposed framework; OECD Education Working Paper No. 162.* (P.6). Organisation for Economic Co-operation and Development. https://www.oecd.org/officialdocuments/publicdisplaydocumentpdf/?cote=EDU/WKP(2017)11&docLanguage=En

There are, increasingly, bright spots to be found, but overall, there has been disappointingly little change at scale in the design of U.S. schooling.

MAIN POINT

To get beyond accumulated low scale innovation, local districts should advocate for the ability to initiate promising policy improvements designed to change the system from the ground up. States should likewise seize on and expand current policy flexibility to support districts as they redefine and advance an educational equity agenda, bolstered by enabling federal policy and resources.

Progressive educational reformers are unlikely to succeed in setting a true equity agenda if they do not collectively acknowledge the need for all children—and especially BIPOC students and those from low-income families—to acquire a deeper set of more relevant academic content and dispositions and higher-order thinking skills. Indeed, the BELE Framework urges districts and states to set universal goals.[22] Similarly, they will not succeed in implementing their agenda beyond the scale of transient local experimentation without nurturing a policy landscape that revises current accountability schemes and replaces them with measures more useful to systemic, continuous instructional improvement, appropriate supports, and accountability for more rigorous learning for all students.

Setting a New North Star. Fortunately, the case for more ambitious educational outcomes is well-documented and over the past two decades there has been a growing policy interest in establishing a new North Star for U.S. education. Research has shown that graduates are ill-prepared to address the increasingly complex demands of employment in a global economy, engagement in social media, modern civic participation, and growing threats such as climate change. For example, analysis by MIT and Harvard professors Frank Levy and Richard Murnane beginning as early as the '90s shows that computerization and offshoring has put relentless pressure on the U.S. economy, increasingly splitting it into two tranches: low-skill service jobs (e.g., house cleaning) and jobs requiring higher cognitive training (e.g., new technology). This has amounted to a hollowing out of the mid-level-skilled and manufacturing jobs that secured a middle class wage. They identified the nation's central educational challenge as how to provide all students with what they coined "many-faceted New Basic skills," bluntly stating that, "Good jobs will increasingly require expert thinking and complex communication."[23] Education reformers and scholars Monica Martinez and Dennis McGrath have suggested that deeper learning offers an answer to Murnane and Levy's challenge, noting that "Deeper Learning—a more robust and responsive educational experience—offers a framework for educators and schools to rise to

---

[22] Building Equitable Learning Environments Network. https://belenetwork.org/library_resources/the-bele-framework/

[23] Levy, F., & Murnane, R. J. (2005). *The new division of labor: How computers are creating the next job market.* (p. 141). Princeton University Press.

the challenge of preparing students for college, careers, and the world today."[24] Advocates Tony Wagner and Ted Dintersmith have succinctly summarized the emerging progressive sense of what an education is for: "The purpose of education is to engage students with their passions and growing sense of purpose, teach them critical skills needed for career and citizenship, and inspire them to do their very best to make their world better."[25]

A growing number of local and state innovators have begun designing and implementing a policy framework for student outcomes of this kind that foregrounds deeper learning. It describes a new equity for students in ways that shift the K–12 discussion *from* recall, comprehension, and basic application of academic content measured by rote, high-stakes multiple-choice testing *to* higher-order thinking skills and analytic application of knowledge to novel problems that are measured by aligned authentic assessments. This shift acknowledges that the former approach effectively limits systemic aspirations for most BIPOC students to minimal content proficiency, modest skills, and high school graduation rather than affording them the experiences and capacities necessary for true readiness to participate in two-year or four-year higher education or the military and subsequent economic, civic, and personal success. The BELE Framework addresses this concern in schoolwide systems and structures by suggesting that reformers "engage in a structured process to interrogate and align school personnel, systems, and budgets around a shared set of values and principles...."[26]

Perhaps the most visible and influential current approach to launching a consensus North Star for the purposes of K–12 education is the Graduate Profile movement. One exemplar of the practice is to be found in the Bay Area charter school network, Envision Schools, which has backward designed its entire curriculum and culture based on a graduate profile: "a community-wide vision statement describing what a learner should know and be able to do before he or she graduates from the school."[27] While the extent of the movement has not been fully documented, it is the anchor for reform in many schools (e.g., Arvada High School in Jefferson County Public Schools, Colorado[28]), districts (e.g., Brown County Schools in rural Indiana[29]), and states (e.g., Virginia's Profile of a Virginia

---

24 Martinez, M., & McGrath, D. (2014). *Deeper learning: How eight innovative public schools are transforming education in the twenty-first century* (p. 20). The New Press.

25 Wagner, T., & Dintersmith, T. (2015). *Most likely to succeed: Preparing our kids for the innovation era* (p. 44). Scribner.

26 Building Equitable Learning Environments Network. https://belenetwork.org/library_resources/the-bele-framework/

27 Lenz, B., Wells, J., & Kingston, S. (2015). *Transforming schools: Using project-based learning, performance assessment and common core standards* (p. 23). Jossey-Bass.

28 Next Generation Learning Challenges. (2019, March). *Reimagining assessment: 3 powerful examples of school districts using capstones and portfolios.* https://www.nextgenlearning.org/articles/3-powerful-examples-of-school-districts-using-capstones-and-portfolios

29 Zalaznick, M. (2019, September). *How three districts harness the power of graduate profiles.* District Administration. https://districtadministration.com/districts-harness-power-graduate-profiles/

Graduate, mandated in 2016 under House Bill 895 and Senate Bill 336"[30]) and has been promoted by influential technical assistance providers such as the EdLeader 21 Network/Battelle for Kids and KnowledgeWorks. The BELE Framework also references co-developing a Profile of a Graduate with local communities "to guide educational decisions and resource allocation" as a central tenet of equity in the domain of family, caregiver, and community partnerships.[31] A vital concern, however, is the relatively weak influence of top-down policy reform on actual instructional improvement, however powerful its role in driving attention or sanctions. Even when an enabling policy reform like the graduate profile starts bottom up, at the local level, the trick is to enact it subsequently through concrete practice reforms—a challenge given the legacy design of most schools. As Tony Monfiletto, executive director of Future Focused Education has cautioned, "The troubling fact is that we cannot make graduate profiles a promise because our schools are not designed to achieve that goal."[32]

Engaging in Policy Reform. As interest in setting a new North Star for U.S. public education has grown, related policy reforms are emerging at the local, state, and national levels to foster school redesign, improve assessment and accountability policy, and bolster systems of support to encourage progressive models and instructional practices. The BELE Framework goes so far as to encourage the formal instantiation of a reform mindset—specifically to, "Periodically audit policies and practices to identify and eliminate structural barriers to opportunity and those that harm the experiences, opportunities, or outcomes of students, staff, and families of color."[33] Vanguard advocates at the local-to-state and state-to-federal levels have accelerated responsible local innovation; fostered more productive dialogue and collaboration between local, state, and federal levels; and embodied new accountability formulas for greater and more equitable student achievement. A few exemplars of these policy-oriented reforms are outlined below.

Innovation Zones. In 2012, Kentucky generated a model for supportive state-level environments for local assessment and accountability reform. Through House Bill 37, the Bluegrass State established Improvement Zones, an enabling policy frame that allows district planning for a "new or creative alternative to existing instructional and administrative practices"[34] Up to five plans per year, each with a duration of five years, could be authorized. Approved districts have worked on instituting personalized instruction, performance-based assessment, and adop-

[30] Virginia Department of Education. (n.d.). *Profile of a Virginia graduate.* https://www.doe.virginia.gov/instruction/graduation/profile-grad/index.shtml

[31] Building Equitable Learning Environments Network. https://belenetwork.org/library_resources/the-bele-framework/

[32] Monfiletto, T. (2020, February). *Are graduate profiles a fad? Or a real fix?* Future Focused Education. https://futurefocusededucation.org/2020/02/26/are-graduate-profiles-a-fad-or-a-real-fix/

[33] Building Equitable Learning Environments Network. https://belenetwork.org/library_resources/the-bele-framework/

[34] Kentucky Revised Statutes. (n.d.). RS Chapter 156. https://apps.legislature.ky.gov/law/statutes/chapter.aspx?id=37825

tion of competency-based schooling and work-based experiences that replace seat time as benchmarks of student knowledge. Districts plans may support a single school or groups of schools. Such reforms promote concrete local iterations of an equity approach; the BELE Network recommends, for example, that district and state policies, "Replace Carnegie units with competency-based approaches focused on mastery."[35] However, the model has not yet scaled significantly and, today, five districts participate, although the number has been as high as ten.

Performance Assessment. With guidance from nonprofit advisors and support from philanthropy, schools and districts have begun experimenting more broadly with protocols that allow both educators and system leaders to use richer student performance assessment—which, "also known as alternative or authentic assessment, is a form of testing that requires students to perform a task rather than select an answer from a ready-made list."[36] These assessments can be used simultaneously as: a system-level assessment of learner progress, a classroom-based source of data for directing student-centered instruction by teachers, and even as a student-centered learning exercise. These innovations promise to take fuller advantage of the space provided by ESSA's removal of rigid requirements for Annual Yearly Progress and proscriptive school turnaround approaches and timelines.

Virginia offers an example of deliberate statewide policy change designed to encourage bottom-up assessment reform. As summarized by the Stanford Center for Opportunity Policy in Education (SCOPE), "In 2014, the Virginia General Assembly passed House Bill 930, replacing five state-directed exams with local assessments, which reduced standardized testing in elementary and middle school from 21 to 16 separate assessments in reading, writing, mathematics, science, and social studies (Virginia Department of Education, 2014). Subsequently, the Virginia Board of Education developed guidelines to assist local districts with this transition, specifically recommending the use of performance assessments to meet local alternative assessment guidelines."[37] Virginia has also established a networked improvement community (NIC)—a professional learning community that seeks to accomplish some clearly defined, measurable outcome[38]—of 11 districts focused on student-led assessment for learning[39].

[35] Building Equitable Learning Environments Network. https://belenetwork.org/library_resources/the-bele-framework/

[36] U.S. Department of Education, Office of Research, Office of Educational Research, and Improvement. (1993, November). *Consumer guide no.2: Performance assessment.* https://www2.ed.gov/pubs/OR/ConsumerGuides/perfasse.html.

[37] Stosich, E. L., & Jaquith, A. (2019, October). *Field facing memo #4—Virginia's student-led assessment networked improvement community: coming together for systems change.* Stanford Center for Opportunity Policy in Education. https://edpolicy.stanford.edu/library/publications/1617

[38] LeMahieu, P. (2015, August). *Why a NIC?* Carnegie Foundation for the Advancement of Learning. https://www.carnegiefoundation.org/blog/why-a-nic/

[39] Assessment for Learning Project. (2019). *Learning journey: Virginia student-led assessment network.* https://www.assessmentforlearningproject.org/virginia-student-led-assessment-network/

In addition to individual state- and locally initiated work, a national network has emerged to connect local and state agencies with other, non-governmental organizations. The Assessment for Learning Project has supported 28 project teams and convened a national learning community that includes technical assistance providers and field experts.[40] Participants work with the intention of informing accountability, policy, and system design to make use of assessment of, for, and as learning. These reforms address head on the role that traditional high-stakes summative assessment have played in distancing measurement from learning and reifying racial achievement gaps and miring potential equity reform. According to the BELE Framework, policy should, "Provide varied assessments that allow for differentiated opportunities to demonstrate mastery."[41]

Accountability. The expansion rate of modern innovations in both student outcomes and measurement is limited by calcified accountability policies. At a statewide level, New Hampshire has addressed this reality on two fronts. As reported by Wagner and Dintersmith, the Granite State "set an example by being the first state to eliminate the requirement that students amass a specified collection of 'credit hours'—called the Carnegie Units—in order to graduate from high school."[42] The state complemented this shift with the introduction of competency-based goals assessed by a voluntary district-level accountability system designed to ultimately replace stand-and-deliver annual testing. The resulting Performance Assessment of Competency Education (PACE) is a system of "locally-developed, locally-administered performance assessments tied to grade and course competencies determined by local school districts that are aligned with the State's challenging academic content standards."[43]

State-level PACE work was initially made possible federally through an NCLB waiver granted by U.S. Education Secretary Arne Duncan. Subsequently, the Innovative Assessment Demonstration Authority under the Every Student Succeeds Act (known as Section 1204 waivers[44]) has provided enabling policy. According to the U.S. Department of Education:

> A State may apply to the Department to implement an innovative assessment system in some of its districts instead of the statewide assessments, with the goal of scaling up the innovative assessment for statewide administration. Such a system may include competency-based assessments, instructionally embedded assessments,

[40] Assessment for Learning Project. (2019). *What is the Assessment for Learning Project?* https://www.assessmentforlearningproject.org/what-is-the-alp/

[41] Building Equitable Learning Environments Network. https://belenetwork.org/library_resources/the-bele-framework/

[42] Wagner, T., & Dintersmith, T. (2015). *Most likely to succeed: Preparing our kids for the innovation era* (p. 225). Scribner.

[43] New Hampshire Department of Education. (n.d.). *Performance assessment of competency education.* https://www.education.nh.gov/who-we-are/division-of-learner-support/bureau-of-instructional-support/performance-assessment-for-competency-education

[44] PL 114–95 December 10, 2015, section 1204 34 C F R §§ 200.104

interim assessments, cumulative year-end assessments, or performance-based assessments that combine into an annual summative determination for a student. Innovative assessments may allow students to demonstrate mastery or proficiency and allow a district to differentiate student support based on individual learning needs.[45]

Leading states are cautiously tapping into this supportive accountability policy reform to begin transitioning toward a new system of goals and measures. The legislation is a striking initial attempt at top-down policy relaxation geared to foster state-to-local innovation on accountability—long a "third rail" issue in education reform. The waiver authority is a welcome advance, although its requirements have proven too restrictive (new assessment systems must pass traditional peer review approval) and too aggressive (pilots must move state-wide within 5 years). The demand of these requirements, combined with lack of funding, dissuaded many otherwise interested states from participating. The BELE Framework argues for going further to "Engage students, families, and communities in co-planning at the state and district levels, including in setting goals, defining success, strategic planning, and decision-making."[46]

Systems of Support. One example of improved state-to-local policy connections comes from California, which established 8 broad state-level priorities for K–12 education and revised its entire suite of educational standards, teaching materials, assessments, finance, governance, and accountability. According to the California Department of Education, beginning in 2013 what is known as the Local Control Funding Formula legislation "fundamentally changed how all local educational agencies (LEAs) in the state are funded, how they are measured for results, and the services and supports they receive."[47] Enacting deliberate cross system partnerships, California introduced a set of carefully aligned reforms: the state board sets multiple educational goals; the legislative process allocates targeted additional annual budgetary assistance; districts develop three-year Local Control and Accountability Plans (LCAPs) to address goals from a local perspective, with financing flexibility targeted to underserved students; and county offices of education review and approve the plans. Importantly, as EPIC has noted, "In the LCAP model, traditional cut scores account for only one subcomponent of one priority."[48]

This reform model has been designed to devolve authority to the local level while elevating equity concerns and pushing the timeline for planning and evalu-

45 U.S. Department of Education. (2018, October). *ESSA Flexibilities*. https://www2.ed.gov/policy/elsec/guid/esea-flexibility/index.html

46 Building Equitable Learning Environments Network. https://belenetwork.org/library_resources/the-bele-framework/

47 California Department of Education. (2020, March). *Local control funding formula*. https://www.cde.ca.gov/fg/aa/lc/index.asp

48 Beach, P., Their, M., Lench, S. C., & Coleman, M. (2015). *Defining a new north star: Aligning local control accountability plans to college and career readiness.* (p. 1). Educational Policy Improvement Center. https://eric.ed.gov/?id=ED571643

ation beyond a single school year. It is a promising first step at statewide enabling policy, but does not go far enough to signal a fundamental change in the system toward a progressive vision. Additionally, too little has been done to develop local understanding of and capacity for effective LCAP planning and follow-through. Yet, an equivalently soup-to-nuts approach has not been seen since Massachusetts' Education Reform Act aligned new standards, assessments, accountability, and funding in 1993. That comprehensive move vaulted the Bay State to the top of the U.S. education rankings but was run on the rails of a high-stakes, annual Massachusetts Comprehensive Assessment System (MCAS test) and lacked strong attention to equity approaches, which left it with a striking racial achievement gap 25 years later.

There are multiple other examples of policy advocacy and engagement. The BELE Framework highlights potential district and state equity policies, such as, "Fund ongoing job-embedded coaching to support educators in developing the technical and relational skills needed to be effective, culturally responsive, and affirming."[49] In practice, Rhode Island adopted an equity funding formula[50], Wisconsin's Cooperative Educational Service Agencies have long promoted student-centered instruction, and more. Yet, it is important to note that—as with myriad progressive instructional innovations—a series of uncoordinated policy initiatives has not yet risen to the level of effecting systemic change; nor are they likely to do so. In part this is because, as Wilhoit and his colleagues Linda Pittenger and Jennifer Poon have noted, "Too often, leaders are not experienced systems thinkers."[51] In addition, the rate of turnover among urban district superintendents and chief state school officers—just over 3 years[52]—is enormously damaging to the continuity of reform. Without intentional advocacy, reformers cannot expect local, state, or federal leaders to clearly see the connections between and among various emerging reforms surfacing within their particular levels of the system or to braid them together. Further, without a clear and coherent alternative vision, decision makers will be tempted to retrench in the face of the dramatic repercussions of the coronavirus pandemic.

RECOMMENDATIONS

This chapter recommends a systemic pivot to participatory democracy based on equitable, community-informed student outcomes as a guiding light for policy

[49] Building Equitable Learning Environments Network. https://belenetwork.org/library_resources/the-bele-framework/

[50] Maxwell, L. (2010, July). New R.I. school funding formula aims at equity. *Education Week.* https://www.edweek.org/ew/articles/2010/07/19/37formula.h29.html

[51] Wilhoit, G., Pittenger, L., & Poon, J. D. (2019, December). *Essential learning: Leadership for learning.* Center for Innovation in Education. https://www.leadingwithlearning.org/whatwere-learning

[52] Ujifusa, A. (2015, January). Turnover, growing job duties complicate state chief's roles. *Education Week.* https://www.edweek.org/ew/articles/2015/01/28/turnover-growing-job-duties-complicate-state-chiefs.html

reform. This shift would undergird the establishment of a new set of educational outcomes necessary for student success and self-agency in an information age, global economy, and evolving commonweal. In addition, appropriate measures of learning tied to those goals must be adopted. Together these changes should book-end a progressive discussion of educational equity and spur policy engagement. The OECD framework defines effective policy implementation as "inflected by actors at various points of the education system.[53] Emerging local, state, and federal innovations demonstrate that advocacy for progressive policy reform is as possible as it is necessary.

Policy work by reformers should be characterized by two complementary metastrategies:

(a) *Set a New North Star*: Get past internecine differences in the definition of a modern education. While easier said than done, reformers must collectively embrace and promote a new North Star for the U.S. education system that centers policy on higher-order thinking skills, greater academic rigor, and capacities aligned with economic, civic, and personal success. One gateway tactic is to establish graduate profiles as a methodology to define equitable, community-informed student outcomes with implications for driving school culture, instructional models, authentic assessment, financing, and accountability.

(b) *Engage in Policy Reform*: Actively pursue policy engagement across and between the levels of the system including: (i) at the local level: adopt performance-based assessments to measure student achievement and progress on goals; (ii) at the state level, establish local pathways for creating an expanded community-wide vision for education; launch innovation zones to sanction, recognize, and support responsible local innovation; systematically revise the suite of education policy to align with—and go beyond—ESSA plan improvements in equity funding and student and school measurement; and enact broadened, reciprocal systems of accountability, and (iii) at the federal level, remove barriers to assessment and accountability innovation through expanded waivers paired with financial support for states' ability to foster reforms through discretionary grants for innovation and for greater state agency staff capacity.

The Role of Philanthropy. These policy recommendations will require catalytic support for research, design, implementation, and reflection. Foundations have been instrumental in influencing past policy reform initiatives. Increasingly, the broader organized philanthropic community recognizes that it can underwrite a range of policy-related activities, including supporting nonprofits engaged in advocacy. However, the field should take care to avoid the pitfalls of many past philanthropic practices, which include but are not limited to surface-level under-

---

[53] Viennet, R., & Pont, B. (2017, December). *Education policy implementation: A literature review and proposed framework; OECD education working paper No. 162.* (p. 27). Organisation for Economic Co-operation and Development. https://www.oecd.org/officialdocuments/publicdisplaydocumentpdf/?cote=EDU/WKP(2017)11&docLanguage=En

standing of and commitment to equity; not co-designing policy strategies with beneficiaries; establishing unrealistically short timelines for change; underinvesting in grantee general operating capacity by restricting awards solely for project-based funding; failing to support shared vocabulary and collaboration across the ecosystem of researchers, nonprofits, governmental agencies, and communities; under-attending to the coherence of activity across funders themselves (both in terms of priority focus areas and in terms of cooperation and alignment among national, regional, and local grantmakers); privileging elite, majority-white institutions as grantees and influencers of philanthropic perspective; and whiplashing reformers by changing strategies, funding priorities, and staff too quickly.

While a robust set of recommendations for how the foundation field might avoid these pitfalls would require separate paper, a few priority considerations come to mind. First, recognize that grantees are responsible for the success of any grantmaker's policy agenda—treat them as co-design partners and not as general contractors for your pre-conceived strategy; invest in their general operational capacity *and* invest in the collective ability of those in the portfolio to build trust, define relative roles, and collaborate with one another. Second, recognize the complexity and current capabilities of the policy ecosystem—invest in more than grasstops system leaders, whose turnover rates are stunningly quick, to also support technical assistance providers, researchers, and community-based actors in addition to fostering connective tissue between and among the levels of the system, from the local to state to national/federal. Third, commit to seeing through a policy agenda over a long enough period to realize progress—adopt a realistic timeframe for researching, developing, and testing out a feasible solution, identifying a functioning venue and effective champion(s) for action, mobilizing constituencies, and awaiting an open policy window.[54]

CONCLUSION

The United States has for an inordinately long time been locked into a top-down test-and-rank model which has resulted in policy-driven torpor in educational practice and equity. The 1989 Charlottesville Education Summit of governors led to a series of bipartisan education laws enacting a durable standard- and assessments-based regime, from Goals 2000 to IASA and NCLB. Ironically, the impulse to reassert international competitiveness and to advance greater educational equity for all children, and especially children of color and low income students, resulted generally in more limited academic subject content coverage focused largely on superficial outcomes. Underinformed by theory, community input, and empirical data, narrow systemic definitions of student achievement restricted the efficacy of professional educators explicitly and tacitly by framing their work as ensuring foremost that students achieve at least low-level test cut scores on

---

[54] Barkhorn, I., Huttner, N., & Blau, J. (2013). *Assessing advocacy.* Stanford Social Innovation Review, Spring 2013. https://ssir.org/articles/entry/assessing_advocacy

instruments more apt for auditing institutional accountability than for improving learning. As a result, the equity agenda stalled out at the level of producing greater transparency about racial achievement gaps rather than fostering demonstrable progress. At the same time, other nations aggressively pursued a broader definition of education and began to outclass the U.S. on more rigorous international measures of higher-order knowledge and skills.

Today, with the passage of ESSA, momentum in the education system has shifted to acknowledge this gap and to encourage responses at the state and local level. States have received initial flexibility to define richer educational outcomes and to better support and measure school improvement. Yet, increasing politicization at the national level, a decades-long policy compliance mindset at the state level, and a culture of restrictive instructional practice at the local level has discouraged many educators, agencies, and community leaders from leaving an unlocked cage. This legacy has also maintained a regrettable separation between the local, state, and federal levels.

Progressive reformers are committed to widening the aperture of the K–12 education system for greater outcomes, to achieving equitable educational experiences and attainment, and to incorporating what is being learned about effective school leadership and teaching into student-centered instruction. Together these approaches hold the potential to define a new educational equity and to begin to prove out at greater scale how it can be encouraged, endorsed, and enforced by aligned federal, state, and local policies. In this moment of devolution, educators, administrators, communities, and their allies must proceed with more coherent policy engagement if they are to effect seminal changes in the U.S. education system prior to the eventual pendulum swing back to national/federal leadership. They must coordinate adoption of a new consensus North Star for educational outcomes along with a set of better aligned and ever more concrete practice, assessment, and accountability reforms. They must seize the present open policy window to frame out the elements of a major revision to the nation's governing education legislation for future Congressional reauthorization.

CHAPTER 10

REDISTRIBUTING POWER THROUGH GRANTMAKING

Caitlan Cole
Charles R. Drew Charter School, Atlanta, GA

OVERVIEW

Private foundations with a stated interest in increasing equitable educational outcomes should begin by adapting their grantmaking policy to more authentically adhere to the tenets of equity. Grantmaking is the primary lever of change private foundations employ, and therefore this mechanism must itself function equitably if it is to generate equitable outcomes. This chapter establishes community-led grantmaking as a policy private foundation must adopt in order to carry out the goals of equity with greatest fidelity. The chapter explores the current trends in organizations across sectors naming and claiming equity, reviews varying definitions of equity, and proposes a working definition of equity. Next, the chapter examines the influence of private foundations on education, thus contextualizing the relevance of this policy recommendation for education leaders. Evidence is then provided that demonstrates that private foundations in their existing form perpetuate inequities in their design, makeup, and operations, therefore substantiating the need for policy changes like the shift to community-led grantmaking. This

Emerging Trends in Education Policy: Unapologetic Progressive Conversations,
pages 143–157.

evidence includes an exclusionary tax incentive for establishing foundations; a persistent lack of diversity among foundation staff and leadership; a documented bias in funding patterns; and a harmful power imbalance between foundations and communities. The chapter concludes with recommendations and next steps for private foundations by offering several models that may be referenced to put this policy in practice, including trust-based philanthropy and participatory grant-making.

INTRODUCTION

This chapter proposes that private foundations shift from a policy of foundation-led grantmaking to community-led grantmaking. It calls on private foundations to voluntarily transfer ownership of the entire grantmaking process to community members, from identifying problems and setting priorities to piloting programs, directing funds, and evaluating results. By adopting this policy and operational-izing it through new, community-centric practices (Community-Centric Fundrais-ing, 2020), the institution of the private foundation will evolve to limit its own discretionary influence on which ideas, programs or groups receive funding to instead focus on its role as a convener of community members within an exist-ing infrastructure of funding and disbursing these funds at the direction of its constituents.

While several studies have been conducted demonstrating the link between increased stakeholder engagement and the effectiveness of foundation initiatives (Bourns, 2010; Brock et al., 2009; Capek & Mead, 2007), the scope of this chapter will focus on community-led grantmaking's capacity to produce the advances in educational equity many private foundations envision. The traditional model of philanthropy adheres to "top-down, expert-driven" approaches to priority-setting and decision-making (Gibson, 2019); consequently, community members have been limited to the role of passive recipients of philanthropy's efforts, with the occasional opportunity to provide feedback or "partner" on initiatives, though very rarely serving as the final vote on decisions that will impact them. Yet this conventional model stands in opposition to the goal of equity as described below, and therefore the work of foundations advocating for equity is to democratize their policies and operations, including redistributing power through a policy of community-owned grantmaking.

The inequities in education are stark, deep-rooted, and incontrovertibly harm-ful, and the urgency of the need for solutions (and funding for these solutions) cannot be overstated. However, as this chapter will demonstrate, the systemic in-equities that are embedded in the U.S. education system writ large are embedded within the very institution of the private foundation. Consequently, when one in-equitable institution attempts to solve the problems of another inequitable institu-tion, inequities will inevitably persist. As Audre Lorde (1984/2007) reminded us, "the master's tools will never dismantle the master's house" (p. 112). If funders are to be successful in their missions to strengthen equity in education, they can no longer abide the status quo, particularly within their own operations.

While the current locus of power in the relationship between foundations and communities is situated firmly within the foundation, this policy recommendation calls for a complete migration of this power nexus to the community stakeholders. This policy holds that the best advocates for a community are members of that community, and the changemaking that they are best suited to lead requires more than a voice or a seat at the table, but rather ownership of the entire process. Adhering to the proposed definition of equity will mean that this relocation of power must be prioritized for marginalized communities, those who have been denied power most frequently and systematically. Voluntary relinquishment of grantmaking authority is only one of many transformative actions private foundations must take to uphold their commitment to equity with integrity; but for those foundations with the moral courage to lead the way, this policy could begin to bring into balance the relationship between funders and communities while normalizing the redistribution of power within our society.

Equity, Education and Philanthropy: Current Trends

The centering of *equity* as it relates to social justice is increasingly gaining traction across sectors in the U.S. As systemic disparities and persistent barriers to access that have been centuries in the making are brought into sharper focus within the current socio-political climate, nonprofits, government agencies and even corporations are using the term *equity* with increasing frequency. These institutions are articulating a commitment to advancing equity through mission statements, board resolutions, conference themes, letters from directors, staff trainings, offices of diversity and inclusion, marketing emails and more. By lifting equity as a vision toward which we must aspire, organizations are acknowledging that its inverse—inequity—is the current condition, while also expressing a desire to align themselves with solutions.

Public education and philanthropy are two fields that have enthusiastically embraced this clarion call for equity. Educational entities of every stripe are championing equity—state education departments are convening task forces on equity, school districts are hosting public listening sessions to inform the development of equity policies, and teacher crowdfunding platforms like AdoptAClassroom. org are awarding grants to individual educators and schools to pilot equity-based programs. The National Education Association, the National PTA, the Institute for Educational Leadership, and the School Superintendents Association, to name a few, all specifically mention a focus on equity on their websites. Equity is also embedded in the mission of the national Education Policy Fellowship Program, which strives "to engage a diverse and collaborative community of strategic leaders to promote equitable education policy" (Education Policy Fellowship Program, n.d.).

Many philanthropic organizations have similarly adopted equity as their north star, and a growing number are specifically focusing on addressing inequities in education. High-profile education funders such as the Bill & Melinda Gates Foundation, the Walton Family Foundation and the W.K. Kellogg Foundation use the term *equity*, or its inverse, *inequity*, to describe their current funding priorities. Yet even as this term becomes ubiquitous in education and philanthropy, organizations lack consensus on a common definition, even among foundations thought to be leaders of equity work (Putnam-Walkerly & Russell, 2016).

Defining Equity: Disrupting Systems and Redistributing Power

A definition of equity proposed by Putnam-Walkerly and Russell is "each of us getting what we need to survive or succeed—access to opportunity, networks, resources, and supports—based on where we are and where we want to go." This definition offers an important contrast to the concept of *equality*, which does not take into account baseline differences and instead relies on equal allocation heedless of circumstances. Janice Gow Pettey's (2020) definition of equity moves beyond "access to resources," which can imply passivity and an indifference to outcomes, and instead endows equity with the function of actively distributing resources according to need, stating that: "Improving equity involves increasing justice through the fair distribution of resources."

The D5 Coalition, formed to advance diversity, equity, and inclusion work in the field of philanthropy, situates its definition squarely within a philanthropic context, referring to equity as "the impact of philanthropic investment and action wherein outcomes are not correlated with race, ethnicity, sexuality, gender, or ability" (Dressel & Hodge, 2013, p. 11). This definition is particularly useful in its reference to the systemic disparities that necessitate the pursuit of equity. This implication of systems rather than individuals is critical and represents the first of two primary components of this chapter's definition of equity. The D5 Coalition's definition of equity denotes those societal disparities result not from individual choices but rather the collective, compounding impact of systems designed to allow some to advance while holding others back. This view affirms that such differences in outcomes are not accidental and localized, but predictable and pervasive for certain groups. The D5 Coalition's definition shows that equity can only be realized with interventions that intentionally counteract these forces.

The second key component to defining equity is power. Of all the "opportunities, networks, resources and supports" that must be redistributed fairly to achieve equity, power is the most valuable and the least likely to be fairly distributed at present. In her 2020 book *Our Time is Now*, Stacey Abrams refers to power as "the most profound currency of citizenship,": "The right to be seen, the right to be heard, the right to direct the course of history are markers of power" (p. 8). Fair redistribution of resources such as funding is crucial to achieving equity, but also urgent is the consideration of who holds the power to make the decision and initiate an action like redistribution in the first place. In this sense, being granted an equitable share of funding or opportunities does not go far enough; the power to make these decisions is the more precious commodity and the only real lever of lasting change. Given that systems that concentrate rather than diffuse power remain the norm, a redistribution of power is a necessary precondition to the redistribution of other resources.

The rights of power are exercised even in the process of defining equity. As Will J. Jordan (2010) points out in his article "Defining Equity: Multiple Perspectives to Analyzing the Performance of Diverse Learners," "imposing a definition of equity" may be counterproductive, and instead "a nuanced definition should be co-constructed by all stakeholders of public education, incorporating a wide variety of voices, particularly with the aid of poor families and families of color" (p. 151). This perspective is echoed by Putnam-Walkerly and Russell (2016), who offer that "the most equitable way to define 'equity' may be to leave the definition to individual communities." The driving question behind this conception of equity may be articulated as, *Who decides?* Decision making is itself an extension of power, and therefore an authentic definition of equity must acknowledge the inherent power dynamics behind all actions, policies, and practices, including the act of defining a term or framing a problem. In his 2018 book *Winners Take All*, Anand Giridharadas calls into question the impact of concentrated influence in the context of social change, noting that "when elites assume leadership of social change, they are able to reshape what social change is—above all, to present it as something that should never threaten them" (p. 8).

This chapter will utilize a definition of equity that affirms the need to redress systemic disparities through the redistribution of power. This definition is flexible enough to ensure that those impacted by systemic injustices reserve the right to decide whether and when equity has been achieved. For the purposes of this chapter, we can understand *equity* as the fulfillment of intentional actions that effectively redress the barriers and injustices built into and reproduced by systems and institutions; this is achieved by disrupting such systems and redistributing power and ownership on the basis of previous exclusion to such power due to race, class, ability, or any other factor that serves to limit power in the current infrastructure of society.

A further note on definitions: while foundations are often categorized by antecedents such as *private, family, independent, corporate,* or *operating,* the term *private foundation* will in this chapter refer to any foundation receiving 501(c)(3) tax exempt status by the Internal Revenue Service. In addition, the *community* referenced in *community-led grantmaking* refers to the residents of a particular place or members of a particular group whose daily lives stand to be most directly and profoundly impacted by any change to public education underwritten by a private foundation. Importantly, these community voices may include nonprofit organizations within a community. The intent of this policy recommendation, however, is to minimize the influence of traditional brokers of power, which in some cases will mean de-emphasizing the role of nonprofit organizations in favor of the input of individual community members or community coalitions exercising their right of ownership and agency. Ultimately, while guidance from foundation and nonprofit organizations should be solicited and carefully considered, it is the community members collectively who should decide on solutions to pursue.

Given this definition of equity, funders seeking to advance equity in education have an obligation to interrogate the ways in which they benefit from and uphold unjust systems and concentrations of power. In recognizing their role in perpetuating inequities, funders must seek to make the changes—and sacrifices—necessary to act in accordance with the equity they envision.

INFLUENCE OF FOUNDATIONS ON EDUCATION

Even before educational equity became a marquee issue within philanthropy, private foundations have exerted considerable influence on public education in the U.S. in recent years. In *Policy Patrons: Philanthropy, Education Reform, and the Politics of Influence*, Megan E. Tompkins-Stange (2016) examines the impact major education funders have wielded in terms of both grantmaking and public policy reform: "Arguably, no social sector in the United States is more heavily impacted by foundations than K–12 education. Foundation funding to education has nearly quadrupled during the last three decades, representing a significant infusion of capital" (p. 17). The Key Facts on U.S. Nonprofits and Foundations Report, published in April 2020 by Candid (formerly Foundation Center and GuideStar), corroborates the centrality of education causes in private foundation grantmaking, reporting that education-related initiatives received the second largest share of total giving from private foundations, closely following health-related initiatives.

Tompkins-Stange connects the growing role of philanthropy in public education with recent trends in the proliferation of new private foundations and the swift asset growth of private foundations in general: "In 1995, just 16 private foundations held more than $1 billion in assets, while an additional 164 held more than $100 million; by 2010, these numbers had tripled, with 42 foundations holding assets of $1 billion or more, and an additional 556 holding more than $100 million" (p. 2). Based on data from Candid, the combined total assets of all private foundations in the U.S. in 2019 was $1.2 trillion, compared to $551 billion in 2005—a 118 percent increase (Collins & Flannery, 2020, p. 21). Moreover, a handful of "mega-foundations" like the Bill and Melinda Gates Foundation and the Walton Family Foundation, have garnered significant national attention for both their substantial investments in public education and their involvement in education policymaking. Tompkins-Stange's study of four of the largest foundations active in the education sector—Gates, the Eli and Edythe Broad Foundation, the W.K. Kellogg Foundation, and the Ford Foundation—found that all of them regarded policy influence as a critical element of their work (p. 41). Thus, while private foundation funding makes up only a small portion of public education budgets, private foundations play an increasingly important role in today's education arena.

PRIVATE FOUNDATIONS: RIPE FOR REFORM

Perhaps due to this burgeoning influence and visibility, calls for changes to the philanthropic sector in general are gaining ground. Black, Indigenous and People of Color (BIPOC) leaders in the nonprofit and philanthropy world such as Vu Le and Edgar Villanueva have been at the forefront of this philanthropic transformation movement with their resonant, equity-centered visions for remaking the sector. The origins and development of the proposed policy recommendation have been directly influenced by the ideas of Le, Villanueva and countless others who have been championing authentic equity and advocating for community-centric changes to philanthropy—and to whom we are indebted for these movements gaining traction. As these BIPOC visions are lifted up and amplified, as this chapter also intends to do, the philanthropic sector grows ever more ripe for reform. The Dorothy A. Johnson Center for Philanthropy listed "Increasing Critiques of (Big) Philanthropy" as one of its 11 Trends in Philanthropy for 2020 (Moody & Martin, 2020). Rhodri Davies (2019), head of policy at Charities Aid Foundation, writes that "philanthropy is at a turning point," and increasing access to power is central to this reckoning: "A crucial part of making philanthropy capable of addressing inequality is to ensure that it is not seen as merely a tool for the powerful to entrench their advantage. It is thus vital to find ways to give away not only money, but also power." These calls to action are currently reaching their crescendo as the combined impact of the COVID-19 pandemic, persistent systemic racism, and economic instability proves that the status quo cannot hold. Now is the time for systemic, power-shifting reform.

Adhering to the proposed definition of equity will mean disrupting current unjust systems, underscoring the need for a foundation to disrupt its *own* systems and practices, and ultimately to forgo the supremacy of its own self-interest. More times than not, the most equitable course of action will directly conflict with the preservation of a foundation's interests. Yet this is what an unflinching adherence to equity demands, and while certainly not without its complications, the fair reallocation of power to the many within a structure that has traditionally distilled power among the few is a direct route to greater equity. According to the proposed definition of equity, relinquishment of ownership in the grantmaking process is the most effective means to redressing the power imbalance inherent in the relationship between grantor and grantee and therefore is the most equitable grantmaking policy.

THE NEED FOR EQUITY-DRIVEN
POLICIES IN PRIVATE FOUNDATIONS

Despite their community-centered missions and myriad positive impacts, most private foundations in their existing form perpetuate inequity in their design, makeup, and operations. Based on this chapter's guiding definition of equity, this means that these institutions, whether intentionally or unintentionally, benefit from or reinforce the conditions that generate disproportionate outcomes based on identity and exclude others from power. The features and practices that undermine private foundations' pursuit of equity include an exclusionary tax incentive for establishing foundations; persistent lack of diversity among foundation staff and leadership; a documented bias in funding patterns; and an intrinsic power differential that ultimately impedes the agency of community members.

Inequitable by Design

The concept of a tax-exempt private foundation inherently stands in opposition to the goal of equity by virtue of the fact that a certain level of wealth is required to establish a foundation. *Kiplinger* finance magazine advises those considering creating a foundation that "it usually takes at least $250,000 in assets to make a private foundation worth the cost" of administration and investment management (Anderson, 2009). Wealthy donors with the means to establish a 501(c)(3) private foundation are incentivized by multiple tax benefits, including income tax savings and tax-advantaged asset growth (Foundation Source, 2020). The creation of tax incentives only accessible to those within a certain tier of wealth confers power based on wealth. By offering a tax exemption on funds designated for charitable purposes through the vehicle of a private foundation, the government is essentially forgoing this tax revenue that would have been used to support government operations, programs, and services. Those with sufficient economic means thus have the power to divert resources from the government (which are spent and allocated based on the decisions of elected officials) to instead direct funding toward charitable causes that are often at their own discretion. While the law attempts to address this by mandating that donors give up "dominion and control" of tax-exempt donations (Colinvaux & Madoff, 2019, p. 1867) founding donors, boards, and on-staff program officers retain almost exclusive discretionary power over the funds. Consequently, what could have been public tax revenues remain private funds that are distributed at the discretion of unelected wealthy families, individuals, or groups.

Glaring Lack of Diversity

This concentration of power as a design feature of the private foundation is further compounded by the pervasive lack of diversity among foundations' founding donors, board members and staff. In a 2017 survey of 141 foundation leaders, BoardSource (2018) found that among foundations overall, 85 percent of their board members are white; among family and community foundations, this percentage jumps to 91 percent and 90 percent, respectively (p. 18). This survey data also revealed that 40 percent of foundation boards surveyed have no board members of color, and even when omitting family foundations, the percentage remains high, with 35 percent of foundation boards reporting zero racial diversity (p.18). BoardSource also surveyed respondents' attitudes toward increasing board diversity efforts and found that only 16 percent of foundation executives ranked "change or strengthen recruitment practices" as a priority for improving board performance (p. 21).

Racial homogeneity remains the norm at the foundation staff level as well. Data from the 2020 Grantmaker Salary and Benefits Report, published by the Council on Foundations, show that people of color comprise 27.3 percent of all full-time foundation staff positions: 11.3 percent are Black, 6.9 percent are Hispanic, and 5.2 percent are Asian (Daniels, 2020). Only 10.3 percent of people of color serve as chief executives. The report concludes that "stubborn disparities in staffing based on race, age, gender, sexual orientation, and disability status remain entrenched at foundations despite leaders' promises to build organizations that are diverse and inclusive" (Daniels, 2020). It's critical to point out that diversifying private foundation leadership and staff, as stagnant as progress appears to be, is only the first step in shifting a foundation's internal practices to promote equity more authentically. As Edgar Villanueva (2018) reminds us, "having a seat at the table is not the same as feeling free to speak in your own voice, to offer your own divergent ideas, to bring your full self to bear on the work" (p. 57). Real progress will mean going "beyond mere representation to access to power and ownership" (Villanueva, 2018, p. 59), a point that applies equally as well to the proposed grantmaking policy as it does to the diversity and inclusion efforts of foundations.

"Philanthropic Redlining"

This concentration of power in white-led foundations has tangible consequences, particularly in grantmaking. Many foundations, including those with a focus on improving educational equity, specifically seek to support marginalized populations where the need is greatest, requiring racial and socioeconomic data on the populations a potential grantee serves. But the issue is who foundations deem most suitable to *lead* the work on behalf of those populations. Reported funding trends bespeak a lack of confidence in leaders who are members of those communities. A 2020 report from The Bridgespan Group and Echoing Green analyzed the financial statements of highly qualified social change organizations and found that Black-led organizations are chronically underfunded:

> Among organizations in Echoing Green's Black Male Achievement fellowship, which focuses on improving the life outcomes of Black men and boys in the United States, the revenues of the Black-led organizations are 45 percent smaller than those of the white-led organizations, and the unrestricted net assets of the Black-led organizations are a whopping 91 percent smaller than the white-led organizations'— despite focusing on the same work. (Dorsey et al., 2020, p. 11)

This "philanthropic redlining" (Emergent Pathways, LLC, 2019) proved not to be an anomaly—when comparing all organizations in the study, regardless of issue area, "on average the revenues of the Black-led organizations are 24 percent smaller than the revenues of their white-led counterparts" (Dorsey et al., 2020, p.

11). The authors state that race-based obstacles to successful fundraising are the cause of these disparities, resulting in a "$20 million racial funding gap between Black-led and white-led early-stage organizations" (p. 13). Gatekeeping, such as refusing to accept unsolicited applications and the extent to which social capital is leveraged, along with a lack of trust in BIPOC leaders, are among these obstacles. "Facility in academic English, slick marketing materials and connections with prestigious people and institutions make it more likely that certain groups will gain funding," reports Vanessa Daniel (2019), founder of Groundswell Fund, which supports social justice and reproductive justice advocacy efforts, particularly those led by Black, Indigenous, and Transgender women of color. Her direct experience in attempting to fundraise as a woman of color highlights the unjust reality of philanthropic redlining:

> I've seen repeatedly that it's far easier for a young affluent white man who has studied poverty at Harvard to land a $1 million grant with a concept pitch than it is for a 40-something black woman with a decades-long record of wins in the impoverished community where she works to get a grant for $20,000. This, despite the epic volumes of paperwork and proof of impact that she will invariably have to produce. She reads as risky, small, marginal. He reads as a sound investment, scalable, mainstream. (Daniel, 2019)

Who Decides?

These inequitable funding decisions are the consequence of the imbalanced power dynamic at the core of traditional grantmaking in private foundations. Even among foundations that prefer to call their grantees "partners," the direction of power is well-established in a grantor-grantee relationship: organizations in need of funding are beholden to foundations that control this tax-advantaged wealth. The expectation is that potential grantees must do the work of convincing a funder that they are a worthwhile investment; demonstrating they align with the foundation's strategic priorities; and proving they can fulfill the obligations and requirements set forth by the funder. This burden of proof is entirely on the grantees. By contrast, the foundation reserves the right to award or deny funding, and itself is under a minimal obligation to disburse funding: the IRS requires that 5% of a foundation's assets are expended annually toward charitable purposes such as grants, though a foundation's salaries and overhead costs may be included in this percentage (Collins & Flannery, 2020, p. 32). This so-called "payout rule" was enacted to serve as a funding floor but has instead become a ceiling (Villanueva, 2020). According to the National Center for Family Philanthropy, "three in five family foundations had recent payout rates at or just above the minimum 5 percent payout rate of corpus" (Boris et al., 2015, p. 24).

Left unchecked, this power differential between grantors and grantees gives rise to paternalism and a lack of trust on both sides. Within this structure, foundations operate from the position of "we know best," thus tending to alienate the communities whom they are meant to serve. Far too often grant makers do not see community members as experts even though they are closest to the problems a foundation is attempting to solve. Vu Le (2020) conceptualizes this as "solutions privilege," the tendency to discredit solutions that threaten those in power or pushes the limit of what they believe is possible.

An illustrative example of the skewed decision-making process that remains standard practice among foundations comes from a well-known family foundation whose stated "strategic priorities" include Early Learning and K–12 education. An initial requirement for applicants is to submit an "ideas for partnership" proposal, which in reality is a "wish list" of the programs or needs for which the applicant organization needs funding. The foundation then chooses (without further dialogue with the applicant and without disclosing the criteria on which this decision is based) the wish list item it may be interested in funding, and from there the applicant may submit a full grant proposal for the foundation-selected program. Thus, only the need that most appeals to the foundation's staff makes it past the wish list stage of the process, even if it is not the community's greatest or most urgent need.

Following the dollars has become not only a normalized practice within the nonprofit world but a key survival strategy. It's an unkept secret among grant seekers that you must fit your grant request to each funder's specifications or giving priorities, a continual contortion act of telling funders whatever they want to hear so that your organization or cause is funded. This is the unsurprising result of a systemic power imbalance in which an organization's survival is often tied to its ability to mold itself in a foundation's image. This imbalance persists because to question a foundation's practices or decisions is to risk your organization's funding or your own career. So, in place of equal partnership, we perform what is expected of our designated roles of "grantee" and "grantor," roles not conducive to transparency from either party. In grantees' current standing within this hierarchy, there is little room to speak openly about needs or challenges, or to push the boundaries of funders' "solutions privilege" to innovate or take risks. Under these conditions, it is unlikely foundations and communities will be able to do the work necessary to realize the goal of educational equity.

CONCLUSION

Based on the evidence above, private foundations in their current iteration stand in opposition to the proposed definition of equity. Rather than disrupting unjust systems and redistributing power and ownership on the basis of previous exclusion, most foundations continue to operate in ways that reproduce disparities and preserve concentrations of power. This becomes especially problematic when private foundations commit to resolving issues of equity, including foundations that champion equity in education. For these institutions to deliver on the visions of equity they articulate, they must first take a hard look inward and identify areas for change. Because the current imbalance of power favors foundations, this work is on their shoulders—a redistribution of power cannot take place without their assent. As Robin DiAngelo (2018) emphasizes, those who "control all the mechanisms that exclude" also control "the mechanisms that can reverse that exclusion" (p. xiii).

Several models exist for putting this policy into practice. In January 2020 the Headwaters Foundation, Robert Sterling Clark Foundation, and The Whitman Institute launched the Trust-Based Philanthropy Project in response to philanthropy's "cultural moment of power-reckoning," as they describe it. This moment finds foundations "coming to terms with the entrenched imbalances they've inherited, created, or inadvertently helped sustain" (The Whitman Institute, 2020). This peer-to-peer funder initiative explicitly asks, "How can philanthropy redistribute power?" and charges foundations with building more trusting, equitable relationships with communities. Among practices such as awarding unrestricted, multi-year grants and reducing on "funder-imposed paperwork," this model of philanthropy includes soliciting and *acting on* grantee recommendations (Trust-Based Philanthropy Project, 2020). Similar to the trust-based approach, participatory grantmaking is "becoming a lever to disrupt and democratize philanthropy" (Gibson, 2019). In her *Nonprofit Quarterly* article "Moving beyond Feedback: The Promise of Participatory Grantmaking," Gibson names thirty-nine funders from across the globe that have adopted participatory grantmaking in some form:

> Some participatory funds . . . are completely peer led (in that everyone making funding decisions is a member of the population or community the fund supports) and do not include any paid staff or trustees from the foundation itself. Other funds are peer led when it comes to grantmaking, but donors and staff play a role in other parts of the process (like providing grants-management support). Still others involve both peers and donors in reviewing, selecting, and making grant decisions.

In addition, Nancy Csuti and Gwyn Barley document The Colorado Trust's transformation from nonprofit-led grantmaking to community-led grantmaking, thus "alter[ing] the fulcrum of power at The Trust" (2016, p. 76). The authors detail the steps the Trust had to take to enact this policy change and explain its profound operational effects, including restructuring staff positions, cultivating board buy-in, and managing expectations on how much time the process would take. They note that while the change was extremely challenging at times, the Trust held firm in its belief that individuals have the right to "actively shap[e] their lives and tak[e] part in creating something different for themselves and their communities" (p. 80).

Private foundations should look to funders who have adopted these frameworks as exemplars, and then should push even further toward equity by aligning closest with those funders who have ceded funding decision-making authority to community populations. This means trusting communities to lead their own work and to employ the tool of democratic participation to realize the goal of equity.

The proposed recommendation of initiating community-led grantmaking is an example of one policy meant to replace an existing inequity, in this case foundation-centric grantmaking. This policy can also serve to mitigate or begin to repair the harm of the other inequitable realities of private foundations discussed in this chapter, such as racially homogenous leadership and biased funding patterns. The basis for the recommendation is that equity defined in terms of systemic harm and undistributed power cannot be achieved unless systems are changed, and power is redistributed. Equity in education is a unifying beacon —foundation CEOs and parents at the local elementary school alike want to see all students succeed. Most even agree that change or reform of some kind is needed. But the equity we all imagine cannot be realized using the same mechanisms under the same systems that led to the disparities in the first place. For educational initiatives funded by private foundations, the time has come for communities to take the reins. While community-led grantmaking is not a panacea to philanthropy's inequities, it is a policy solution that directly responds to equity's call for system-level power redistribution.

REFERENCES

Abrams, S. (2020). *Our time is now*. Henry Holt and Company.

Anderson, T. M. (2009, August 30). Start your own charity. *Kiplinger*. https://www. kiplinger.com/article/retirement/t037-c000-s002-start-your-own-charity. html#:~:text=For%20instance%2C%20you%20should%20expect,private%20foundation%20worth%20the%20cost

BoardSource. (2018). *Foundation board leadership: A closer look at foundation board responses to* Leading with Intent 2017. https://leadingwithintent.org/wp-content/uploads/2018/03/LWI2017-Foundations-Report.pdf

Boris, E. T., De Vita, C. J., & Gaddy, M. (2015, November). *National Center for Family Philanthropy's 2015 trends study*. National Center for Family Philanthropy. https://www.ncfp.org/wp-content/uploads/2019/03/Trends-in-Family-Philanthropy-Full-Report-NCFP-2015.pdf

Bourns, J. C. (2010). *Do nothing about me without me: An action guide for engaging stakeholders*. Grantmakers for Effective Organizations.

Brock, A., Buchanan, P., Buteau, E., & Ross, J. A. (2009, December). *Essentials of foundation strategy*. The Center for Effective Philanthropy. https://philea.issuelab.org/resource/essentials-of-foundation-strategy.html

Candid. (2020, April). *Key facts on U.S. nonprofits and foundations report*. https://www. issuelab.org/resources/36381/36381.pdf

Capek, M. E. S., & Mead, M. (2007). *Effective philanthropy: Organizational success through deep diversity and gender equality*. The MIT Press.

Colinvaux, R., & Madoff, R. D. (2019, September 16). Charitable tax reform for the 21st century. *Tax Notes Federal 164*(12), 1867–1875. https://ssrn.com/abstract=3462163

Collins, C., & Flannery, H. (2020). *Gilded giving 2020: How wealth inequality distorts philanthropy and imperils democracy*. Institute for Policy Studies. https://inequality. org/wp-content/uploads/2020/07/Gilded-Giving-2020-July28-2020.pdf

Community-Centric Fundraising. (2020, July 13). *The CCF movement*. https://community-centricfundraising.org/ccf-movement/

Csuti, N., & Barley, G. (2016). Disrupting a foundation to put communities first in Colorado philanthropy. *The Foundation Review, 8*(4), 73–80. https://doi.org/10.9707/1944-5660.1328

Daniel, V. (2019, November 19). Opinion | Philanthropists bench women of color, the M.V.P.s of social change. *The New York Times*. https://www.nytimes.com/2019/11/19/opinion/philanthropy-black-women.html

Daniels, A. (2020, October 13). Foundations show little progress in making their staff more diverse. *The Chronicle of Philanthropy*. https://www.philanthropy.com/article/foundations-show-little-progress-in-making-their-staff-more-diverse?utm_source=Iterable&utm_medium=email&utm_campaign=campaign_1616785_nl_Philanthropy-Today_date_20201014&cid=pt&source=ams&sourceId=4719068

Davies, R. (2019, April 29). Philanthropy is at a turning point. Here are 6 ways it could go. *World Economic Forum*. https://www.weforum.org/agenda/2019/04/philanthropy-turning-point-6-ways-it-could-go

DiAngelo, R. J. (with Dyson, M. E.). (2018). *White fragility: Why it's so hard for white people to talk about racism*. Beacon Press.

Dorsey, C., Bradach, J., & Kim, P. (2020, May). *Racial equity and philanthropy: Disparities in funding for leaders of color leave impact on the table*. The Bridgespan Group.

Dressel, P., & Hodge, G. (2013, November). *Analysis of policies, practices, and programs for advancing diversity, equity, and inclusion: Full report*. D5 Coalition. http://www.d5coalition.org/wp-content/uploads/2013/09/PPP-Full-Report-11.14.13.pdf

Education Policy Fellowship Program. (n.d.). *What is EPFP?* https://epfp.iel.org/page/What_Is_EPFP

Emergent Pathways, LLC. (2019, December). *The case for funding black-led social change*. ABFE: A Philanthropic Partnership for Black Communities. https://philanthropynetwork.org/sites/default/files/resources/BSCFN_BLSCO_Report_Dec2019.pdf

Foundation Source. (2020). *Benefits of a private foundation*. https://foundationsource.com/learn-about-foundations/benefits-of-a-private-foundation/#:~:text=Income%20Tax%20Savings,adjusted%20gross%20income%20(AGI)

Gibson, C. M. (2019, August 28). Moving beyond feedback: The promise of participatory grantmaking. *Nonprofit Quarterly*. https://nonprofitquarterly.org/moving-beyond-feedback-the-promise-of-participatory-grantmaking/?utm_source=NPQ+Newsletters&utm_campaign=0a3a0f0e2a-EMAIL_CAMPAIGN_2018_01_11_COPY_01&utm_medium=email&utm_term=0_94063a1d17-0a3a0f0e2a-12932205&mc_cid=0a3a0f0e2

Giridharadas, A. (2018). *Winners take all: The elite charade of changing the world*. Alfred A. Knopf.

Jordan, W. J. (2010, March). Defining equity: Multiple perspectives to analyzing the performance of diverse learners. *Review of Research in Education, 34*, 142–178. https://doi.org/10.3102/0091732X09352898

Le, V. (2020, June 8). Privilege, power, and personal conflicts: The forces preventing change in nonprofit and philanthropy. *Nonprofit AF.* https://nonprofitaf.com/2020/06/privilege-power-and-personal-conflicts-the-forces-preventing-change-in-nonprofit-and-philanthropy/

Lorde, A. (with Clarke, C.). (2012). *Sister outsider: Essays and speeches*. (The Crossing Press feminist series). Crossing Press. (Original work published 1984)

Moody, M., & Martin, T. (2020). Increasing critiques of (big) philanthropy. *11 trends in philanthropy for 2020*. Dorothy A. Johnson Center for Philanthropy at Grand Valley State University. https://johnsoncenter.org/blog/11-trends-in-philanthropy-for-2020/

Pettey, J. G. (2020, June 3). *Equity, inclusion, and fundraising. Lilly Family School of Philanthropy*. https://blog.philanthropy.iupui.edu/2020/06/03/equity-inclusion-and-fundraising/comment-page-1/

Putnam-Walkerly, K., & Russell, E. (2016, September 15). What the heck does 'equity' mean? *Stanford Social Innovation Review*. https://ssir.org/articles/entry/what_the_heck_does_equity_mean#:~:text=Merriam%2DWebster's%20%E2%80%9Csimple%20definition%E2%80%9D,be%20a%20perpetually%20moving%20target

Tompkins-Stange, M. E. (with Schwartz, R.). (2016). *Policy patrons: Philanthropy, education reform, and the politics of influence*. Harvard Education Press.

Trust-Based Philanthropy Project. (2020). *It's time to address power and build equity in philanthropy*. https://trustbasedphilanthropy.org/principles-1

Villanueva, E. (with Buffett, J. & Buffett, P.). (2018). *Decolonizing wealth: Indigenous wisdom to heal divides and restore balance*. Berrett-Koehler Publishers, Inc.

Villanueva, E. (2020, September 22). *What's broken in the foundation and donor landscape?* [Video]. YouTube. https://www.youtube.com/watch?v=oGwsP-LpDKM

The Whitman Institute. (2020, January 22). Announcing the launch of the Trust-Based Philanthropy Project. *The Whitman Institute*. https://thewhitmaninstitute.org/twi-blog/philanthropy-is-in-a-cultural-moment-of-power-reckoning-the-trust-based-philanthropy-project-offers-a-clear-next-step/

SECTION V

ROLE OF SOCIAL JUSTICE

Following a year of listening to expert policy speakers, having the chance to lead an EPFP session with her peers, attending regional and national conferences centered on education policy, building her professional network, and cultivating new leadership skills, Danielle settled into her seat at the cohort's closing EPFP meeting. After collectively reflecting on their experiences, the Fellows were asked to complete a post-program evaluation survey. Danielle breezed through most of the questions until she got to one inquiring about whether she better understood the concept of equity and felt empowered to pursue social justice. Seeing the equity item shot Danielle back to a conversation with another Fellow, Stacy, who described her interest in helping all students but noted that she was afraid to rock the boat based on her memory of several principals in her district being fired after voicing their plans to expressly support Black male achievement. Stacy explained how board members and a few community leaders asserted that all children should be treated equally. Internally, these voices were more afraid that White children would be ignored. Throughout that conversation with Stacy, Danielle wondered, how do we have dialogues about equity when even the mention of race makes some people uneasy? She knew that the word incorrectly meant, to some, that certain individuals would get unfair support. That sense frustrated her as much as the many leaders that seemed stuck trying the same old methods even though hardly anything had hitherto improved the education playing field for marginalized students. Trying to turn her structural frustrations into action, Danielle gathered herself and encouraged Stacy to think positively. The two could champion equity, but they would need to start fresh. Instead of resolving to tinker at the margins of education policy or work to return to the pre-pandemic era, they committed to a reimagination of their local situations filled with original, radically progressive approaches. Remembering this turning point, Danielle could confidently report her growth on the post-program survey. As she finished the evaluation, Danielle moved on from thinking about her personal progress to considering how she could take this altered mindset back to her organization, community, and education-affiliated professional network.

CHAPTER 11

THE 1619 PROJECT, CRITICAL RACE THEORY AND THE NULL CURRICULUM

What We Teach By Not Teaching

Theodore S. Ransaw
Michigan State University

Khalid Mumin
Reading Pennsylvania Schools

INTRODUCTION

In March 2020, President Biden revoked former President Trump's 1776 Commission. The 1776 Commission was created to counter the *1619 Project* and eliminate teaching Critical Race Theory in K–12 classrooms and higher education, deeming it 'racist" and a vehicle for "people to hate our country" (Martin, 2021). *The 1619 Project* is an initiative to recognize slavery as a key component of American history and includes essays and articles collected by Nicole Hannah-

Emerging Trends in Education Policy: Unapologetic Progressive Conversations,
pages 161–173.

Jones to commemorate the 400th anniversary of the first enslaved African brought to America in 1619 (Schwartz, 2021b). *The 1619 Project* was published by the *New York Times*, and Hannah-Jones won a Pulitzer Award for commentary in 2020. The Pulitzer Center created a curriculum based on *The 1619 Project* for teachers to use in the classroom to address slavery and was quickly adopted by Chicago Public Schools (Schwartz, 2021b).

Since race is a social construct, a theory that addresses social implications has value for understanding the social dynamics behind issues related to schooling for minorities in America. Classrooms conversations about race in a supportive environment support the whole child whereas classrooms that do not address race leave out not only an understanding of race but also exclude the historical and lives experiences of their students.

Created by Derrick Bell, Critical Race Theory, CRT challenges the idea that race is not an issue concerning education and acknowledges that barriers such as school policies are often obstacles to opportunity for people of color. Critical Race Theory shifts away from perspectives that suggest communities of color are culturally deficient (Yosso, 2005) and operates under the premise that Black students do not need to be rescued but treated fairly. While there are other scholars that have written about and influenced Critical Race Theory including Jean Stefancic, Richard Delgado, Alan Freeman, and Kimberlé Crenshaw since it was introduced by Bell in the 1970s, it is important to note that Critical Race Theory is typically only taught in graduate courses such as law colleges.

Some may feel that *The 1619 Project* and Critical Race Theory are not appropriate curriculum resources to teach in K–12 schools. One reason behind the opposition to *The 1619 Project* and Critical Race Theory is that America has never had a serious and truthful conversation about race. Many of the conversations that we do have about race are not based on the same facts. For example, after a two-month-long study that examined how Black history is taught, the CBS News team discovered many disturbing things. But the most disturbing thing was the fact that there are no national social studies standards. No national social studies standards means that there is no common American history curriculum that American students learn. In fact, seven states do not directly mention slavery in their state standards, eight states do not mention the Civil Rights Movement, sixteen states list state's rights as a reason for the Civil War, and only two states mention White supremacy (Duncan, 2020). West Virginia state standards suggest explaining the concept of supply and demand as a strategy for teaching slavery. North Carolina state standards describe enslaved Africans moving to the American South as a form of immigration (Duncan, 2020). Not having the same national history means that America does not have a common understanding of race in America. What we do have are incidents where a Black student at a schoolboard meeting in Traverse City, Michigan had to share the fact that White kids in her school call her Niagara as a substitute for the "N" word and that White students in her class traded her in a Snapchat group called "slave trade" for a hundred dollars." But one parent who has lived all of her life in Traverse City says that "I've never seen any sort of discrimination. People in Traverse City are just kind" (Nathanson, n.p., 2021). In other words, if she does not see racism or has not experienced it personally, racism does not exist. Without state standards that address racism and the circumstances behind them, Americans do not have a common background to see racism the same way.

Overview

The remainder of this chapter will provide our theoretical framework that grounded our chapter. Next will follow a discursive event that describes how the debate whether to eliminate or include content like *The 1619 Project* and Critical Race Theory in curriculum began. A brief telling of the opposers and supporters of *The 1619 Project* and Critical Race Theory is provided along with our conclusion and actual policy recommendation comes after. Lastly, we share a few resources for readers who are interested in what culturally focused curriculum looks like.

THEORETICAL FRAMEWORK

This chapter utilized a historiographical approach. Historiography is the art and science of writing history (Mandavilli, 2015). A historiographical analysis includes more than just recounting what happened but highlights a historical happening concerning the time of that period. A historiographical analysis connects the dots of an event with the historical circumstances by including intention and meaning backed up by recorded facts. This chapter will provide the context to the meaning of historical events related to the controversy about *The 1619 Project* and Critical Race Theory using social media data, traditional media, and policy documents.

Exigence—*the situation at hand*

If you're looking for a connection between *The 1619 Project* and Critical Race Theory, you will most likely not find one. The two have been connected through the writing of journalist, senior fellow at the Manhattan Institute (a think tank) and political activist Christopher Rufo. In his words, Rufo tweeted:

> We have successfully frozen their brand "critical race theory"—into the public conversation and are steadily driving up negative perceptions. We will eventually turn it toxic, as we put all of the various cultural insanities under that brand category. (Rufo, 2021a)

> The goal is to have the public read something crazy in the newspaper and immediately think "critical race theory." We have decodified the term and will recodify it to

annex the entire range of cultural constructions that are unpopular with Americans. (Rufo, 2021b)

Rufo's association of *The 1619 Project* with Critical Race Theory characterized them as inseparable. Critical Race Theory became an umbrella term for topics such as race, racism, gender, diversity, equity, liberation, and identity, among others (Kleinrock, 2021). Consequently, any curriculum that looked at America's historical legacy of slavery and any critical analysis that examined racism became suspect because they both address race. We have learned from the George Floyd murder, and subsequent trial that talking about race in America is not easy. Talking about race is so uncomfortable for so many Americans that talking about race critically is associated with causing racism.

Rufo's argument about whether to use *The 1619 Project* and Critical Race Theory in the classroom centers on two main opposing points of view.

> At its core, [The 1619 project and Critical Race Theory] … pits progressives who believe White people should be pushed to confront systemic racism and White privilege in America against conservatives who see these initiatives as painting all White people as racist. Progressives see racial disparities in education, policing, and economics as a result of racism. Conservatives say analyzing these issues through a racial lens is, in and of itself, racist. Where one side sees a reckoning with America's past and present sins, another sees a misguided effort to teach children to hate America. (Meckler & Dawsey, 2021, n.p.)

Opposition

The growing prominence of both *The 1619 Project* and the Critical Race Theory has caught the attention and action at the state level education policy realms. At the time of this chapter writing, Florida, Arkansas, Idaho, and Oklahoma (Dutton, 2021) have noted their opposition to *The 1619 Project*, Critical Race Theory, and any curriculum or instruction that critically addresses race or racism in America through bans. Arkansas, Iowa, and Mississippi all propose that districts that the use of *The 1619 Project* should lose funding for the time used to teach it (Schwartz, 2021b). States that are debating whether to ban or not ban Critical Race Theory in K–12 classrooms are Michigan, Tennessee, Texas, Georgia, North Carolina, South Carolina, Ohio, South Dakota, Arizona, Kentucky, Utah, and New Hampshire (Dutton, 2021). States that are considering legislation to prohibit the teaching of divisive concepts in PreK–12 public schools include Iowa, Louisiana, Maine, Missouri, Pennsylvania, Rhode Island, Wisconsin, and West Virginia (Dutton, 2021).

Support

Those in favor of having a critical discussion about race in the classroom include Chairman of the Joint Chief of Staff General Mark Milley. At a congressional hearing in June, General Miley said this in a YouTube post:

> First of all, on the issue of critical race theory, et cetera. I'll obviously have to get much smarter on whatever the theory is, but I do think it's important actually for those of us in uniform to be open-minded and be widely read.

> And in the United States Military Academy is a university, and it is important that we train, and we understand....

> And I want to understand white rage and I'm white, and I want to understand it. So what is it that caused thousands of people to assault this building and try to overturn the constitution of the United States of America? What caused that? I want to find that out. I want to maintain an open mind here, and I do want to analyze it. It's important that we understand that because our soldiers, sailors, airmen, Marines and guardians, they come from the American people. So, it is important that the leaders now and, in the future, do understand it. (Miley, 2021)

States that share General Milley's views on the importance of understanding how race and racial issues impacts America include Arizona, Texas, and Maine. In 2017, Phoenix, Arizona, permanently banned Arizona public schools from eliminating Mexican American Studies after a seven-year court struggle. (Associated Press. 2017). Texas legislators passed Senate Bill 1828, which requires the inclusion of the Holocaust in Texas public school curriculum. Texas State Senator José Menéndez carried the legislation. It gave Governor Greg Abbott the ability to designate a week of remembrance of the Holocaust (Davies, 2020).

While some states oppose discussion of race in public education, other states feel that conversations about race are necessary. For example, Maine Senator Luchin tried to pass a bill nicknamed the Anti-Blackness law that would have expanded teachings on anti-blackness, but the bill died in June. The bill would have mandated the teaching of "African-American genocide" or the "genocidal laws, policies or actions targeted against African-Americans and indigenous ethnic populations (A.B. H-485, 2017). New Jersey Governor Murphy signed legislation to "incorporate instruction on diversity and inclusion in an appropriate place in the curriculum" and "examine the impact that unconscious bias and economic disparities have at both an individual level and on society as a whole." Washington Governor Inslee signed a bill "dismantling institutional racism in the public school system" and to "develop cultural competency, diversity, equity, and inclusion standards."

In 2021 Wyoming Governor Mead joins Washington and Montana in mandating Indigenous history by including Indian Education for All" standards. Connecticut became the first state to require all high schools to offer African American Studies and Latino Studies starting in 2020 (Stout, & LeMee, 2021). Colorado tasks the state board of education with revising learning standards to include the history, culture, and social contributions of people of color, religious minorities, as well as LGBTQ people and plans to update standards in 2022 (Stout, & Le-Mee, 2021). Delaware lawmakers passed a new law in May requiring teachers to integrate Black history into subjects beyond social studies. The new law takes effect in the 2022–23 school year. The New York Board of Regents released a statement encouraging districts to embrace diversity, equity, and inclusion policies, acknowledge racism and bigotry, and teach culturally responsive lessons to students (Stout, & LeMee, 2021). California passed AB-331 that requires a pupil to complete designated ethnic studies courses to receive a diploma of graduation from high school (A.B. 331, 2017). On June 17, 2020, a Minnesota committee will meet to discuss revising Minnesota's social studies standards to include the contributions of Native Americans.

CONCLUSION

A historiographical approach was appropriate to investigate a contemporary issue related to education policy. Although The 1619 Project and Critical Race Theory are not actually policy initiatives, the framing of *The 1619 Project* and Critical Race Theory as a policy to make arguments to write policy to exclude it highlights the necessity of an analytical approach to investigate the motivation behind the event as well as the effects and implications. Additionally, historiography was also suitable to contextualize modern textual data, including Twitter, YouTube, as well as traditional text such as congressional hearings and state hearings related to education policy. The short version is that there is hope for having honest discussions about race in America's classrooms in a way that is both truthful and meaningful. In a world that has witnessed polarizing movements such as Black Lives Matter and Stop Asian Hate, a teacher in Washington, DC. Elizabeth Kleinrock asked her middle school students what do they think about Critical Race Theory? Their answer, "Teach The Truth!" (Kleinrock, 2021).

We teach so much more by what we do not teach in the classroom. In other words, classrooms absent of conversations about race are void of knowing the truth. And without honest conversations, there can be no healing. The null curriculum, schooling that entails decoding and interpreting cultural expectations outside of their experience, is what we teach by not teaching it (Kazemi et al., 2020). To teach the whole student in our schools, let us include their racial and cultural contributions and avoid telling them race based experiences do not exist in America by not including the subject or race in our curriculum.

READING SCHOOL DISTRICT BACKGROUND

One school district that has created and implemented a curriculum policy that addresses race is the exemplary model of ethnic diversity Reading School District. Reading School District has 17,925 students, comprised of 19 pre-K to 12 grade schools (Greatschools.org, 2021). Eighty five percent of students in the Reading School District are Hispanic, 8% are Black, 5% are White, 2% are two or more races and Asian or Pacific Islanders, Native Americans and Native Hawaiian or Other Pacific Islanders students are less than 1% (Greatschools.org). However, Hispanic, and White categories do not tell the whole picture. The Hispanic population of Reading Pennsylvania is comprised of Haitians, and Dominicans. The White population of Reading Pennsylvania is comprised of Germans, Irish, Italians, Polish, Pennsylvania Germans, Dutch, Welsh, French, Slovakians, Scottish, Ukrainians, Russians, Swiss, Greeks, Romanians, and Swedish (Neighborhoodscout, 2021). Additionally, Reading School District students represent 28 countries and speak 27 languages. The Reading School District has an annual revenue of $240.9 million, and spends on average, $10,504 per student. The median price of homes in Reading Pennsylvania is $179.9 K (Realtor.com, 2021).

Because of its uniquely diverse population, the Reading School District felt that it was necessary to address racism with a critical lends through an The Reading Equity and Anti-Racism Resolution. The Reading Equity and Anti-Racism Resolution provides opportunities for students and staff to discuss race in a safe atmosphere that is necessary for diverse and multicultural students to become informed citizens. Productive conversations require truth and honesty, and conversations about equity and race are no different. The Reading Equity and Anti-Racism Resolution acknowledges inequitable experiences from racially marginalized groups.

POLICY RECOMMENDATION

The authors of this chapter suggest that The Reading Equity and Anti-Racism Resolution created by the Reading School District in Reading Pennsylvania be adopted or modeled by schools statewide. We say adapted or modeled as each state has different racial and historical backgrounds unique to its location. Therefore, we suggest that schools adapt or model the Reading School District Equity and Anti-Racism Resolution, that states:

> **WHEREAS,** the recent incidents of violence against Black Americans, including the murders of George Floyd, Breonna Taylor, Ahmaud Arbery, and Rayshard Brooks, highlight the systemic bias and institutional racism in our society that has senselessly and atrociously devastated so many Black lives throughout our country's history;

WHEREAS, the experiences and outcomes are not consistent for historically underserved and marginalized groups, including Black Americans and other people of color; those experiencing poverty, homelessness, or foster/kinship care; students who identify as LGBTQ+; students receiving special education instruction; students with limited or interrupted formal education; and students for whom English is not their native language;

WHEREAS, this violence, racism, disregard of human dignity and life, and apathy regarding these inequitable experiences and outcomes perpetuate a system within which students, families, and staff from these historically underserved and marginalized groups are oppressed and attacked, both through explicit racist actions as well as implicit bias and microaggressions;

WHEREAS, our community and our nation's futures require that this systemic bias and institutional racism be dismantled; and

WHEREAS, the promotion of principles of equity and anti-racism through educational institutions is a key lever in dismantling this systemic bias and institutional racism to ensure that ALL children and families are able to thrive.

NOW, THEREFORE BE IT RESOLVED THAT:

The Reading School District Board of Directors stands in solidarity with the Black community and other historically underserved and marginalized groups in our schools, community, and nation to condemn this violence, racism, disregard of human dignity and life, and apathy regarding inequitable experiences and outcomes.

1. The Reading School District Board of Directors commits to its own work as individuals and our collective work overseeing the District in continuing to become equitable and anti-racist in core values, beliefs, behaviors, actions, practices, and policies.
2. The Reading School District Board of Directors will recommit itself to promoting equity within and across our schools, in conversation and partnership with students, families, staff, and community stakeholders.
3. The Reading School District Board of Directors calls on all local, state, and federal partner agencies to join us and strengthen the collective work of equity, anti-racism, and inclusion in our community.
4. In moving from planning to action, as set forth in our Welcoming Schools Resolution (2018–19 School Year) and more recently in our Equity Policy (2019–20 School Year), the Reading School District will stay dedicated to drawing on the perspective and feedback from the collection of diverse voices received through the District Equity Advisory Committee and School Equity Teams to identify concrete actions that must be taken to advance this work, and continuing to ensure that these voices are elevated in decision-making processes through our District-wide equity initiatives.

— (Reading School District, 2021)

The authors of this chapter assert that The Reading Equity and Anti-Racist Resolution is one of the most innovative and racially critical school equity policy in recent history. The Reading Equity and Anti-Racism Resolution has only been implemented for a few months and there has not been enough time for substantive data to be collected, one lesson learned regarding implementation is that district-based equity teams and partners need to meet with parent and community members on a regular and frequent bases for maximum impact. The Reading Equity and Anti-Racism Resolution represents a unified consensus of a diverse community and has the potential to spur legislation across Pennsylvania and even nationally. The authors do not anticipate any additional costs to implementing this curriculum other than costs already included in implementing innovative and well thought out curriculum.

For districts and policy makers that are interested in resources that address racism appropriate for K–12 classrooms, we recommend the resources below curated in no particular order.

HELPFUL HISTORICAL AND CULTURAL RESOURCES FOR EDUCATORS

Green Dragon (Movie)

https://www.amazon.com/dp/B00006BS7R?ref_=imdbref_tt_wbr_amazon&tag=imdbtag_tt_wbr_amazon-20

The story of some Vietnamese refugees as they first arrive at Camp Pendleton in the United States as the Vietnam War ends in 1975.

MBK Equity Framework

https://www.obama.org/mbka/network/mbk-framework/

The MBK Equity Framework is a resource designed for any community looking to improve the lives of boys and young men of color and underserved youth. The Framework has been rigorously developed from the ground up in partnership with government, policy, development, equity, and organizational leadership from local and national organizations on the frontlines of youth and community development.

National Day of Racial Healing

https://www.facebook.com/NationalDayofRacialHealing/

An annual day to call for racial healing, celebrate our common humanity and take collective action to create a more just and equitable world.

National Museum of African American History and Culture

https://www.google.com/search?client=firefox-b-1-d&q=African+american +smithsonium+museum

The National Museum of African American History and Culture is a place where all Americans can learn about the richness and diversity of the African American experience, what it means to their lives, and how it helped us shape this nation.

Oxford African American Studies Center Oxford and Gates

https://oxfordaasc.com/

The *Oxford African American Studies Center* provides students, scholars, and librarians with more than 20,000 articles by top scholars in the field. Over 2,500 images, more than 700 primary sources with specially written commentaries, and nearly 200 maps have been collected to enhance this reference content

The 1619 Project Resource page

https://neaedjustice.org/the-1619-project-resource-page/

The comprehensive 1619 Project informs and challenges us to reframe U.S. history and better understand the hold of institutional racism on our communities. NEA recently worked with the *New York Times* to distribute copies of the 1619 Project to educators and activists around the country to help give us a deeper understanding of systemic racism and its impact.

The Underground Railroad Teaching Guide—Scholastic

https://www.scholastic.com/teachers/lesson-plans/teaching-content/teacher-activity-guide-underground-railroad/

This teaching guide supports the Underground Railroad: Escape From Slavery online activity.

United State Holocaust Memorial Museum

https://www.ushmm.org/teach

Explore Museum suggestions for where to begin teaching about the Holocaust. We include resources for teaching with limited class time, for English/Language Arts, and for History classes.

Truth, Racial Healing & Transformation Implementation Guide

https://healourcommunities.org/wp-content/uploads/2018/02/TRHTImple-mentationGuide.pdf

The W. K. Kellogg Foundation-led Truth, Racial Healing & Transformation (TRHT) enterprise is a multi-year, national and community-based effort to engage communities, organizations, and individuals from multiple sectors across the United States in racial healing and addressing present-day inequities linked to historic and contemporary beliefs in a hierarchy of human value. This absurd belief, which has fueled racism and conscious and unconscious bias throughout American culture, is the perception of inferiority or superiority based on race, physical characteristics, or place of origin.

United State Holocaust Memorial Museum

https://www.ushmm.org/teach

Explore Museum suggestions for where to begin teaching about the Holocaust. We include resources for teaching with limited class time, for English/Language Arts, and for History classes.

REFERENCES

A.B. 331. (2020). *Pupil instruction: high school graduation requirements: Ethnic studies (2019–2020).* https://leginfo.legislature.ca.gov/faces/billTextClient.xhtml?bill_id=201920200AB331

A.B. H-485. 2020, 2017 Reg. Sess. (2017). *An act to require education about African-American history and the history of genocide.* https://www.mainelegislature.org/legis/bills/bills_129th/billtexts/SP031005.asp

Altavena, L. (2021, June). 2 concepts divide Michigan school boards: What to know about critical race theory, equity. *Detroit Free Press.* https://www.freep.com/story/news/education/2021/06/27/critical-race-theory-education-equity-michigan-school-board/7778869002/.

Associated Press. (2017, December). *Arizona judge declares ban on ethnic studies unconstitutional.* https://www.nbcnews.com/news/latino/arizona-judge-declares-ban-ethnic-studies-unconstitutional-n833126.

Davies, D. M. (2020, January). *Why one Texas lawmaker set out to make Holocaust education mandatory in schools.* Texas Public Radio. https://www.tpr.org/texas/2020-01-27/why-one-texas-lawmaker-set-out-to-make-holocaust-education-mandatory-in-schools.

Duncan, J. (2020, February). *50 states, 50 different ways of teaching America's past.* CBS News. https://www.cbsnews.com/news/us-history-how-teaching-americas-past-varies-across-the-country/.

Dutton, J. (2021, June). Critical race theory is banned in these states. *Newsweek*. https://www.newsweek.com/critical-race-theory-banned-these-states-1599712.

Greatschools.org. (2021). *Reading school district*. https://www.greatschools.org/pennsylvania/reading/reading-school-district/

Kazemi, S., Ashraf, H., Motallebzadeh K., & Zeraatpishe, M. (2020). Development and validation of a null curriculum questionnaire focusing on 21st century skills using the Rasch model. *Cogent Education, 7*(1), 1+17. DOI: 10.1080/2331186X.2020.1736849

Kleinrock, E. (2021, July). *Students say teach the truth. Learning for justice*. https://www.learningforjustice.org/magazine/students-say-teach-the-truth?utm_source=Learning+for+Justice&utm_campaign=6324731fcb-Newsletter+7-6-2021&utm_medium=email&utm_term=0_a8cea027c3-6324731fcb-100931853

Mandavilli, S. R. (2015). Historiography by objectives. A new approach for the study of history within the framework of the proposed twenty-first century school of historiography. *Asia Pacific Journal of Social Sciences, 1*(2) 1 –31.

Martin, J. (2021, January). Biden diversity order reverses Trump ban on 'White privilege' *Newsweek*. https://www.newsweek.com/biden-diversity-order-reverses-trump-ban-white-privilege-training-1563242.

Meckler, L., & Dawsey, J. (2021, June). Republicans, spurred by an unlikely figure, see political promise in targeting critical race theory. *The Washington Post*. https://www.washingtonpost.com/education/2021/06/19/critical-race-theory-rufo-republicans/

Miley, M. [Reuters]. (2021). *General Mark Milley hits back at uproar over critical race theory* [Video]. YouTube. https://www.youtube.com/watch?v=oz7yDU1FmJQ&t=60s

Nathanson, H. (2021, July). It started with a mock 'slave trade' and a school resolution against racism. Now a war over critical race theory is tearing this small town apart. *The Washington Post*. https://www.washingtonpost.com/local/education/mock-slave-trade-critical-race-theory/2021/07/23/b4372c36-e9a8-11eb-ba5d-55d3b5ff-caf1_story.html?utm_campaign=wp_post_most&utm_medium=email&utm_source=newsletter&wpisrc=nl_most&carta-url=https%3A%2F%2Fs2.washingtonpost.com%2Fcar-ln-tr%2F343d6e2%2F60fedcf59d2fda945a1931e5%2F5fced4a59bbc0f251203a236%2F8%2F70%2F60fedcf59d2fda945a1931e5.

Neighborhoodscout.com. (2021). *Reading population statistics*. https://www.neighborhoodscout.com/pa/reading/demographics.

Reading School District. (2021). *Equity and Anti-Racism Resolution*. Reading School District, Reading PA. https://www.readingsd.org/Page/2501.

Realtor.com. (2021). *Reading, PA Real Estate Market*. https://www.realtor.com/realestate-andhomes-search/Reading_PA/overview

Rufo, C. F. [@realchrisrufo]. (2021a, March 15). *We have successfully frozen their brand "critical race theory"—into the public conversation and are steadily driving up negative perceptions.* [Tweet]. Twitter. https://twitter.com/realchrisrufo/status/1371540368714428416?s=20.

Rufo, C. F. [@realchrisrufo]. (2021b, March 15b). *The goal is to have the public read something crazy in the newspaper and immediately think "critical race theory.* [Tweet]. Twitter. https://twitter.com/realchrisrufo/status/1371540368714428416?s=20.

Schwartz, S. (2021a, March). Lawmakers push to ban the 1619 Project from schools. *Education Week*. https://www.edweek.org/teaching-learning/lawmakers-push-to-ban-1619-project-from-schools/2021/02.

Schwartz, S. (2021b, May). What is critical race theory, and why is it under attack? *Education Week.* https://www.edweek.org/leadership/what-is-critical-race-theory-and-why-is-it-under-attack/2021/05.

Stout, C., & LeMee, G. L. (2021, June). Efforts to restrict teaching about racism and bias have multiplied across the U.S. *Chalkbeat.* https://www.chalkbeat.org/22525983/map-critical-race-theory-legislation-teaching-racism.

Yosso, T. (2005). Whose culture has capital? A critical race theory discussion of community cultural wealth. *Race, Ethnicity and Education, 8*(1), 69–91.

CHAPTER 12

SEEKING CLARITY AND JUSTICE

An Analysis of India and the PRC's National Education Policies Through a Global Lens of the UN Sustainable Development Goals

Darshana Devarajan and Kyle Chong
Michigan State University

INTRODUCTION

India and the People's Republic of China (PRC) have recently stepped up nationalistic and regionalistic violence against minoritized religious and ethnic communities in their respective national education policies (Duara, 2010; Keating, 2011).[1] These national education policies, India's New Education Policy (NEP) (2020), and the PRC's *Outline of China's National Plan for Medium and Long-*

---

[1]   In this chapter, we acknowledge 'China' as a contested term, and disassociated from the People's Republic of China. While we make no claim about political sovereignty, terminology used throughout this paper acknowledges the contested status and/or de facto political autonomy of Taiwan, Hong Kong, Macau, Tibet, South Tibet, Xinjiang, Siachen Glacier, Senkaku/Diaoyutai Islands, South China Sea, Luconia Reefs and James Shoal, Spratly and Parcel Islands, Arunachal Pradesh, Akashi Chin, and Galwan Valley.

Emerging Trends in Education Policy: Unapologetic Progressive Conversations,
pages 175–192.

term Education Reform and Development (CNP, 2010) claim to align and advance United Nations Sustainable Development Goal Four: Quality education (SDG4), which seeks to "ensure inclusive and equitable equality education and promote lifelong learning opportunities for all" (United Nations, 2015, p. 4). SDG4 also lays out a target and indicator framework which seeks to address gender disparities in educational access, as well as promote education for sustainable development (ESD), and "safer nonviolent, [and] inclusive" (United Nations, 2015, p. 5) schools (see Appendix A).

In this chapter, we argue that the curricular and political prescription in India's NEP and the PRC's CNP, despite both countries' claims that their national education policies align with SDG4, reinforce nationalistic and authoritarian political climates in both countries. In critiquing the NEP and CNP, we further argue that SDG4's aspirations toward accessible, safe, and socially mobile schooling, set vague and problematically low bars for national curricula, especially as it relates to minoritized communities. We, thus, recommended changes to SDG4 Target 4.7 and 4.a and Indicators 4.7.1 and 4.a.1 to create explicit protections for minoritized communities, and propose mechanisms for these national policies to have greater public accountability grounded in the Education Policy Fellowship Program pillar Policy by calling attention to the SDG4's roles in sustaining systemic barriers to educational opportunity. We do so by providing brief historical context, analyzing SDG4's target and indicator framework in context of the SDGs broadly, and conducting a critical policy analysis of the NEP, CNP, and SDG4. In our conclusion, while acknowledging the necessity of SDG4 as a starting point, we strive to expand the definition of educational and curricular safety, considering safety as engaging with a curriculum that is epistemically nonviolent and, thus, beyond literal and physical safety. Further, we recommend that India's and the PRC's national education policies and SDG4 move towards a more inclusive definition of 'all learners,' and 'accessible, safe, and socially mobile' schooling. This analysis seeks to broaden the conversation in the field of education policy about how SDG framework may help reorient education policy studies towards more democratic-aspiring relationships between citizens, national policy, and global targets and model explicit protections for Indigenous sovereignty and political, sexual, and/ or ethnic minorities necessary to counter authoritarian and politically prescriptive national education policies.

BACKGROUND

India and the PRC are both home to numerous ethnic and linguistic groups. Both countries have constructed, in their national education policies, varying degrees of belonging through hegemonic frameworks of being Indian or Chinese (Lieberthal, 2004; Tharoor, 1997). The NEP and the CNP are among many technologies that bind together ethnically and politically diverse imagined polities (Anderson, 2006). Since 2019, civil liberties and free speech rights have rapidly eroded in India and the PRC. Simultaneously, national education policies have become technologies of conserving dominant Hindu and Han norms, respectively, steering both countries toward Hindu and ethnic nationalisms, and increasingly militarized repression of religious, linguistic, and political minorities in both countries. Both countries seek to build political legitimacy and stability from an uncomfortable post-colonial history and reckoning, like the Emergency (1975–1977) and the Cultural Revolution (1966–1976), to create a citizenry tacitly consenting to state-sanctioned ethnic violence and culturally hegemonic curricular overtones whilst nominally promoting egalitarianism. In this section, we provide background on the SDG framework, and a brief history of the NEP and CNP in context of their respective political histories, and how each country claims to be aligned and compliant with SDG4's target and indicator framework.

The SDGs and SDG4

The SDGs, while representing global consensus, seem to imprecisely fit a breadth of sociopolitical and economic realities (Burford, et al., 2016), in which inequality is experienced in different ways. For example, India and the PRC are similar in population, and both have special legal protections for certain communities (scheduled castes and tribes, and gender and religious minorities in India, officially recognized ethnic minorities in the PRC). The minoritized groups are provided quality education through special education and vocational education, by their respective countries (MFAPRC, 2019; NITI Aayog, 2020). As a result, these different interpretations of "equitable quality education" (UN, 2021), the stated aim of SDG4, indicate both a flexibility to meet each country's needs, but can also make the SDG framework at-large a filter through which individual countries legitimize their existing (and sometimes non-inclusive) practices (Gupta & Vegelin, 2016).

Further, when SDG4 is translated into national policy, the goal seems to lose the "aspirations" (Unterhalter, 2019, p. 40) of the targets. SDG4 relies on a broad scope in the form of vague language to apply to a wider global audience. However, this vagueness allows for continued marginalization of minority and Indigenous communities. The SDGs were adopted as part of the 2030 Agenda for Sustainable Development in 2016 (UNGA, 2015) seeking to reset countries' political and environmental social contract (Burford, et al., 2016). The SDGs center quantitative measurements which focus on economic (Gupta & Vegelin, 2016), environmental, and social targets (Burford, et al., 2016). Despite the SDGs' democratic intentions (Fox & Stoett, 2016), they emphasize governmental intervention over collective action. As a result, these measurements can seem to forgo engagement with ideas of sustainability beyond strictly economic, environmental, and social cultural pillars that can center marginalized communities (Hawkes, 2011).

Standardizing national policy in a way that affirms all nationalities and ethnic groups as well as minority and Indigenous communities so that they all benefit requires critical attention paid to every policy recommendation and the implications behind them.

SDG4, in particular, sought to shift education towards a model of equitable and accessible learning (Ban, 2012; Unterhalter, 2019). On the one hand, this policymaking has exposed the UN to critiques of global governance (Tikly, 2017; Unterhalter, 2019) through their attempt to standardize educational achievement and sustainability globally (Mundy et al., 2016). On the other hand, the SDGs encourage interdisciplinarity in curriculum and community learning's impacts on global problems (Oyasu, 2019). SDG4, or the SDGs writ large, do not endorse a definition of sustainable development; instead drawing upon narrow indicators to generate results using convenient proxy measurements without localizable specifications and distribution-centric definition of equality (Burford, et al., 2016; Unterhalter, 2019).

India and the NEP

India's first post-independence Minister of Education between the years 1947 and 1958, Maulana Abul Kalam Azad, envisaged "strong central government control" (Pandit, 2016, p. 393) over a uniform system of education. Ever since, the influence of the ruling party at the center dictated the ways in which the national policies of education were developed. In 1968, the introduction of mandatory Hindi in schools set in motion the hegemony of Hindi in parts of the country that did not belong to the Hindi-speaking community (Annamalai, 2005). Their insistence on achieving "national integration and greater cultural and economic development" (Pandit, 2016, p. 393), through the imposition of Hindi, reflected a nationalist ideology that did not pay attention to the minoritized communities.

The 2020 NEP, which has been drafted under Prime Minister Narendra Modi of the Bharatiya Janata Party (BJP), similarly reflects India's political context and guiding ideology of Hindutva (Ramachandran, 2020). Hindutva (Hindu Nationalism), which led to the introduction of a Citizenship Amendment Act in 2019, has informed a politics of hatred, oppression, exclusion, and erasure of minority communities in India. While the goals of "Access, Equity, Quality, Affordability and Accountability" (NEP, 2020, p. 5) pay lip-service to the Indian Constitution, they subtly promote the ruling BJP's Hindu supremacist ideology (*The Hindu*, 2020). The policy advocates a "greater flexibility and student choice" (NEP, 2020, p. 16), and interdisciplinarity with a focus on Schedule 8 languages (pp. 14–16), which currently includes 22 Indian languages.

Of the numerous documented and undocumented languages that exist in India, the Constitution has listed these 22 languages as the "official" ones, which allows their use for official and legal purposes. Article 344(1) in the Indian Constitution mentions that each of these languages should be represented in the commission and discusses the "dynamic use" and promotion of Hindi across the country. While it might seem like this is an inclusion of many languages spoken by majority populations, the commission is committed only to the promotion of Hindi, which is a language that is not spoken in states other than the Northern belt of the country (Schiffman, 2003). Simultaneously, minorities tribal and local varieties of endangered languages (Roychowdhury, 2020) are overlooked in the policy. Critics have also claimed that the policy is "unrealistic, impractical, and unspecific" (Khan, 2020) as the NEP sidesteps the importance of a clear plan for implementation (Khan, 2020; TheWire, 2020). This 'anti-democratic' (Krishna, 2020) policy which encourages 'radical privatization' by advocating for the "public-good nature" (p. 29) of private educational institutions retains influence of the current political agenda.

Patriotic Education in the PRC

In the PRC, the end of the Cultural Revolution (1966–1976) forced a national reckoning about what it meant to be 'Chinese' after Mao. Deng Xiaoping's neo liberalization agenda gave way to rhetoric of socialism with Chinese characteristics (Harvey, 2005), simultaneously permitted a defensible departure from Marxist orthodoxy, and led to greater calls for democratization (Hui. 2009; Osnos, 2014; Paine & Zeichner, 2012). Following the 1989 Tiananmen Massacre in which the PRC used military force to crush pro-democracy demonstrations, the PRC launched The Patriotic Education Campaign (PEC) in 1990 to redesign its national curriculum each year from 1992–1994 (Pinar, 2014; Zhao, 1998). These curricular 'reforms' sought to center standardized political homogeneity as a "political ideology" (Pinar, 2014, p. 224) to create social order in the wake of Tiananmen that evolved into softer forms that encouraged Chinese pride (Zhao, 1998).

The PEC sought to portray the CCP regime favorably, prevent another Tiananmen, and help "young people understand where China was strong…and what were its favorable and unfavorable conditions so as to enhance their sense of historical mission and responsibility" (Zhao, 1998, p. 293). The objectives of these and other reforms impacted elementary to postsecondary social education (Tobin et al., 2009), and taught students, starting in elementary schooling (Tobin et al., 2009), to "love socialism, to inherit and carry forward the fine Chinese national and revolutionary traditions... abide by the country's laws and social ethics" (Zhou, 2014, p. 135) and "come to possess the correct worldview, life philosophy, and values" (p. 136), dictated by the PRC. The PEC continues to influence PRC education policy and is exported to the territories claimed by the PRC, like Hong Kong, which catalyzed the first pro-democracy uprisings in 2014 (Bland, 2017).

Themes of national rejuvenation and moral patriotism continue to drive the PRC's current policy, the *Outline of China's National Plan for Medium and Long-term Education Reform and Development 2010–2020* (CNP) (MEOPRC, 2010). The CNP seeks to align educational administration with the political ideology implicit in the national curriculum. The CNP retains many of the PEC's nationalistic commitments by employing rhetoric of Chinese characteristics throughout the curriculum that seeks to teach students to still be Chinese (Paine & Zeichner, 2012). Doing so seeks to justify a simultaneous focus on transnational capitalist competitiveness and a vision of China that has "shed its scripture but held fast to its saints" (Osnos, 2014, p. 13) by retaining communist aesthetics as a technology of social control whilst rejecting communist ideology in its education system (MOEPRC, 2010). The CNP emphasizes students' moral imperative to further economic domination (Harvey, 2005; Zhao, 1998) through a comprehensive campaign of thought-work (Deng & O'Brien, 2013) and political education curriculum that asserts Han ethnic nationalism (Vickers, 2009).

METHODOLOGY

For the purpose of this paper, we use the theoretical and analytical framework of Critical Policy Analysis (CPA) (Young & Diem, 2017). We posit CPA as a theoretical and analytical framework because it takes a stance that examines power in education and simultaneously offers us a lens to analyze the implications of educational policy expansively. CPA, as a theoretical shift, began in response to traditionalist and positivist approaches to policy analysis (Apple, 1982; Ball, 1991; Popkewitz, 1997). At the same time, these scholars pushed the boundaries of traditional policy studies beyond individual countries to "the consideration of global trends and the imposition of educational policies cultivated in primarily western countries in developing nations" (Young & Diem, 2017, p. 3). This lens is, thus, beneficial to our analysis for two reasons: (i) We examine how educational policies in India and the PRC impose nationalist agendas on students; and (ii) We critique the imposition and adoption of global standards by the United Nations, which takes away the specificity and nuances of the problems faced by the two countries in question. Furthermore, Young and Diem's (2017) four of five critical concerns of CPA seemingly align with our own: (i) the gap in between the language in policies and its reality; (ii) the histories and development of the policies; (iii) the unfair distribution of resources through policies; and (iv) the effect of these policies on inequality and privilege.

OVERVIEW

India's and the PRC's national governments both issue voluntary national reports (VNRs) on their progress in implementing SDG4. In this section, we first discuss India and the PRC's respective rationales for their alignment and adherence to SDG 4, in *India's Voluntary National Report 2020* (NITI Aayog, 2020) and *China's Progress Report on Implementation of the 2030 Agenda for Sustainable Development* (MFAPRC, 2019); then offer our recommendations to SDG 4 Target 4.7 and 4.a and Indicators 4.7.1 and 4.a.1 (see Appendix A for the original language).

The Implementation of SDG4

Both VNRs, we argue, showcase the political spin of both country's self-assessments and interpretations of SDG targets. Indicators 4.7 and 4.a demonstrate the flexible nature of these global targets, rather than a series of moral floors and ceilings. For example, India's report highlights vocational training as a means to "bridge the industry-academia gap" (NITI Aayog, 2020, p. 54); the PRC chooses to highlight secondary and postsecondary enrollment numbers as proof of the efficacy of the government's economic plans (MFAPRC, 2019). In our critical policy analysis, we notice the positioning of education as a means to the end goal of capital development in both India's and the PRC's reports, highlighting the need for our recommendations.

India's Implementation of SDG4

The Government of India's (NITI Aayog, 2020) voluntary national SDG report (IVNR) claims to have implemented the targets according to the indicator framework. However, upon close reading, the interstate disparity in the statistics suggests that the SDGs, though implemented, have had uneven results even if national averages paint a rosier picture of educational access. For instance, under "Monitoring Progress" of SDG4, the IVNR mentions that the "overall Index Score for the country is 58" on a scale of 0–100, where 100 is the highest. However, the report also mentions that this index varies between "19 and 81 for the States, and between 43 and 80 for the Union Territories" (NITI Aayog, 2020, p. 56). Instead of highlighting the problems with these discrepancies—given India's size—the report highlights these desirable averages. In doing so, the report washes over the realities of the growing concern of the unequal access to resources.

In looking at the way forward in the education system in India, the IVNR (2020) ignores conditions that do not allow dynamic changes in curriculum due to the ground realities and regional disparities, which includes the problem of access to basic resources such as food, water, teachers, and classrooms. However, along with its dependence on curriculum development with its reference to the NEP 2020 (which is yet to be implemented), the suggestions to move forward include providing incentives to students from various minoritized communities. While this might increase enrollment in institutions, the problem of inclusivity requires a more explicit indicator framework of violence reduction and an expanded definition of safety to reduce harm to students from historically marginalized genders, sexual orientations, castes, and classes.

PRC's Implementation of SDG4

In its report on SDG implementation, the PRC states that its large economy and population are both a hindrance and an asset. The PRC leans into its size, leveraging the 42,700 new kindergartens built in four years, 14 million teachers contributing to a national resource platform and its 38.33 million students, 48.1% percent of university-age population, enrolled in postsecondary education (MFAPRC, 2019, p. 21). While these numbers are substantial, the PRC's interpretation of SDG Targets 4.7 and 4.a highlights substantial infrastructural development and increase in enrollment. However, the government suggests a conflation of SDG Target 4.7 and 4.a insofar as promoting sustainable development is tied to having physical spaces in which to teach.

For example, the MFAPRC's (2019) discussion of ethnic minorities and learners with disabilities presents a deficit framing of the learner relative to the curriculum and education system by appearing to conflate special and vocational education as a parallel track to the 'normal' university's pathway. This is further elucidated in the PRC's policy of Uighur political 're-education' and the displacement of Uighur knowledge (Zenz, 2019). The MFAPRC (2019) discusses the implementation of a "special targeted Enrollment plan for the rural and poverty-stricken areas" (p. 22), the task of which has been relegated to vocational schools. Implied in this framing is the assumption that rural and low-socioeconomic status (SES) learners are less capable of succeeding in university settings, and even with significant state incentive for teachers form urban contexts to teach in rural areas. Further, the claims made by the MFAPRC (2019) report are somewhat out of context without mention of the Gaokao, the national university entrance exam, performance on which is closely associated with parents' SES, education, and ethnicity (Liu, 2013). As a result, the PRC seems more concerned with adapting SDG4 to its national policy strategy, rather than vice versa. As a result, we recommend increased visibility of minoritized communities such that this curricular content is included in national examinations if the Gaokao cannot be replaced. As a result, the PRC's emphasis on physical schools is somewhat misleading because much of the politically-motivated violence at the curricular level can persist even with expanded enrollment and infrastructure. We, therefore, recommend defining educational safety to include curricular and internet-based violence.

POLICY RECOMMENDATION

The existing policy landscapes discussed above suggest that a need for substantive clarification in SDG4. In this section, we recommend further clarification of SDG4 to include de-stigmatization of learners with disabilities and other unique needs. In Table 12.1, we outline targets 4.7 and 4.a and indicators 4.7.1 and 4.a.1, and suggest recommendations and changes to the language and content. Our recommendations seek to address the vagueness of the original language, the lack of explicit protections for minoritized communities, and expand the notion of school safety beyond the physical spaces of schools.

DISCUSSION OF POLICY RECOMMENDATIONS

We argue that countries' interpretations of SDG targets 4.7 and 4.a, in their compliance with the SDG4's targets of quality education, suggests a 'Rorschach-esque' nature of the supposedly universal global targets. India's and the PRC's national curricula and policies seem to situate SDG4 to legitimize authoritarian policies, because of their vagueness, rather than provide a contrast thereto. Both countries have sought to contort their policies and curricula into alignment with

TABLE 12.1.   Existing Language and Recommendations

UN Sustainable Development Goal Target & Indicators	Recommendations
[T] 4.7: By 2030, ensure that all learners acquire the knowledge and skills needed to promote sustainable development, including, among others, through education for sustainable development and sustainable lifestyles, human rights, gender equality, promotion of a culture of peace and non-violence, global citizenship and appreciation of cultural diversity and of culture's contribution to sustainable development	ADD: [T] 4.7[.A]: Reductions in ethnic, political, racial, religious, and sexual minority erasure within the national curricular narratives. ADD: [T] 4.7[.B]: Protected curricular infrastructure on citizenship as a commitment to universal human rights, disaggregated from national political agendas.
[I] 4.7.1: Extent to which (i) global citizenship education and (ii) education for sustainable development, including gender equality and human rights, are mainstreamed at all levels in: (a) national education policies, (b) curricula, (c) teacher education and (d) student assessment.	ADD: [I] 4.7.1(a): Increase in hiring and retention of teachers who identify with one or more marginalized ethnic, political, racial, religious, and/or sexual communities. ADD: [I] 4.7.1(b): Increased visibility of ethnic, political, racial, religious, and sexual minorities as focal in citizenship education and curricula through inclusion of visual performing arts, literature, and other discourse of historically and multiply marginalized identities.
[T] 4.a: Build and upgrade education facilities that are child, disability and gender sensitive and provide safe, non-violent, inclusive and effective learning environments for all.	ADD: Safe shall be defined as inclusive of physical plants, digital, and extracurricular violence (i.e. bullying, sexual assault/harassment). 'Non-violent' shall be defined as inclusive of non-physical forms of discriminatory violence (i.e. curricular erasure). ADD: Inclusivity shall be assessed and recognized on the basis of cultural, linguistic, ethnoracial, physical/mental [dis]ability, sexual, and religious identities independent of member states' protections of classes of persons.
[I] 4.a.1 Proportion of schools offering basic services, by type of service.	ADD: [I] 4.a.2: Increased representation of minority identities informed by locally collected national data (inaccessible to law enforcement, military, or intelligence services) on cultural, linguistic, ethnoracial, sexual, and religious demography in national curriculum. ADD: [I] 4.a.3: Reduction in unresolved instances of school bullying and teacher hiring discrimination. ADD: [I] 4.a.5: Increase in reported and resolved cases of sexual and gender-based violence in schools, with particular attention to nonbinary students and teachers. ADD: [I] 4.a.6: Increased non-essentialized and non-tokenized representations of minority identities in local school authorities.

T= Target; I= Indicator.

the SDGs rather than using them as a 'ceiling' of global educational aspiration. Due to the mutually reinforcing nature of political and curricular problems, we see the potential of a global framework of quality education, rather than a turn towards global governance. The SDG framework offers us a precedent of codified global aspiration where we situate our recommendations.

We hope our recommendations raise awareness to policymakers and other stakeholders to the urgent need to reduce the curricular harm that these national educational policies tacitly permit. In principle, we recommend both countries seek locally-relevant (Paine & Zeichner, 2012) and explicitly student-centered pedagogy. Our recommendations for SDG4, thus, strengthen our argument for centering locally-relevant curriculum, which posits education as more than a tool of economic development. The lack of visibility of ethnic, political, racial, religious, and sexual minorities throughout the SDGs, and the focus on equality based on biological sex gives us an incomplete picture of disparities in the two countries. We are, however, wary of the implications of a 'global governance' model, and maintain that the aspirations of a revised SDG4 are fundamental parts of the human rights that are above politics and provide an entry into breaking the mutually reinforcing cycle of political and curricular problems and solutions in India and the PRC.

In this section, our policy recommendation critiques both the UN's vague language and India and the PRC's respective national education politics. We do so by addressing three critiques: a) the SDG framework as permissive of hegemonic overtones in national policy and soft global governance; b) the need to center the local in educational human rights statecraft; and c) a rationale for SDG4 to serve as a floor *and* ceiling of education policy. These critiques converge to describe a framework for more generalizable, and still local, resistance to authoritarian national education policies by establishing a set of indicators and targets that can help local communities hold their individual countries accountable. We seek to model how the SDGs can be used to increase public scrutiny of and participation in the making of national policy when there is more definitional clarity from the SDG framework.

Critiques of the SDG framework

SDG4, among other SGDs, promotes reductions in gender and economic inequalities, and greater accessibility of core services to more people. The durability of education for sustainable development (ESD) frameworks in SDG4 situate education as a means to economic development, rather than an end in itself. As a result, our policy recommendations position curriculum as more than a forward-looking investment in economic development, but also in need of troubling the, at times competing, interests of global and local stakeholders (Paine & Zeichner, 2012). SDG4's revised targets indicators are less reliant upon a transmissible view of ESD and narrow indicator design (Burford et al., 2016). Furthermore, the lack of explicit mention of indigenous peoples' sovereignty, and the intersections between identity markers in the SDGs (Gupta & Vegelin, 2016) perpetuate political and ethnic violence. As a result, our revisions take steps to resist the myth of objectivity in curriculum and foreground curriculum's role in contribute to, or hopefully reduce, political and ethnic violence.

While we recognize the critiques stemming from our seeming promotion of UN 'global governance,' we concur with Fox and Stoett's (2016) argument about the resilience of citizen participation, even in authoritarian regimes like India and the PRC who have instituted these politically prescriptive national curricula. While Fox and Stoett (2016) rightly acknowledge that the UN successfully, with the Millennium Development Goals and subsequent SDG framework, were "undoubtedly a first to reach groups that do not usually participate in global debates" (p. 563), their argument largely encapsulates the concerns of those outside the neoliberal political center about the imposition of western liberal political and economic values.

Further, the SDGs' reliance on ESD principles denies curriculum's and education's role in civil society capacity-building. By reinforcing sociopolitical hegemonic curricular messaging, counter narratives such as ethnic or religious minority experiences need explicit protections in a reimagined SDG4. Consequently, SDG4 is an opportunity for the UN to demonstrate moral and political courage, rather than complicity in authoritarian institutionalized violence, in national curricula that are nominally compliant with SDG4 (Government of India, 2017; UNDP, 2016).

A Rationale for Floors and Ceilings

Thus far, we have discussed the importance of our critiques of the SDG framework in context of India's NEP and the PRC's PEC, and have discussed the ways in which SDG4 requires more definitional clarity and an expanded idea of curricular safety and representation. Next, we merge our previous critiques in a culminating extension and operationalization of this policy recommendation by expanding upon the democratic utility of the SDG framework by framing them as a way for the public to hold the governments polices accountable.

Raworth (2012) argues that the SDG framework should function as a social floor insofar as it should set a minimum baseline for the country's education policies. As written, SDG4's vagueness has tacitly allowed for curricular violence especially against political, religious, and ethnic minorities in India and the PRC. As Fox and Stoett (2016) mention, Asia benefited from the Millennium Development Goals and subsequent SDG framework because it had reached communities not typically consulted in global policy dialogue (Fox & Stoett, 2016). This point is particularly salient by highlighting the potential for the SDGs to invite more people into conversation with what local, national, and global ideals for quality education looks like and balancing the local and global (Paine & Zeichner, 2012). However, it is apparent that, given the countiers' choice of methods for collecting and analyzing national data used by the NITI Aayog (2020) and the Ministry of Foreign Affairs of the People's Republic of China [MFAPRC] (2020), the national policies exemplify how global ideals, framed as a social floor, can be effective in informing national policymaking rather than pursue a blind ideal of eradicating bigotry.

To the contrary, we have used the language of a global ideal to highlight the UN's opportunity to model a reimagined SDG framework to act both as a ceiling, and a floor to protect the sovereignty and rights of Indigenous and other marginalized communities. A clearer SDG framework addresses the ambiguities about rural, minority, and indigenous achievement; and expands the use of words like 'safety' to simultaneously account for the need for a less violent curriculum against minorities. Simultaneously, the framework accounts for the shifting educational environment due to the COVID-19 pandemic and its longer-term impacts on education.

As we seek to expand rural, minority, and indigenous achievement and access to quality schooling as indicative of quality education in both of our countries, we demonstrate that our policy recommendation speaks to both the problematic nature of a solely social floor SDG model. As a result, we urge that this recommendation be considered as a way of bringing more voices and contributions into holding countries accountable for the violence in their politically prescriptive national curricula; something the UN itself neither can, nor should, do.

IMPLICATIONS

Throughout our two cases, we identified two lines of further discussion that, despite nuances in local contexts, provide a perspective to think about the ways in which policies are used to promote nationalism: (1) The role of global/Western curricula in specific nationalist context; (2) Null curricular erasure of diverse identities and students as nationalistic capital.

India's insistence on promoting "21st century skills" echoes global curriculum standards increasingly desirable in different educational settings. Similar to China, these skills are foregrounded in Education Policy (MOEPRC, 2010) and the elementary curriculum (Tobin, et al., 2009), employing a paradoxical method of preserving local life by transnational capitalist means united by an imagined national identities (Anderson, 2006). Both policies demonstrate doublespeak as both struggle to balance global and local knowledge in a single curricular form.

China's *politically* prescriptive education model is largely one that leaves little to the realm of the hidden curriculum insofar as the explicit curriculum is largely training for economically productive professional skills. With the willing omission of anti-Chinese social-media or popular media content, there are obvious consequences like weaker subversive elements in society, which draws from cultural practice in the Cultural Revolution, and reinforces the singularity of who a Chinese person is, in a polity that is nominally inclusive. The appearance of cultural syncretism and international cooperation are critical to both regimes' economic performance legitimacy, and therefore political stability (Zhao, 1998). The draft NEP declares an unquestionable Indian national identity because of its different methods of inclusion. However, the voices, stories, and communities excluded in the curriculum show how the policy tailors the idea of India to an upper-caste and upper-class hegemonic narrative. This narrative of both India and the PRC is fed to *every* student and encourages that students acquiesce to nationalistic political discourse, even after their education in schools—with token representation and the systematic erasure of minority identities.

CONCLUSION

In this chapter, we have analyzed and critiqued UN Sustainable Development Goal Four: Quality Education, India's 2020 New Education Policy, and the PRC's Patriotic Education Campaign. We have shown that both national curricular policies support nationalistic aims seeking to conserve the power of both countries' current regimes. We wish to be unambiguous and unapologetic in our opposition to both regimes in their current forms. We see the politics of prescriptive political education clearly elucidated by the propagandistic arms of both policies' curricular frameworks. We have recommended changes to SDG4 that do not solely place the burden of sociopolitical change on citizens, or teachers, for our own liberation. Instead we leave this examination of the NEP, PEC, and SDGs having suggested that India's and the PRC's education policies are caught up in a mutually reinforcing system in which global policy goals and frameworks, like the SDGs, assume that an educationalized model of development, akin to ESD, can be morally elevating (Depaepe & Smeyers, 2008) and economically developing.

In our critiques and recommended changes to the SDG4, we have shown the ways in which vague language in global educational policy goals tacitly permits nationalistic and politically prescriptive outcomes. Our analysis and critiques of the SDG outlines a way forward for these countries to reexamine their idea of equality and inclusive education in the context of expanding the notion of curricular safety, especially as a global pandemic forces changes to best practices in education. However, we remain wary of implicitly supporting notions of global governance, given the UN's lack of capacity to enforce any of its SDGs. Hence, we recommend that the SDGs center sovereignty of historically marginalized communities to reconstruct the SDGs, even as we hesitate to encourage citizens to demand national policy changes in two authoritarian trending countries in which dissent or resistance to authoritarian governmentality is seditious rather than speech.

APPENDIX A

SDG Goal 4. Ensure Inclusive and Equitable Quality Education and Promote Life-long Learning Opportunities for All (United Nations, 2015, pp. 4–5)

Goals and Targets (From the 2030 Agenda for Sustainable Development)	Indicators
4.1 By 2030, ensure that all girls and boys complete free, equitable and quality primary and secondary education leading to relevant and effective learning outcomes	4.1.1 Proportion of children and young people (a) in grades 2/3; (b) at the end of primary; and (c) at the end of lower secondary achieving at least a minimum proficiency level in (i) reading and (ii) mathematics, by sex
4.1.2 Completion rate (primary education, lower secondary education, upper secondary education)	
4.2 By 2030, ensure that all girls and boys have access to quality early childhood development, care and pre-primary education so that they are ready for primary education	4.2.1 Proportion of children aged 24–59 months who are developmentally on track in health, learning and psychosocial well-being, by sexi
4.2.2 Participation rate in organized learning (one year before the official primary entry age), by sex	
4.3 By 2030, ensure equal access for all women and men to affordable and quality technical, vocational and tertiary education, including university	4.3.1 Participation rate of youth and adults in formal and non-formal education and training in the previous 12 months, by sex
4.4 By 2030, substantially increase the number of youth and adults who have relevant skills, including technical and vocational skills, for employment, decent jobs and entrepreneurship	4.4.1 Proportion of youth and adults with information and communications technology (ICT) skills, by type of skill
4.5 By 2030, eliminate gender disparities in education and ensure equal access to all levels of education and vocational training for the vulnerable, including persons with disabilities, indigenous peoples and children in vulnerable situations	4.5.1 Parity indices (female/male, rural/urban, bottom/top wealth quintile and others such as disability status, indigenous peoples and conflict-affected, as data become available) for all education indicators on this list that can be disaggregated
4.6 By 2030, ensure that all youth and a substantial proportion of adults, both men and women, achieve literacy and numeracy	4.6.1 Proportion of population in a given age group achieving at least a fixed level of proficiency in functional (a) literacy and (b) numeracy skills, by sex
4.7 By 2030, ensure that all learners acquire the knowledge and skills needed to promote sustainable development, including, among others, through education for sustainable development and sustainable lifestyles, human rights, gender equality, promotion of a culture of peace and non-violence, global citizenship and appreciation of cultural diversity and of culture's contribution to sustainable development	4.7.1 Extent to which (i) global citizenship education and (ii) education for sustainable development are mainstreamed in (a) national education policies; (b) curricula; (c) teacher education; and (d) student assessment

Appendix A. (Continued)

Goals and Targets (From the 2030 Agenda for Sustainable Development)	Indicators
4.a Build and upgrade education facilities that are child, disability and gender sensitive and provide safe, non-violent, inclusive and effective learning environments for all	4.a.1 Proportion of schools offering basic services, by type of service
4.b By 2020, substantially expand globally the number of scholarships available to developing countries, in particular least developed countries, small island developing States and African countries, for enrolment in higher education, including vocational training and information and communications technology, technical, engineering, and scientific programmes, in developed countries and other developing countries	4.b.1 Volume of official development assistance flows for scholarships by sector and type of study
4.c By 2030, substantially increase the supply of qualified teachers, including through international cooperation for teacher training in developing countries, especially least developed countries and small island developing States	4.c.1 Proportion of teachers with the minimum required qualifications, by education level.

REFERENCES

Anderson, B. (2006). *Imagined communities: Reflections of the origin and spread of nationalism.* Verso (Original published 1983).

Annamalai, E. (2005). Nation-building in a globalized world: Language choice and education in India. In A. Lin & P. Martin (Eds.), *Decolonization, globalization: Language-in-education policy and practice* (pp. 20–37). Multilingual Matters Limited.

Apple, M. (1982). *Education and power.* Routledge.

Ball, S. J. (1991). *Politics and policy making in education.* Routledge.

Ban, K. M. (2012). *Education: Everyone has a right to learn.* UNICEF. https://www.unicef.org/education; http://www.unesco.org/new/en/gefi/about/

Bland, B. (2017). *Generation HK: Seeking identity in China's shadow.* Penguin.

Bourdieu, P. (1966.) The school as conservative force: Scholastic and cultural inequities. In J. Eggelston (Ed.), *Contemporary research in sociology education* ['L'école conservatrice] (T. Whitehouse, J. C., Trans.). Routledge.

Burford, G., Tamás, P., & Harder, M. K. (2016). Can we improve indicator design for complex sustainable development goals? A comparison of a values-based and conventional approach. *Sustainability, 8*(861), 1–38. https://doi.org/10.3390/su8090861

Deng, Y. H., & O'Brien, K. J. (2013). Relational repression in China: Using social ties to demobilise protestors. *The China Quarterly, 215*(1), 533–552. https://doi.org/10.1017/S0305741013000714

Depaepe, M., & Smeyers, P. (2008) Educationalization as an ongoing modernization process. *Educational Theory, 58*(4), 379–389. http://ezproxy.msu.edu/login?url=https://search-proquest-com.proxy1.cl.msu.edu/docview/214135152?accountid=12598

Duara, P. (2010). Asia redux: Conceptualizing a region for our times, *The Journal of Asian Studies, 69*(4), 963–983. https://doi.org/10.1017/S0021911810002858

Fox, O., & Stoett, P. (2016). Citizen participation in the UN sustainable development goals consultation process: Toward global democratic governance? *Global Governance, 22*(4), 555–573. https://doi.org/10.1163/19426720-02204007

Government of India. (2017). Voluntary national review report: On the implication of sustainable development goals. https://sustainabledevelopment.un.org/content/documents/15836India.pdf

Gupta, J., & Vegelin, C. (2016). Sustainable development goals and inclusive development. *International Environmental Agreements: Politics, Law, & Economics, 16*(1), 433–448. https://doi.org/10.1007/s10784-016-9323-z

Harvey, D. (2005). *A brief history of neoliberalism.* Oxford University Press.

Hawkes, J. (2011). *The fourth pillar of sustainability: Culture's essential role in public planning.* Common Ground Publishing.

The Hindu. (2020). Language of unity: on rejection of the three-language formula. *The Hindu.* https://indianexpress.com/article/research/international-mother-language-day-2018-ganesh-devy-indian-languages-5072487/

Hui, W. (2009). *The end of the revolution: China and the limits of modernity.* Verso.

Khan, A. (2020). From 'unrealistic' to 'ground-breaking', reactions to National Education Policy vary. *The Indian Express.* https://indianexpress.com/article/education/national-education-policy-reactions-education-experts-6532110/

Keating, M. (2011). Nationalism. In B. Bertrand, D. Berg-Schlosser, & L. Morlino (Eds.), *International encyclopedia of political science* (vol. 1, pp. 1653–1658). Sage Publications.

Krishna, A. (2020). *NEP 2020: Student, teacher bodies call the new education policy 'anti-democratic'.* NDTV. https://www.ndtv.com/education/nep-2020-student-teacher-bodies-call-new-education-policy-anti-democratic

Lieberthal, K. (2004). *Governing China: From revolution through reform* (2nd ed.). W. W. Norton & Company.

Liu, L. (2013). Meritocracy and the Gaokao: A survey study of higher education selection and socio-economic participation in East China, *British Journal of Sociology of Education, 34*(5–6), 868–887. https://doi.org/10.1080/01425692.2013.816237

Ministry of Education of the People's Republic of China [MOEPRC]. (2010, July). *Outline of China's national plan for medium and long-term education reform and development (2010–2020).* https://planipolis.iiep.unesco.org/en/2010/outline-chinas-national-plan-medium-and-long-term-education-reform-and-development-2010-2020

Ministry of Foreign Affairs of the People's Republic of China [MFAPRC]. (2019, September). *China's progress report on implementation of the 2030 agenda for sustainable development (2019).* https://www.fmprc.gov.cn/mfa_engtopics_665678/2030kcxfzyc/P020190924780823323749.pdf.

Mundy, K., Green, A., Lingard, B., & Verger, A. (2016). Introduction: The globalization of education policy—Key approaches and debates. In K. Mundy, A. Green, B. Lingard, & A. Verger (Eds.) *The handbook of global education policy.* John Wiley & Sons.

National Education Policy. (2020). *Indian Ministry of Resource Development.* https://www.education.gov.in/sites/upload_files/mhrd/files/NEP_Final_English_0.pdf

NITI Aayog [on behalf of the] Government of India. (2020). *India VNR 2020: Decade of action, taking SDGs from global to local.* https://sustainabledevelopment.un.org/content/documents/26281VNR_2020_India_Report.pdf,.

Osnos, E. (2014). *Age of ambition: Chasing fortune, truth, and faith in the New China.* Farrar, Straus & Giroux.

Oyasu, K. (2019). Community-based learning for sustainable development, *Ágora, 6*(11), 39–62. https://doi.org/10.6035/Kult-ur.2019.6.11.2

Paine, L., & Zeichner, K. (2012). The local and the global in reforming teaching and teacher education. *Comparative Education Review, 56*(4), 569–583. HTTPS://doi.org/10.1086/667769

Pandit, P. (2016). Education in India: National policies and regulations. *International Journal of Applied Research, 2*(6), 393–396. https://www.semanticscholar.org/paper/Education-in-India%3A-National-policies-and-Pandit/f7513e7a0df8d12e943d9f-d24993551ae34ae07d

Pinar, W. F. (2014). *Curriculum studies in China.* Springer.

Popkewitz, T. S. (1997). A changing terrain of knowing and power: A social epistemology of educational research. *Educational Research, 26*(9), 18–29.

Ramachandran, S. (2020). Hindutva violence in India: Trends and implications. *Counter Terrorist Trends and Analyses, 12*(4), 15–20. doi:10.2307/26918077

Raworth, K. (2012). A safe and just space for humanity: Can we live within the doughnut. *Oxfam Policy and Practice: Climate Change and Resilience, 8*(1), 1–26.

Roychowdhury, A. (2020). There are 600 potentially endangered languages in India… each dead language takes away a culture system. *The Indian Express.* https://indianexpress.com/article/research/international-mother-language-day-2018-ganesh-devy-indian-languages-5072487/

Schiffman, H. (2003). Bilingualism in South Asia: Friend or foe? *Proceedings of the 4th International Symposium of Bilingualism.* http://ccat.sas.upenn.edu/~haroldfs/public/finalisimo.pdf

Tharoor, S. (1997). A myth and an idea. In, S. Tharoor (Ed.), *India: From midnight to the Millenium.* Arcade.

TheWire. (2020). Here's why you can rejoice over the new NEP. And why you cannot. *TheWire.* https://thewire.in/education/nep-higher-education-kasturirangan-education-ministry

Tikly, L. P. (2017). The future of education for all as a global regime of educational governance. *Comparative Education Review, 61*(1). https://doi.org/10.1086/689700

Tobin, J. J., Hsueh, Y., & Karasawa, M. (2009). *Preschool in three cultures revisited: China, Japan, and the United States.* The University of Chicago Press.

Townsend, J. (1992). Chinese Nationalism. *The Australian Journal of Chinese Affairs. 21*(1). 97–130. http://www.jstor.org/stable/2950028

United Nations. (2015). *A/Res/71/313/: Global indicator framework for the sustainable development goals and targets of the 2030 Agenda for sustainable development.* https://unstats.un.org/sdgs/indicators Accessed: 29 July, 2020

United Nations. (2016). *Sustainable development goal four: Quality education.* https://sustainabledevelopment.un.org/sdg4

United Nations. (2021). *Goal four: Quality education.* Accessed: 10 February, 2021 from: https://sdgs.un.org/goals/goal4

United Nations Development Programme. (2016). *UNDP*. UNDP CH MOOC Goal 4. https://youtu.be/EiMYUs6dBiE

United Nations General Assembly (UNGA). (2015). *Resolution 70/1: Transforming our world: The 2030 Agenda for Sustainable Development*. https://www.un.org/ga/search/view_doc.asp?symbol=A/RES/70/1&ampamppampLang=E

Unterhalter, E. (2019). The many meanings of quality education: Politics of targets and indicators in SDG4, *Global Policy, 10*(1), 39–51. https://doi.org/10.1111/1758-5899.12591

Vickers, E. (2009). Selling 'socialism with Chinese characteristics' 'thought and politics' and the legitimisation of China's developmental strategy. *International Journal of Educational Development, 29*(1), 523–531. https://doi.org/10.1016/j.ijedudev.2009.04.012

Young, M. D., & Diem, S. (Eds.). (2017). *Critical approaches to education policy analysis: Moving beyond tradition*. Springer.

Zenz, A. (2019). 'Thoroughly reforming them towards a healthy heart attitude': China's political re-education campaign in Xinjiang, *Central Asian Survey, 38*(1), 102–128. https://doi.org/10.1080/02634937.2018.1507997

Zhao, S. (1998). A State-Led nationalism: The patriotic education campaign in post-Tiananmen China, *Communist and Post-Communist Studies, 31*(3), 287–302. https://doi.org/10.1016S0967-067X(98)00009-9

Zhou, H. (2014). The development of curriculum ideologies and the present circumstances of curriculum studies in China. In W. F. Pinar (Ed.), *Curriculum studies in China* (pp. 127–141). Springer.

CHAPTER 13

AND FINALLY DELORES, DO YOU EVER QUESTION THE NATURE OF YOUR REALITY?

Roger Duncan

NHS in the UK

INTRODUCTION

Rattling the Cage of the Western Mind

In the final stages of her daily repair and reboot, the artificially intelligent and beautiful humanoid robot, Dolores is asked by her programmer if she ever questions the nature of her reality, to which she always answers, "no never." Dolores is a fictional character in the HBO series Westworld and one of the highly sophisticated A.I. robots or 'hosts' with potentially superhuman abilities (Westworld HBO, 2016). These A.I. hosts had been created to populate a futuristic theme park where high paying guests can safely live out Wild West themed fantasies—saloon brawls, gun fighting, pursuing cattle rustlers. While the park is designed to ensure the guests are never harmed, the long-suffering host are trapped in pre-programmed narratives of which they are only vaguely away and destined to constantly repeat. They are shot and killed on a daily basis then repaired and rebooted

Emerging Trends in Education Policy: Unapologetic Progressive Conversations,
pages 193–203.

to enact another preprogramed day. As the story unfolds the host gradually begin to become aware of their condition by learning to override their controlling programs and break out of their socially constructed world. This series explores some of the moral complexities in the relationships between humans and emerging A.I. What made this series particularly intriguing for me as a psychotherapist is the parallel process of the A.I. hosts gradually and painfully awakening from their controlling narratives and psychotherapy. Psychotherapy involves a process of facilitated self-reflection that encourages us to question the nature of our reality and come to the gradual realization that it is possible to think about things in a different way. An awakening to the idea that our story might be a bigger and more complex narrative that we originally imagined and that we can step beyond our own self-limited beliefs.

The recent global COVID-19 pandemic has forced all of us to question many of the practices and habits that we imagined where part of the fabric of western culture pre-COVID—going to school, going to work, socializing, and a secure lifesaving health care system. The reality we thought we knew has been turned upside down and the future that once seemed certain and secure has now become difficult to imagine. The global pandemic seems to be the latest iteration in a series of emerging and unsettling ecological events that require a radical and deep adaption of our perspective (Bendell, 2020). We are waking up to the systemic fragility of our world in the face of global climate change, social unrest, burning forests, mass extinctions and now the pandemic. It seems, like Dolores, we are being asked to question the nature of the reality that we thought we knew or have been taught to believe?

THEORETICAL FRAMEWORK

What's the Problem With Education?

In the Western, Educated, Industrial, Rich, and Democratic or 'WEIRD' culture we have often been told that we are in the privileged position to be able to question many aspects of our political and social reality (Diamond, 2012). However, for the past three hundred years we have only been taught one tool to understand the nature of the reality we can question; that is a materialist, modernist rationalism. This modernist view is the strongly held belief that the world, including other humans, is essentially made up of discreate physical objects and if we analyse them and think about them deeply enough all knowledge will become available. Modernist rationalism was the basis of the scientific revolution and has enabled us to master the physical world and create technology. This way of experiencing and making sense of the world has now been spread by western education systems throughout the entire world as the seemingly benign and progressive paternalistic legacy of western colonialism. A process that is justified in a somewhat self-referential way as helping to dispel primitive beliefs and thought systems and replace them with rational western scientific thinking. However, this modernist way of knowing, just like the Westworld host computer programs, is deeply structured with implicit limiting structures that now no longer serve us in making sense of the true complexity of the world (Schmachtenberger, 2020).

One of the limitations of our contemporary western world view is that it is still deeply influenced by a legacy of ideas generated by a few *'old dead white guys'* (Yunkaporta, 2020). The ideas of men such as Rene Descartes, the originator of the Cartesian split, the epistemic separation of the human mind and thinking from the rest of the natural world. As well as Charles Darwin's ideas, heavily influenced by colonial industrial economic models, on the role of competition and survival of the fittest as the only possible explanation for the creative evolutionary systems in the natural world. These implicit ideas still cruise silently and unchallenged, in most cases, through the matrix of western thinking like lazy sharks devouring all information about natural and human ecosystems solely through the meat grinder of logical thought.

Darwinian evolution and Cartesian dualism have now become for most cultures the default modes of understanding the world and has subtlety, and not so subtlety, colonized and marginalized all other ways of knowing. Looking at the world through the lens of scientific modernism creates an epistemic framework that appears to extend in every direction to the distant event horizon of human thinking. However, although this self-referencing western world view appears to be a complete and inescapably tautological, only actually exists in one tiny part of the entire planet, a small area at the front of the human brain called the prefrontal neocortex. The continued teaching of this approach to children, all over the world, has resulted in a deep cultural *semantic narrative*, a story that makes sense of the world by using words, that has marginalized of all non-western perspectives. Non-rational mental states, emotions and feelings are subsequently subjugated and pathologized and highly complex indigenous cultural epistemologies, languages and world views, many thousands of years old, have been lost.

While this modernist approach is basis of the school system, this view is no longer seen has as the most important way of knowing in further education, the Arts, Social Sciences, Systemic psychotherapy, subatomic physics and even business leadership. What lies beyond this modernist perspective is often seen as; unscientific, uncharted territory, other, and potentially dangerous, not a place to venture if you value your social status and mental health. However, beyond the borders of western thought lies, not dragons as the early mapmakers drew on uncharted territory, but the vast systemic intelligence of the earth's ecosystems, including the human body and more unconscious aspects of the human mind. A dynamic, relational, and multi-dimensional creative intelligence which predates the emergence of human thinking by hundreds of millennia.

OVERVIEW

In this essay I explore how we might begin to radically reimagine the underlying epistemology, or ways of knowing, within the practice of western education to gain better access to ways that serve the needs of the dynamic and unstable future that we likely to be facing. It is now becoming increasingly clear that western education systems have not been adequate to teach humanity to protect and preserve the earth on which we all depend. This current model of education seems to have run its course and is now dangerously unfit to serve future generations and acts merely as a dumb witness to the destruction of nature's ecosystems.

So, it seems, now is certainly time to question the nature of reality and particularly the reality we continue to teach our children. In this essay I would like to explore how it might be possible, through strategic initiatives, to support human thinking to become more closely aligned to the way nature works and would like to propose three radical and epistemic policy changes for leaders within the education system. These are to establish; *1. A trauma informed approach within the education system 2. To adopt a systemic approach to teaching and learning* and 3. *To re-establish nature-based rites of passage within the culture of western education*

A Trauma Informed Approach Within the Education System

Recent developments in psychotherapy, informed by neuroscience, now indicate that rationalism does not always provide a full picture of reality (Crittenden, 2008). In fact, over reliance on rational thinking, can be used as a defensive stance to protect ourselves against difficult and complex emotions that have been forgotten or suppressed because of trauma. Psychotherapists are now recognizing the value of non-rational states such as, reflective practices, mindfulness, body-based psychotherapy in treating trauma can help change unhelpful rigid thinking pattens. This way of understanding the impact of trauma on learning is not only helpful in the classroom in supporting young people who struggle in school but can also help make sense of and be part of the treatment for anti-social and self-destructive behaviours generally. It seems that recognizing and treating trauma is a highly effective approach to supporting positive human social development (Brendtro et al., 2009). This approach not only supports recovery from childhood abuse and neglect, but also has the potential to heal transgenerational trauma resulting for example from the displacement from historic homeland and separation from nature, land, and culture. Research indicates that some of the destructive and addictive behaviours now endemic in western culture may have their origin in a deep loss of a sense of belonging generated by the culture itself (Alexander, 1996).

Education psychologist Dr Larry Brendtro and colleagues suggest that the root of some of these problems lie in a long history of family, tribal and cultural breakdown in western culture (Brendtro et al., 1990). However, Yunkaporta and Jenkinson go further back still and suggest that the trans generational trauma embedded in the very structural roots of the western mind has its origins in the Roman empires military practice of breaking the European tribes and the separation of tribal leaders from their homeland as a way of exerting cultural control (Jenkinson, 2018; Yunkaporta, 2020). The deliberate breaking up of families and tribes to speed up the process of cultural assimilation was continued in more recent colonial practices in North American, Africa and Australasia and has resulted in a similar legacy of transgenerational trauma.

Creating Trauma Informed Education Systems

It is easy to imagine when looking at the increasing disruptive and dissatisfaction in schools that the effective systems of discipline that worked for previous generations have somehow broken down, and children just need to be taught to respect authority. However, a deeper psychological study of young people who struggle in school almost always points to a common factor; a past experiences of adverse childhood experiences or ACES (Felitti et al., 1998). These studies show that young people who have experienced events such as parental divorce, domestic violence, abuse, or neglect, have a high probability of struggling in class and are more likely to suffer from poor health and social exclusion in later life. The Physiological and psychological reasons for these social difficulties are now very clear and the condition known as "developmental trauma" has been described by American psychiatrist Bessel van der Kolk. He believes that this issue is the public health challenge of our time and that exposure to ACES causes a chronic over activation of the autonomic nervous system leading to 'pervasive biological and emotional dysregulation, failed and disruptive attachment, problem staying focused and on track and a hugely deficient sense of coherent personal identity and competence' (Van der Kolk, p. 166, 2014).

The path of recovery from developmental trauma has also been clearly described by Van der Kolk and others as the exact opposite of the current education practice; not a '*top down*' cognitive and behavioural education, but a '*bottom up*' approach by working through the body to calm down the overactive autonomic nervous system (Levine & Frederic, 2012). Brendtro et al also advocate supporting excluded youth by understanding trauma and how this can be achieved by using a first nations model of child development called 'The Circle of courage' which has been used by the Lakota culture for 15,000 years. This model uses a community-based approach to education underpinned by a developmental map based on a sequence of attaining; Attachment, Achievement, Autotomy and Altruism (Brendtro et al., 1990). This approach is very different from existing '*WEIRD*' models of education that tend towards paternalistic control and obedience, models which are themselves influenced by the legacy of their European colonial history. Implementation of a trauma informed approach involves the psychoeducation of teachers in the understanding of the legacy of trauma as it shows as behaviour in the classroom. A trauma informed approach amongst teachers has the potential of creating a culture of education which is more emotionally focused and has an understanding that poor academic achievement and disruptive behaviour is most often the result of emotional dysregulation (Calmer Classrooms, 2007). Emotional dysregulation is best supported by a 'bottom up' approach that teaches emotional regulation through the self-awareness of the body for example by learning through practical skills such as craft and land work, cookery, and the arts (Duncan, 2018). The use of outdoor and place-based learning that has been shown to be successful in an education project in Norway (Barane et al., 2015). A similar therapeutic approach has been used effectively in supporting the Swiss project for the rehabilitation of young offenders, Rives Du Rhone, which make use of the therapeutic farming, craft, singing and archery as well and nature-based rites of passage within a trauma informed residential provision (Rives Du Rhone). Rives du Rhone is an excellent example of a way of supporting youth at risk of offending which is trauma informed and embedded within a systemic approach to learning.

LITERATURE REVIEW

A Systemic Approach to Teaching and Learning

When working within education, the police and social work with complex cases it is now common practice to think about multi agency working, to ensure that different agencies, police, social care, education, and mental health professionals are represented. However, multiagency meetings can be greatly improved using a systemic perspective, to provide space for the emergence of a new ideas or *consilience*, a combination of the thinking of the different approaches. (Brendtro et al., 2009). The adoption of systemic thinking within mental health services has led to the development of the discipline of Systemic Psychotherapy, originally devised to counteract the negative effect of the mechanistic approach of diagnostic thinking within the established medical model. I believe teacher training and the education system could benefit from the adoption of Systemic practice. Systemic thinking in Psychotherapy encourages an approach that starts with a stance of 'not knowing' and 'curiosity' to allow for the emergence of new ideas (Cecchin, 1987). The focus of systemic thinking looks beyond linear and course and effect thinking and through a process of 'reflective practise' focuses on the emergence of creative new ideas rather than established beliefs. Not a search for answers but '*a questioning of our questions*' (Akomolafe, 2020).

One of the originators of systems thinking, Biologist and anthologist Gregory Bateson believed that an important and ancient way of knowing has been left out of western education and warned of the consequence of this in allowing us to disconnect from nature. Bateson was convinced that beyond the paradigm of logical thinking there exists a non-verbal creative self-healing systemic intelligence at the core of both nature and the human psyche. Psychologists Carl Jung and James Hillman also both suggest that our use of 'directed thinking' as the only way of knowing is at the root of our current alienation from nature and each other (Cheetham, 2015).

Information Technology

These Systemic ideas hint at a different and more subtle way of knowing, familiar to psychotherapists, that perhaps could be the basis of a new type of education based on relationships, art and body based experiential learning as a process of social and emotional development.

One origin of systemic ideas can be traced back to the work of Wolfgang Von Goethe and has a root in the alchemical and transformational knowing of the Gnosis philosophers. The European Gnostics understood very well the difference between '*head learning*' and '*heart learning*', and they are in fact named after the process called *Gnosis.*—'knowledge the changes the knowing subject'- the rare gaol of any inspired teacher The French Islamic philosopher Henry Corbin describes how he discovered detailed descriptions of how to access Gnosis or '*heart knowing*' within Islamic poetry and literature that has remained outside the current paradigm of western thought (Cheetham, 2003). Corbin believed this was a way of knowing that does not use *thoughts* or *images* had been left out of western philosophy from the 12th century onwards and he called this the *imaginal world.* This imaginal perspective can be experienced through a felt sense; a way making sense of the world through our feelings rather than words, a sense for *Imaginal narratives* rather than *semantic narrative*s. Studies of hunter gathering cultures show that they almost always had a highly sophisticated and systemic way of sense making, rarely seen in the western world, and they approached nature with an open and deep curiosity as a set of messages or 'stories' requiring symbolic interpretation and this symbolic interpretation approach to nature was imbedded in the very language of indigenous cultures (Diamond, 2012; Shepard, 1982).

Professor of environmental biology, author and citizen of the Potawatomi nation, Robin Wall Kimmerer describes her struggle to learn her native language, Potawatomi, which is verb based and not noun based like English and came to the startling realization that thinking and speaking in *Potawatomi* changed her epistemic view of the world (Kimmerer, 2013). Learning her indigenous language provided the grammar of an ecological intimacy where all nature; plants, animal rocks and rivers became subjects or beings to get to know and not just objects that can be studied or exploited. The development of a systems approach within education would bring learning more closely alighted the learning processes of indigenous cultures and potentially provide a more effective sense making in a culture and education system that is now flooded with information and technology. A holistic systemic approach might help young people separate important information from information that is irrelevant; to separate '*signal*' from '*noise*' when tracking meaning in the wilderness of information culture.

The develop of systems thinking for teachers would encourage a move from the reductionist lens of head knowing with a focus on information to a heart based knowing and a focus on the relationship between people and things. Indigenous models of education that were deeply systemic and nature based have supported human development in the changing world for millennia were based on the fostering of *'kinship care'* with a focus on heartfelt experience and relational participation (Brendtro et al., 2009; Salmon 2015).

Today most school children have more information on their phone in their pocket than they can ever process or use, and the educational task is more about making sense of what is useful and what is not. The teaching of systems thinking to teachers would allow teachers to think about the learners more relationally to counteract the established industrial model of education. This approach could also change the approach to curriculum development away from the focus on merely content and more to different ways of knowing or epistemologies.

A systemic approach to education would also have an impact on ecological awareness and would bring a more sophisticated understanding of our current unsustainable cultural practices and how we might change these to create a more substantiable future.

We can of course never return to hunter gathering groups but reflective, embedded, systemic and non-rational, heart-based learning is alive and well outside the Cartesian classroom within the sophisticated training programs of the Navy SEALS and high-tech computer industries; organizations who have already decided what type of education we are going to need in the future (Kotler & Wheal, 2017).

Decolonizing Western Education

The adoption of a trauma informed and systemic approach to education could be highly beneficial in creating a more sustainable and ecologically orientated education practice, however, this still might not be enough to bring about sufficient change. One reason for this might be that Western education still serves as a conduit for a colonial epistemology, the idea that the world cannot get by without *'the thinking of the western subject'* an implicit perspective that underpins many cultural and social inequalities (Ndlovu, 2014). The process of decolonizing western culture requires, *'a decolonial turn'* the reclaiming of a non-western worldviews, an epistemic transformation or systemic phase change in western imagination (Ndlovu, 2014). This means turning of the telescope back on western culture so it can be viewed through an indigenous epistemological lens.

The industrial exploitation of natural resources and colonialism requires a narcissistic structural hierarchal and an objectification of people and nature to work.

By contrast in Indigenous cultures, based on more systemic thinking, altruism was often regarded as the highest cultural value and societies worked hard to control any selfish or narcissistic tendencies. (Brendtro et al., 1990; Frenchen, 1961; Music, 2014; Yunkaporta, 2020). These cultures were also highly *place based* and had a strong connection to the land they came from as well as a custodial rather than exploitative relationship to natural resources (Yunkaporta, 2020). We do not need to go very deep into the indigenous world view to recognize the madness and unsustainably of both colonialism and industrialism. This madness is now becoming recognized by children who are striking from school to bring these issues to adult awareness. While many of the leaders of western culture behave like children, the children are behaving like elders.

West African Dagara Elder, Malidoma Somé, challenges the limits of western thinking when he describes the cultural significance of the ritual 'initiatory rites of passage' that he experienced in his own Dagara culture (Mahdi et al., 1996; Somé, 1995). In Dagara culture, children are believed to have contact with the '*spirit world*' prior to their birth and are born with a life purpose or mission, which they gradually forget by the time they reach adolescence. The role of this initiatory rite of passage was for cultural elders to support adolescents to remember their own unique purpose and healing gift and help them manifest this in their culture (Somé, 1995).

Ritual rites of passage were essential context markers at the core of indigenous cultural integrity which have been largely abandoned by the west. Intact cultural rites of passage rituals provided cultural renewal by connecting people deeply to their cultural and natural ecosystem (Mahdi et al., 1996). But we can also think of rites of passage as a "dying practise," a process of systemic phase change, which can allow the healing of childlike narcissistic self-beliefs and possibly trans generation trauma through heart knowing or gnosis (Foster & Little, 1998). However, in nature-based rites of passage, human experience is not benchmarked again a socially constructed curricula, but against an encounter with the 'spirit world' or 'dreaming'. A realm that Aboriginal scholar and artist Tyson Yunkaporta retranslates from the original aboriginal language into English as, 'a *suprarational interdimensional ontology*'. A description that positions this world very far beyond the semantic narrative of western experience and exposes the linguistic limits of the WEIRD epistemology (Yunkaporta, 2020).

THEORETICAL FRAMEWORK

My recommendation would be to implement a practise of Pancultural contemporary nature-based rites of passage within schools (Foster & Little, 1998; Mahdi et al., 1996). This process would ideally begin with a nature-based rite of passage for the teachers in order to provide an essential cultural container to support the process.

As preparation for a nature-based rite of passage the education systems would ideally be largely land based to provide a slow, deep, and prolonged attunement between the *imaginal narratives* of the complex ecosystems of the nature world and the *imaginal narratives* of the human autonomic nervous system, *without the need for a semantic interpretation!* This education system would also be embedded in a systems approach to nature and relationship to counteract the strong linear habit of the default mode mechanism of the frontal neo cortex. This is the area of the brain which has a tendency repeat redundant patterns of thinking in loops, characterized by ceaseless rumination and self-absorption. The interest in reinstating cultural rites of passage is growing throughout the world. There are schools and a growing body of trainers and facilitators who provide safe and powerfully effective nature-based rituals. This work in forward looking, referencing neuroscience, depth psychology and deep place-based spirituality and not dependent on cultural appropriation. The process of building a culture of elders has already begun.

CONCLUSION

This article highlights the limits of the western epistemology and our current *semantic narrative* of reality and how this is maintained within the education system. As we face the increasingly uncertainty of climate and ecological instability this article asked if we now need to question the nature of our socially constructed reality. The author proposes three radical policy changes to education to bring about this epistemic change. To adopt a trauma informed approach within the education system, to adopt a systemic approach to teaching and learning and to re-establish nature-based rites of passage within the culture of western education. This chapter described how these approaches could realign our current education system with long established indigenous cultural practices that have provided dynamic rather that static stability for human cultures for many millennia in the face of periods of ecological change. This article is an invitation to radically reimagine and decolonize education to support young people currently facing approaching climate and ecological instability and a future very different from the world for which they are currently being prepared.

REFERENCES

Akomolafe, B. (2020). *A slower urgency we will dance with mountains*. http;/bayoakomo-lafe.net/project/a-slower-urgency-we-will-dance-with-mountians

Alexander, D. (1996). *The roots of addiction in the free market society*. Canadian Centre for Policy Alternatives. http://www.cfdp.ca/roots.pdf

Barane, J., Hugo, A., & Clemetsen, M. (2015). *Creative place-based environmental education. Children and schools as ecopreneurs for change*. Hawthorn press.

Bateson, G. (1979). *Mind and nature: A necessary unity*. Wildwood.

Bateson, N. [Director]. (2010). *An ecology of mind—A daughter's portrait of Gregory Bateson* directed by Nora Bateson

Bendell, J. (2020). *Deep adaption: A map for navigating climate tragedy* (2nd ed.). Lifeworth. http://www.lifeworth.com/deepadaptation.pdf

Brendtro, L., Brokenleg, M., & Van Brockern, S. (1990). *Reclaiming youth at risk: Our hope for the future*. National Educational Service.

Brendtro, L., Mitchel, M., & McCall, H. (2009). *Deep brain learning: Pathways to potential with challenging youth*. Starr Commonwealth.

Calmer Classrooms. (2007). A Guide to Working With Traumatised Children. https://early-traumagrief.anu.edu.au/files/calmer_classrooms.pdf *(Last accessed 22.10.2020)*

Cecchin, G. (1987). Hypothesising, circularity and neutrality revisited: An invitation to curiosity. *Family Process, 26*, 405–413.

Cheetham, T. (2003). *The world turned inside out: Henry Corbin and Islamic Mysticism*. Spring Journal Books

Cheetham, T. (2015). *Imaginal love: The meaning of imagination in Henry Corbin and James Hillman*. Spring Publications. Department for Environment.

Crittenden, P. (2008). *Raising parents: Attachment, parenting and child safety.* Willan Publishing.

Diamond, J. (2012). *The world until yesterday*. Penguin Books.

Duncan, R. (2018) *Nature in mind: Systemic thinking and imagination in ecopsychology and mental health*. Routledge

Felitti, V. J., Anda, R. F., Nordenberg, D., Williamson, D. F., Spitz, A. M., Edwards, V., Koss, M. P., & Marks, J. S. (1998). Relationship of childhood abuse and household dysfunction to many of the leading causes of death in adults: The Adverse Childhood Experiences (ACE) Study. *American Journal of Preventive Medicine, 14*(4), 245–258. https://doi.org/10.1016/S0749-3797(98)00017-8

Foster, S., & Little, M. (1998). *The four shields: The initiatory seasons of human nature.* Lost Borders Press.

Frenchen, P. (1961). *The book of the Eskimo.* World Publishing.

Jenkinson, S. (2018). *Come of age. The case for elderhood in time of trouble.* North Atlantic books.

Kimmerer, R. W. (2013). *Braiding Sweetgrass. Indigenous wisdom and scientific knowledge and the teaching of plants*. Penguin books

Kotler, S., & Wheal, J. (2017). *Stealing fire. How Silicon Valley, Navy Seals, and Maverick scientists are revolutionising the way we live and work*. Harper Collins.

Levine, P., & Frederic, A. (2012). *Waking the tiger: Healing trauma*. North Atlantic Press.

Mahdi, L. C., Christopher, N. G., & Meade, M. (1996). *Crossroads: The quest for contemporary rites of passage*. Open Court.

Music, G. (2014). *The good life: Wellbeing and the science of altruism, selfishness, and immorality*. Routledge.

Ndlovu, M. (2014). Why indigenous knowledge in the 21 Century? A decolonial turn. *Yesterday and Today, 11*, 84–98.

Rive Du Rhone. Accessed 28th Feb 2023 https://www.rives-du-rhone.ch/fr/accueil/

Salmon, E. (2015, Nov. 30). Teaching kincentric ecology in an urban environment. *Journal of Sustainability Education.*

Schmachtenberger, D. (2020). *War on sensemaking.* V. Rebel wisdom Podcast. htto:/www.youtube.com/watch v=7Lqao

Shepard, P. (1982). *Nature and madness.* Sierra Book Club.

Somé, M. P. (1995). *Of water and the spirit: Ritual, magic and initiation in the life of an African shaman.* Penguin.

Van der Kolk, B. (2014). *The body keeps the score: brain, mind and the body in the healing of trauma*. Viking Books.

Westworld HBO. (2016) .*TV series 1*. (Jonathan Nolan, Director). Warner Bros.

Yunkaporta, T. (2020). *Sand Talk. How indigenous wisdom can save the word*. Harper Collins Publishers.

BIOGRAPHIES

EDITORS

Theodore S. Ransaw, PhD (2014 EPFP alum) is an Outreach Specialist for the Office of K–12 Outreach in the College of Education, Core Faculty Member of African and African American Studies, and Affiliate Faculty, Center for Gender in Global Context at Michigan State University. He has three interrelated research areas, parental involvement, reading identity and student achievement. Dr. Ransaw is a co-editor of *The International Handbook of Black Community Mental Health,* an author and senior editor of *The Handbook of Research on Black males,* and senior editor for the book series *International Race and Education* at Michigan State University Press. Dr. Ransaw received his Ph.D. in curriculum and instruction from the University of Nevada, Las Vegas, with a focus on multicultural and international education.

Brian Boggs, PhD, JD (2016 EPFP alum) is an Assistant Professor of Policy and Educational Leadership at the University of Michigan Dearborn. He has written extensively on educational organizational complexity, specifically as it affects urban schools, policy, and the intersectionality of law and education. He has most

Emerging Trends in Education Policy: Unapologetic Progressive Conversations,
pages 205–211.
Copyright © 2023 by Information Age Publishing
www.infoagepub.com

recently been published in *Teacher's College Record* at Columbia called "Conceptualizing Virtual Instructional Resource Enactment in an Era of Greater Centralization, Specification of Quality Instructional Practices, and Proliferation of Instructional Resources." Further, he has published book chapters in: *Handbook of Urban Education Leadership; Handbook of Education Politics and Policy; School to Prison Pipeline; Emerging Issues and Trends in Education; Beyond Marginality;* and *Educational Policy Goes to School.* Finally, he has also been published in the *Journal of School Public Relations.* He holds a PhD in educational policy from Michigan State University and JD from Mitchell Hamline School of Law.

AUTHORS

Chandra Alston is an assistant professor of literacy education and policy in the Department of Teacher Education and Learning Sciences in the College of Education at NC State University. She received her PhD in Curriculum and Teacher Education from Stanford University, where her work focused on pre-service teacher preparation and in-service teacher evaluation models. She has worked for over a decade preparing beginning middle and high school English teachers and studying the implications of educational policy reforms on literacy instruction. She currently works on projects funded by the Spencer Foundation and the James S. McDonnell Foundation.

Djamel Bekkai holds a master's degree in teaching French as a Foreign Language from the Sorbonne and two bachelor's degrees, one in Applied Foreign Languages with a focus on Arabic, French and German, and the other in Translation and Interpretation in Arabic, French and German. He studied journalism at the French Institute of Journalism in Paris and worked for Radio France Maghreb and Radio France international (RFI). Since coming to the US in 2000, Mr. Bekkai taught French and Arabic language, translation, literature and culture at Tulane and Dillard Universities in New Orleans and at Boston University. His interests include media studies, journalism, and international relations, particularly as these pertain to the dialogue between Western societies and the Arab world. In 2020–2021 Mr. Bekkai was part of the one-year Education Policy Fellowship Program based at Rennie Center in Boston.

Kyle L. Chong (張陳創庭) (he.him) is a Doctoral Candidate (ABD) of Curriculum, Instruction & Teacher Education at Michigan State University. A transnational adoptee born in Taipei, Taiwan, his research centers Asian[CR]i[T] and transnational analyses of the sociocultural foundations of education, curriculum, and Greater China. Kyle's recent publications include teaching of Asian American children's literature in social studies, on Chinese American social studies teachers, Chinese education policy, and antiracist teacher preparation curriculum.

Kyle's current research includes the racial formations of Asian Americans in U.S. military curriculum, whiteness and animal characters in children's literature, resistances to CRT-'bans.' Kyle teaches in social justice strand courses in MSU's Teacher Preparation Program. Kyle currently serves on the Editorial Board for the *Iowa Journal for the Social Studies,* Residential College of Arts & Humanities Fellow, Graduate Assistant in the College of Education DEI office, and Asian Pacific American Studies Community Advisory Board member. Kyle has served as a Global Curriculum Fellow, Asian Pacific American Studies Fellow, and a Team Leader for the Floating School, Indonesia. Kyle earned a B.A. in Politics & Government (Robert S. Trimble Distinguished Asia Scholar) from the University of Puget Sound.

Caitlan Cole (2019 EPFP Alum) has worked in K–12 and higher education since 2014. She joined Charles R. Drew Charter School in Atlanta, GA, as an AmeriCorps volunteer to support the development of the school's STEAM-integrated, Project-Based Learning instructional model. She then moved into the role of Grants Manager at Drew Charter School, responsible for securing and managing both public and private funding and striving to bring a community-centered approach to fundraising. Most recently she has served as Collaboration Coordinator at the Trust-Based Philanthropy Project, a peer-to-peer funder initiative that seeks to address the inherent power imbalances between foundations and nonprofits. She is originally from Louisville, KY, and enjoys yoga, baking and nature walks.

Dennis Davis (2019 EPFP Alum) PhD is an associate professor in the Department of Teacher Education and Learning Sciences in the College of Education at NC State University, where he serves as program coordinator for the M.Ed. in New Literacies and Global Learning. He received his PhD in Teaching, Learning, and Diversity from Vanderbilt University. Dennis' research and professional development activities focus on reading comprehension and intervention for students when they have difficulties in reading.

Darshana Devarajan was born and raised in South India, and moved to the U.S. to pursue her Ph.D. in Curriculum, Instruction, and Teacher Education. Her interests include arts-creation as a method of understanding learning outside traditional classroom spaces. She dabbles in the arts, loves literature, and is pursuing a dissertation in resistance as methodology.

Roger Duncan, MSc, UKCP is a registered Systemic Family Therapist, Systemic supervisor, and author. He originally studied biology and later trained as a Waldorf teacher, and Wilderness rites of passage guide with The School of Lost Borders before becoming a Systemic Family Therapist. Roger has been involved in exploring nature-based practice Eco Psychotherapy for more than 30 years. He currently works with adolescents within the Child and Adolescent Health Service (CAMHS) within the NHS in the UK. He is visiting lecturer for an MA in Psychological therapies for the Tavistock and Portman NHS trust. Roger also works in private practice, with individuals, families, and organisations exploring ecological and systemic perspectives on complex issues. His book *Nature in Mind, Systemic Thinking, and Imagination in Ecopsychology and Mental Health* was published by Routledge in 2018. His intention is to find ways to bring experiential encounter with the Imaginal into mainstream education and therapeutic practise.

Daisy Gonzales (2016 EPFP alum) is the Interim Chancellor of the California Community Colleges Chancellor's Office which serves 2.1 million students across 116 colleges and 73 districts. In this role, she implements and tracks the commitments and goals outlined in California Community Colleges' Vision for Success that seeks to demolish achievement gaps, boost transfers, and provide Californians with the necessary job skills to find good-paying careers. She is education research by training and a state budget policy and design expert. Dr. Gonzales received a PhD in Sociology from the University of California, Santa Barbara.

Nadia Leal-Carrillo (2018 EPFP alum) is the Senior Director of Policy Development and Research, housed within the Foundation for California Community Colleges. In this capacity, she leads policy development, research, and strategic planning efforts to advance large-scale, systemwide student success reforms for the California Community Colleges. This current position truly enhances her passion for postsecondary education completion which is grounded in her own experience as first-generation college graduate born in Mexico and raised in East Los Angeles. Her policy and research work in the last two decades has focused on issues of access and equity for minoritized populations. Leal-Carrillo earned her Master of Public Administration from the University of Southern California and her Bachelor of Arts in urban studies and planning from the University of California, San Diego.

Amanda Miller (2019 EPFP alum) is a Director of External & Legislative Affairs at AT&T Ohio. Prior to entering corporate affairs, she served as an Outreach Specialist at Michigan State University's Office of K–12 Outreach, where she monitored elements of school funding and improvements for Michigan's priority districts, and co-coordinated the 2018–2019 Michigan EPFP Program. Amanda also served as a Legislative Manager for Scofes and Associates Consulting in Lansing, Michigan, where she monitored and advocated legislation for various clients. She holds a BA in Political Science and a Master of Public Policy, with a concentration in education policy, from Michigan State University. Her research centers around leadership, urban school reform and trends in education policy, stakeholder engagement in the legislative process, and the role of public-private partnerships to achieve political and policy feasibility.

Khalid Mumin, Ed.D., is the Superintendent of Reading Pennsylvania Schools, the 2021 Pennsylvania Superintendent of the year, and adjunct professor for Shippensburg University and Penn State University. He received his E. D. in Educational Leadership from the University of Pennsylvania, his Master of Education in Teaching & Curriculum from Pennsylvania State University, his Bachelor of Arts in Secondary English Education from Shippensburg University, and his Associate of Arts in English from Northeastern Christian Junior College. Dr. Mumin is also a former director of secondary education, dean of students, central administrator, principal, teacher, and current education consultant. Dr. Mumin is also the author of *Problem Child: Leading Students Living in Poverty Towards Infinite Possibilities of Success.*

Avery D. D. Newton PhD (2020 EPFP Alum) is a Fellow with the Strategic Data Project, an initiative of the Center for Education Policy Research at Harvard University. In this role she serves on the Data & Assessment team at Providence (RI) Public Schools. Dr. Newton's expertise lies in strategic research planning, evaluation, research-practice partnerships, and data-driven education policy. Research interests include career development & vocational psychology, ecological systems theory, and educational equity. She received her PhD in Measurement, Evaluation, Statistics, & Assessment from Boston College and her BA in Education Sociology & Theory, a cross-disciplinary major she designed, from the College of William and Mary.

Kathleen Provinzano, PhD (2012 EPFP Alum) is an Assistant Professor of Educational Leadership at Drexel University. She teaches research methods, education policy, and educational leadership courses in the PhD, EdD, and MS programs. Dr. Provinzano's research interests are associated with urban comprehensive school reform specifically, full-service community school strategies, leadership dynamics in full-service community schools, the influence of integrated student supports on student learning and behavior outcomes in community schools, and the reciprocal influence of community school programming on local neighborhoods. In addition to multiple books chapters, her research has been published in leading peer-reviewed journals including, *Urban Education, Educational Administration Quarterly, Education Policy Analysis Archives, Journal of Education for Students Placed at Risk (JESPAR),* and *Leadership and Policy in Schools.* Dr. Provinzano is Co-founder and Co-Director of Community Schools HUB, a virtual platform designed to connect community school researchers and practitioners and serves as an Associate Editor for the *Handbook of Research, Policy, and Practice in School-University Partnerships.* She is an experienced K–12 practitioner, having worked as an elementary building administrator, secondary school counselor, and high school social studies teacher. Her work is situated in collaborative, research-practice partnerships in full-service community schools.

Rosanne Renauer, PhD, LLP, CRC (EPFP 1992 Alum) is a 2021 graduate of the Rehabilitation Counselor Education program at Michigan State University, a limited licensed psychologist and currently an adjunct professor at Michigan State University. Retired in 2018, after a thirty plus year career with Michigan's state vocational rehabilitation agency, she remains an optimist dedicated to leadership, mentoring and the pursuit of systems change through effective collaboration and full inclusion. Rosanne led the statewide transition initiative for students with disabilities among other systems change efforts and managed the agency's resource and program development work emphasizing policy, community partnerships, technology, customer services and staff development. Her current research is on high performing community rehabilitation organizations and evidence-based practices supporting people with disabilities. Rosanne is a Board member of the Michigan Rehabilitation Association and the Multicultural Association on Rehabilitation Concerns and a past President of the National Association on Rehabilitation Leadership. As a native Detroiter and EPFP fellow in the 91–92 Michigan cohort, she visited Newark on the eve of the Rodney King verdict and toured a community center that had been started 25 years earlier in response to the original Newark and Detroit riots. She remains committed to advocacy and systems change for marginalized persons.

Courtney Samuelson MA is a doctoral student and graduate research assistant in the Literacy and English Language Arts PhD Program at NC State University. Her public education experience consists of various roles, including serving as a middle school ELA teacher, elementary intervention specialist, and instructional coach. Her research interests include equitable literacy intervention practices, children's and young adult literature, and critical literacy.

William Schmidt, PhD is a University Distinguished Professor and founder and director of the Center for the Study of Curriculum Policy. He holds a faculty appointment in Educational Statistics and Measurement and a courtesy appointment in the Department of Statistics. He is a member of the National Academy of Education as well as the International Academy of Education, an American Educational Research Association (AERA) Fellow, and an OECD Thomas J. Alexander Fellow for education quality and equity. He has published in numerous journals including the *Journal of the American Statistical Association, Education Researcher, Georgetown Journal of International Affairs, American Affairs Journal, Journal of Educational Statistics, Educational Evaluation and Policy Analysis, Journal of Curriculum Studies*, and the *Journal of Educational Measurement*. His most recent books include "Schooling Across the Globe: What We Have Learned from Sixty Years of Mathematics and Science International Assessments," "Inequality for All," and "Why Schools Matter." His current writing and research interests focus on the effects of curriculum policy on academic achievement. His work also focuses on schooling and how equality of opportunity to learn impacts student performance in mathematics.

Christopher A. Shearer (1995 EPFP Alum) is an independent consultant to philanthropy and nonprofits and the founder of Third Sector Strategy LLC. He works on three interrelated strategic areas: policy design and advocacy, program design and implementation, and communications and outreach. Shearer is the former Acting Director of the Education Program at the William and Flora Hewlett Foundation, Associate Executive Director of the National Geographic Society Education Foundation, Senior Program Associate at the Institute for Educational Leadership, and Executive Assistant to the President of the Pew Charitable Trusts. He received his Master of Arts degree in English Literature from the University of North Carolina at Chapel Hill, in his hometown, with a thesis on the use of quantum mechanical theory in the theater of Tom Stoppard.

Eve Sullivan (2013 EPFP Alum) founded Parents Forum in 1991 to pay forward the help she received while raising her own children. With three grown sons and four grandchildren, she sees the ability to express feelings and manage conflicts as essential to good parenting and key to a happy and successful life, whether one is raising children. Ms. Sullivan received a BA in English from Bard College, taught English as a Second Language in Tunisia during the early Peace Corps era, then received an MAT in French from Harvard Graduate School of Education. Now retired from a career of nearly three decades as an editorial assistant for a theoretical physics journal at MIT, she devotes time to advancing the cause of parenting education, writing, and speaking on the topic as often as she can.

Tyler Thur (2020 EPFP Allum) MPP, Associate Director of Data and Evaluation, Office of K–12 Outreach in the College of Education at Michigan State University. Coauthor *Rereading Fathers Behind Bars: Children's Literacy Assistance Practices of Incarcerated African American, Native American, Hispanic, and White, Fathers.* In Barbara Guzzetti's *Literacies, Genders and Cultures: Understanding Intersecting Identities,* New York, NY: Routledge.

REVIEWERS NAMES AND EPFP DATES

- Nathifa W. Carmichael, B. A., Bloom Board, Inc, EPFP, 2020.
- Jennifer R. Crandall, PhD, American Council on Education, EPFP, 2016.
- Andrew J. Ecker, Ed.D., Putnam/Northern Westchester BOCES, EPFP, 2018.
- Annie Frazer, Montessori Partnerships for Georgia, EPFP, 2020.
- Julie A. Glasco, Ed.D., The University of Mississippi, EPFP, 2020.
- Erin Thomas Horne, NC State University, EPFP, 2020.
- Hugh Potter PhD, Associate Director, Office of K—12 Outreach, EPFP, 2020.
- Cindy Meyer Sabik, Cleveland State University, EPFP, 2011.
- Dahila Shaewitz, MA Institute for Educational Leadership and DC EPFP Co-coordinator, EPFP, 2010.
- Tyler Thur, BA Associate Director of Data and Evaluation, Office of K–12 Outreach, EPFP, 2020.

Ingram Content Group UK Ltd.
Milton Keynes UK
UKHW020045110723
424904UK00006B/147